Sketchercises

LONDON

Volume 1

An illustrated sketchbook on London and its people

Mike Green

ISBN 978-0-244-63762-0

www.mikegreenillustration.com
Instagram: @mike_sketches

Cover Image: Boris Bikes on Exhibition Road, Kensington
Below: St Paul's Cathedral from the top of One New Change Shopping Centre

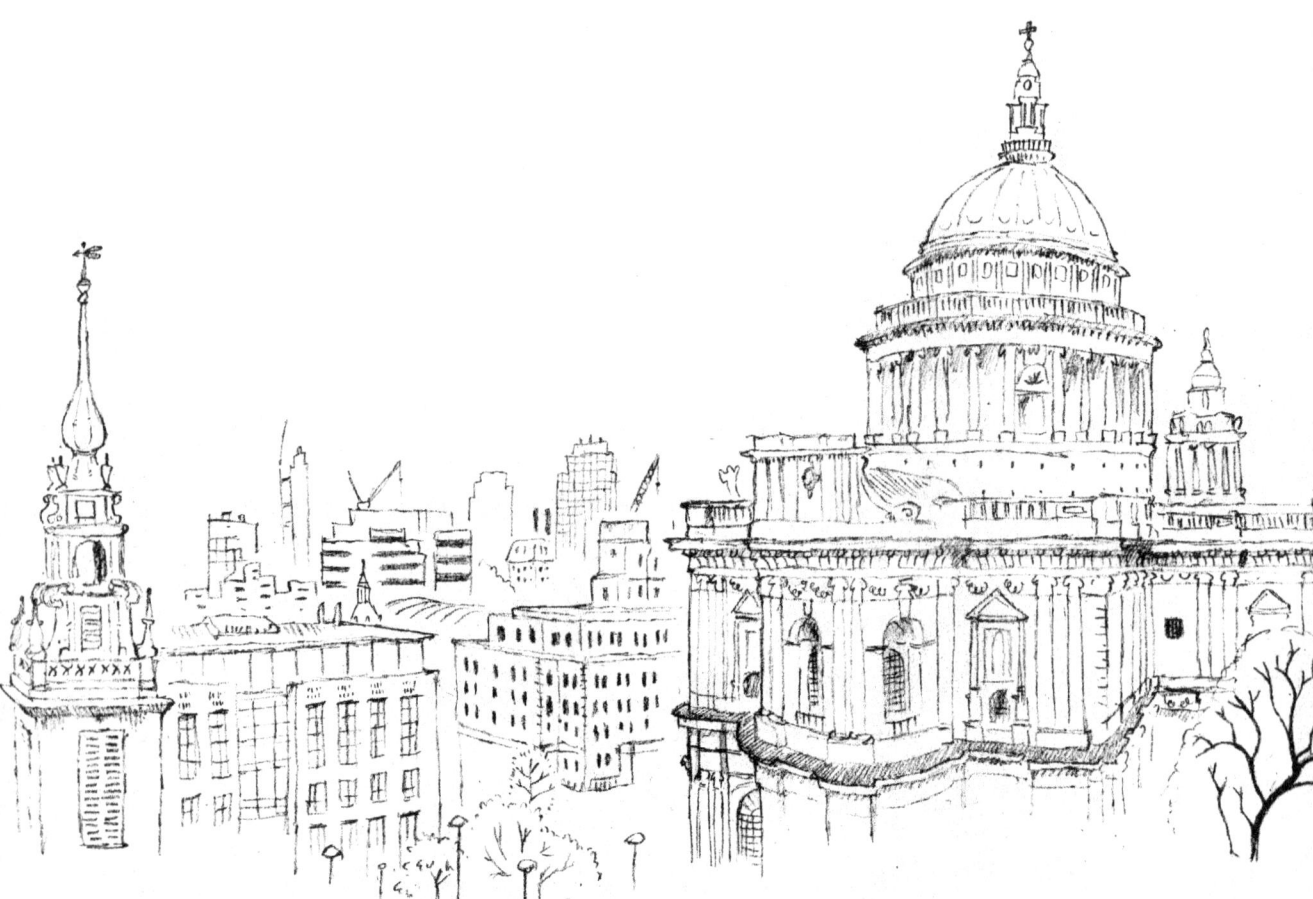

Forward

Sketchercises – exercise for the mind through the activity of drawing.

Following a six year break from sketching after studying illustration at university, I decided early in 2012 to try and get back into it. However I soon discovered, like an unused muscle, my sketching ability was much weaker than it had once been. Thus followed many hours of sketching, seeing, staring, studying, meditating, eating, drinking, shivering, sweating, walking, driving, tube-ing, caffeinating, rehydrating, aching, stretching, pondering, nibbling, leaning, learning and meeting a lot of good, like-minded people.

The collection of sketches in this book, made between 2012 – 2015, are the result of all these ing's.

Mike

Inner London Boroughs

Camden

Islington

Hackney

City of
Westminster

City of
London

Tower
Hamlets

Kensington and
Chelsea

Southwark

Greenwich

Wandsworth

Lambeth

Lewisham

Contents

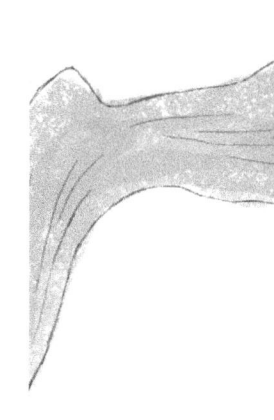

Kensington and Chelsea

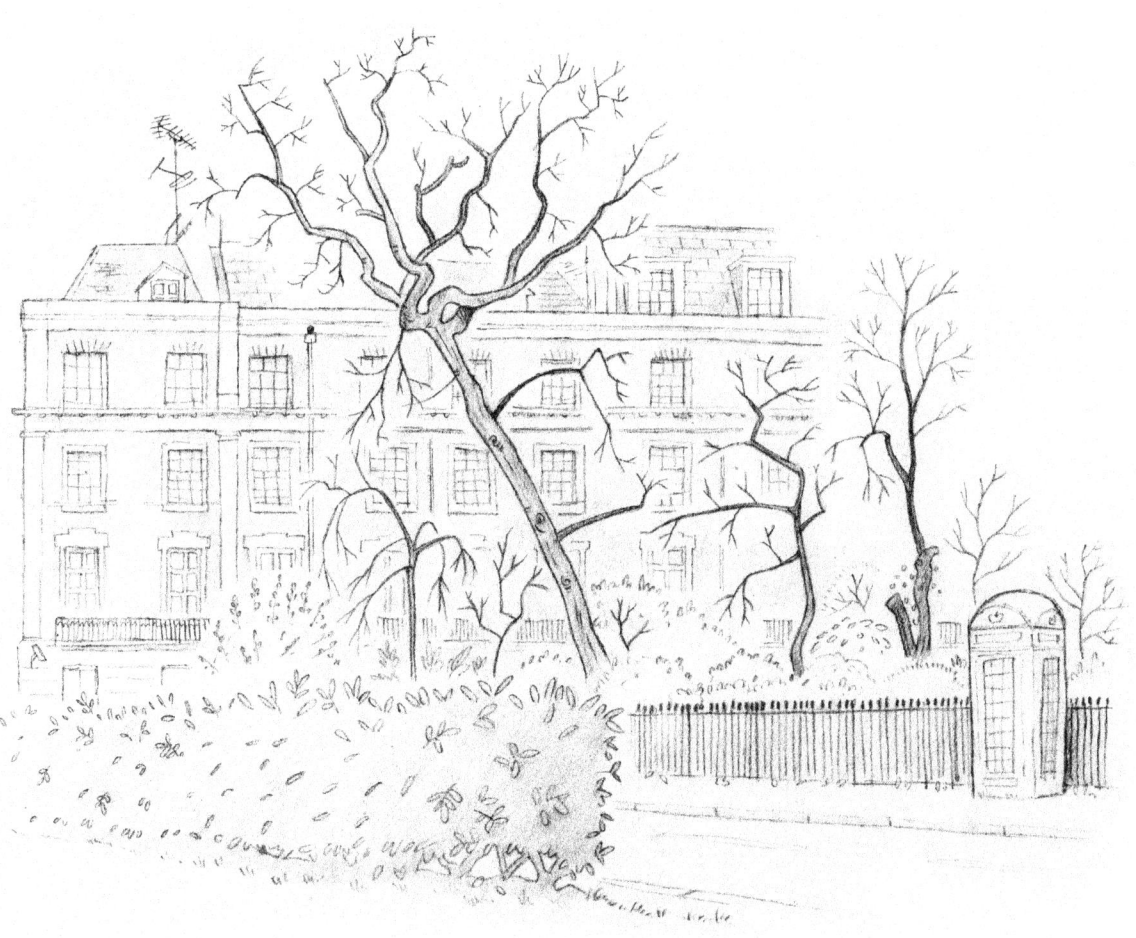

Thurloe Square Gardens and the Republic of Kazakhstan embassy

Christie's Auction House: 'Out of the Ordinary'

In September 2013 Christie's held an auction for unusual items. Among those for sale were the objects on these two pages. So now you know how much someone is prepared to pay to own a real 65 million year old dinosaur skull. It must be quite something to bring home, a real conversation starter. It would make a great hat stand too :)

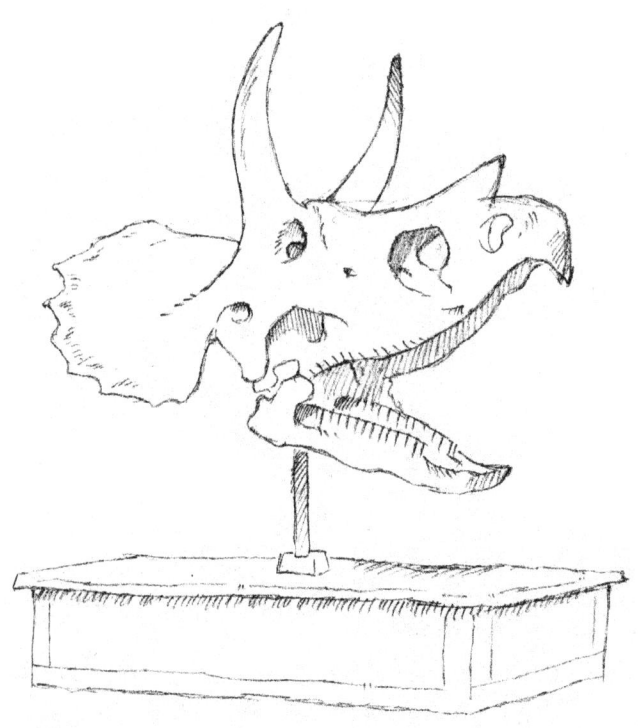

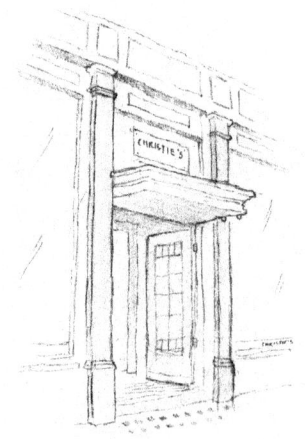

85 Old Brompton Rd

99: Triceratops Scull, Hall Creek Formation. Montana
    Estimate: £150 – 250,000, Realised: £193,875

103: The Tooth of a Tyrannosaurus-Rex, Montana
          Estimate: £5 – 8,000, Realised: £9,375

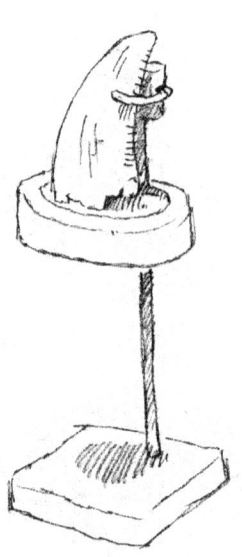

96: Large Megalodon Tooth (one of two)
Estimate: £6 - 9,000, Realised: £7,500

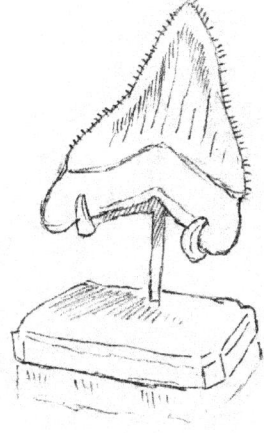

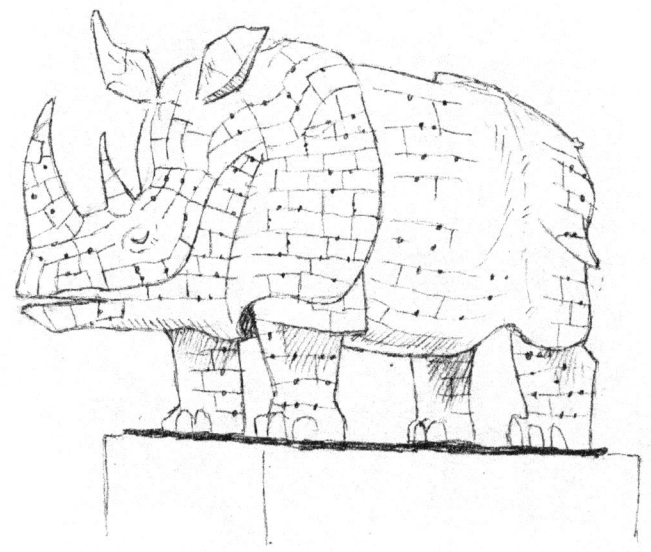

46: Large Illuminated Pierced Brass Sculpture of a Rhino
Estimate: £8 - 10,000, Realised: £10,000

98: Large Double-Curved Woolly Mammoth Tusk
Estimate: £30 - 50,000, Realised: £77,500

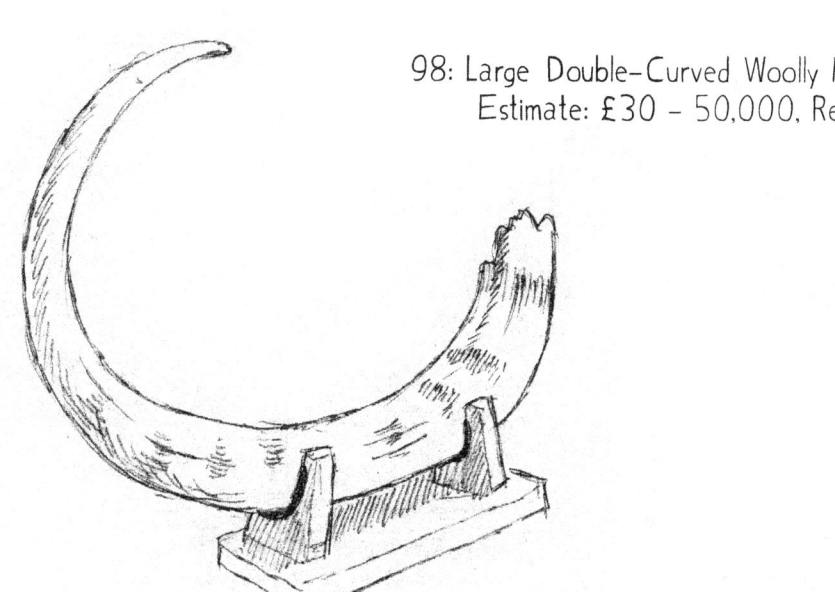

The Natural History Museum

A grandiose building with plenty of nobly bits (or Romanesque features to give its proper architectural term). Buildings like these, with distinct silhouettes and many details actually make them slightly easier to sketch, at least in the sense it has more features that make it unique. Most children could make a recognisable drawing of Tower Bridge for example. As for drawing the items inside, skeletons pose a similar challenge to buildings; you are attempting to piece together a structural puzzle. Adding a bit of character always helps too. I'd imagine this museum is not such a bad place for a skeleton to live.

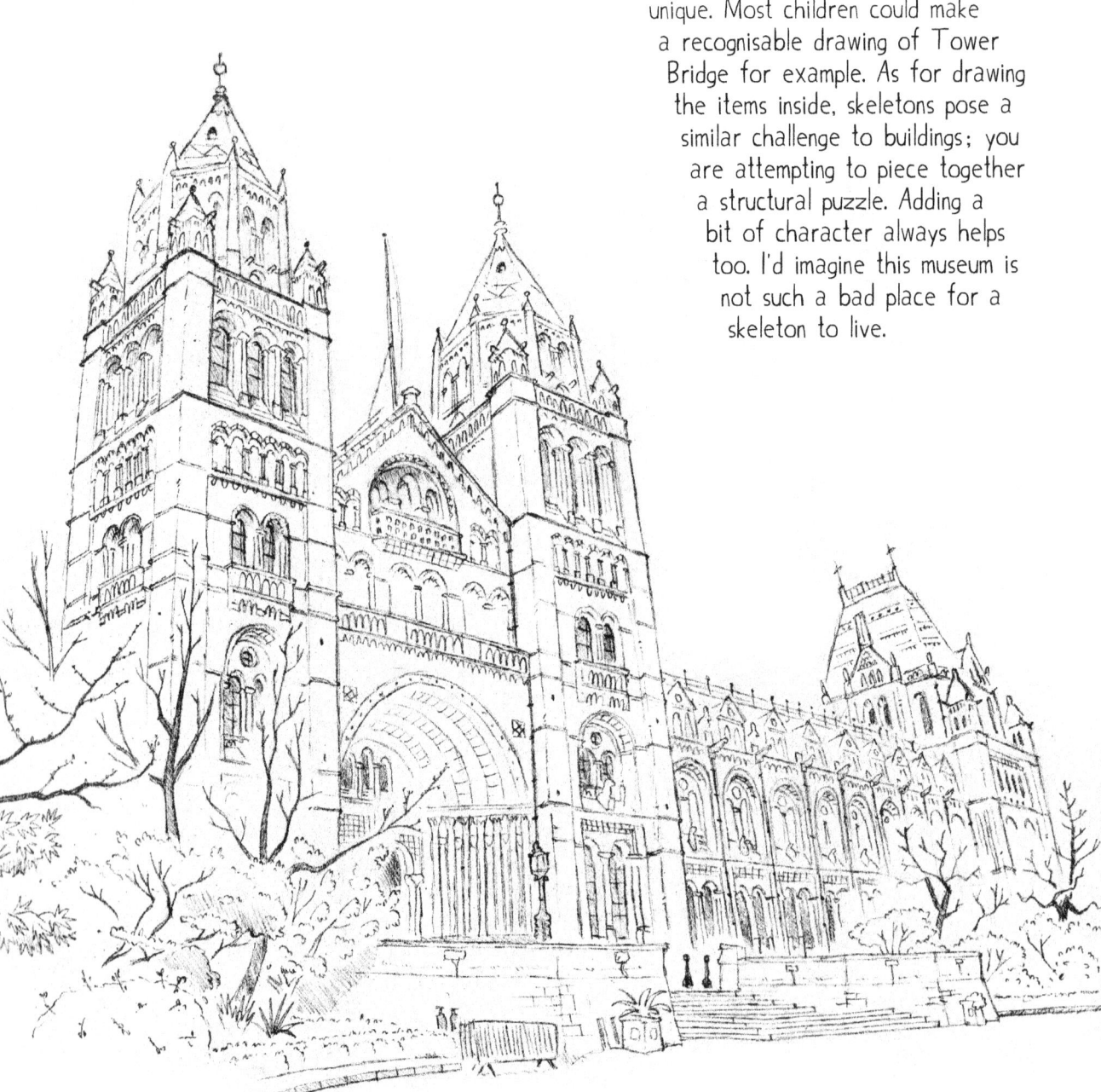

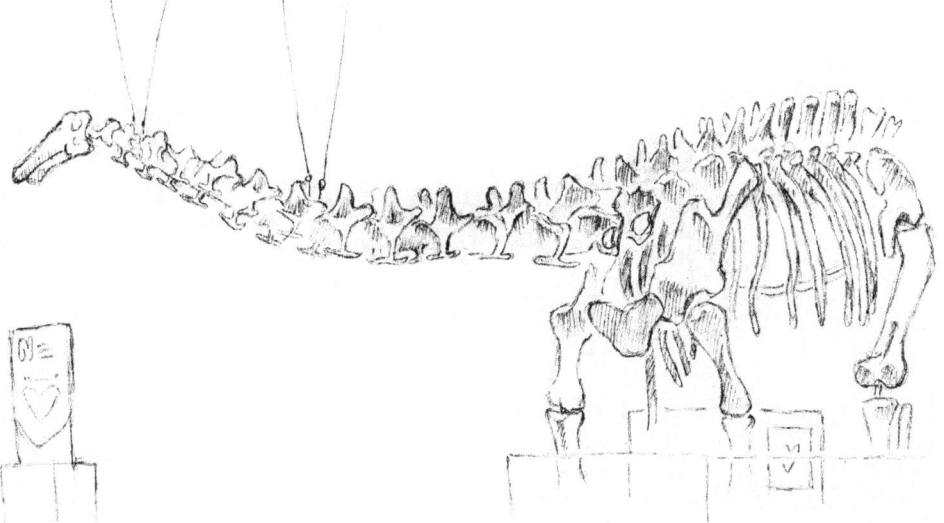

Diplodocus (Dippy), 150 million years

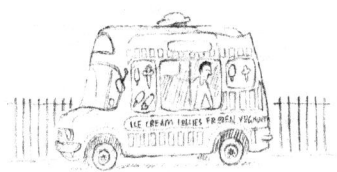

Ice cream van in
the museum garden

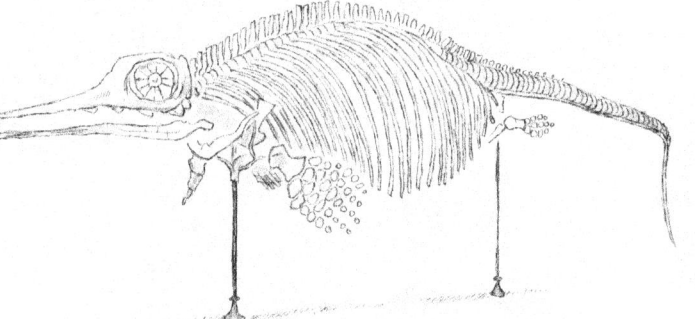

Ophthalmosaurus Icenius, 165 million years

Megatherium Americanum,
8000 BC

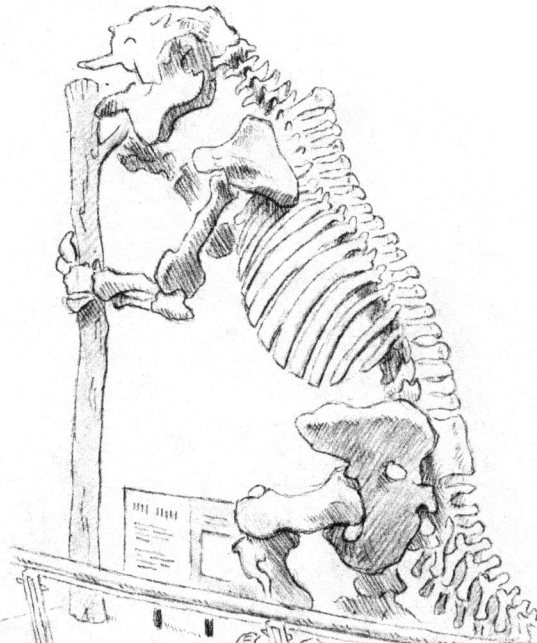

The Science Museum

Originally part of the South Kensington Museum, the current building was constructed between 1913 - 1928. This museum attracts nearly 3 million visitors a year.

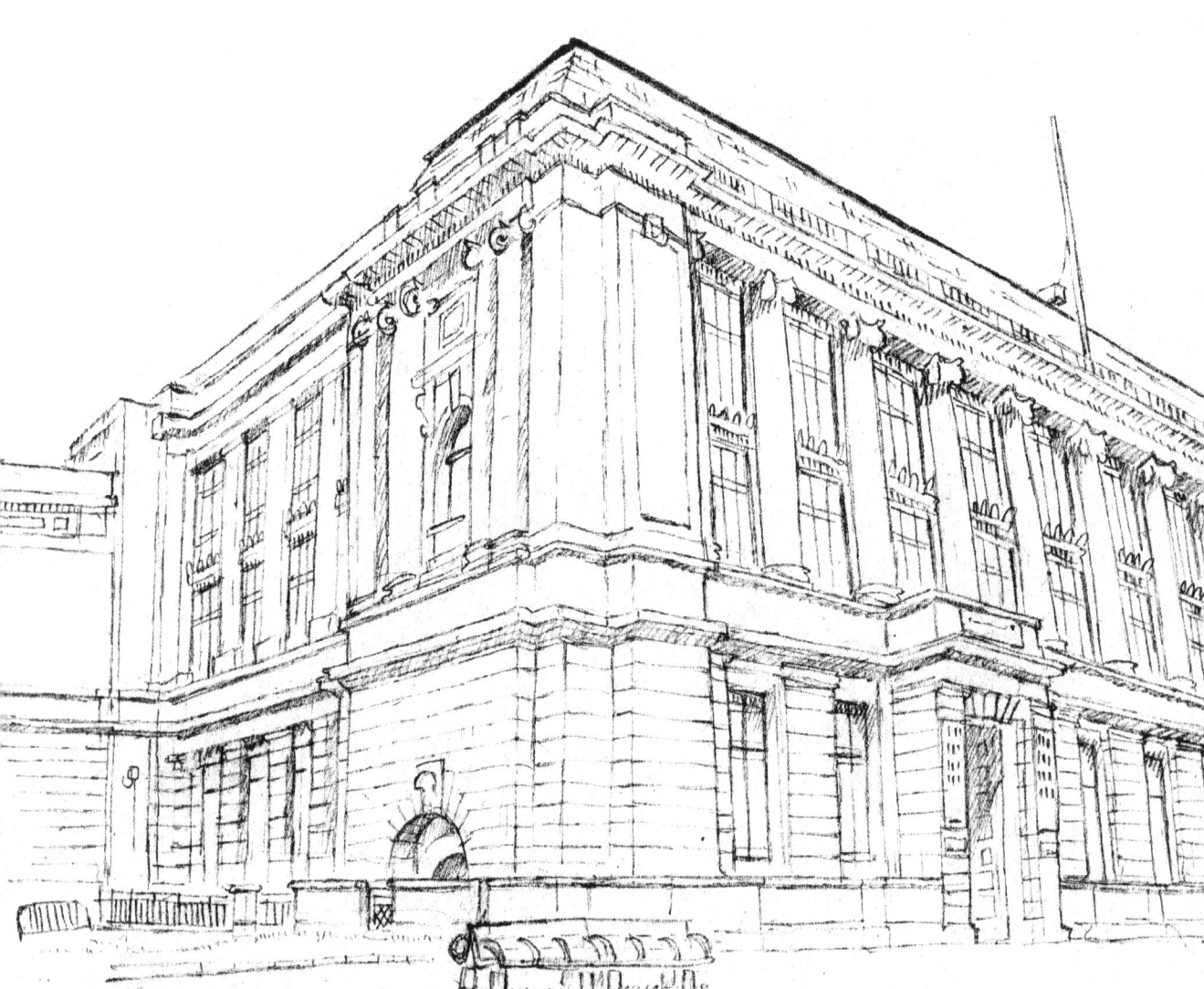

Although the museum houses over 300,000 items covering all areas of science, for some reason I stuck to drawing the automobiles. Along with planes & trains, they are often the most aesthetically pleasing. It would be good to sketch in the rooms dedicated to space exploration, which contain some very interesting objects. Unfortunately itss pretty dark in there. Ill have to take a head torch in next time.

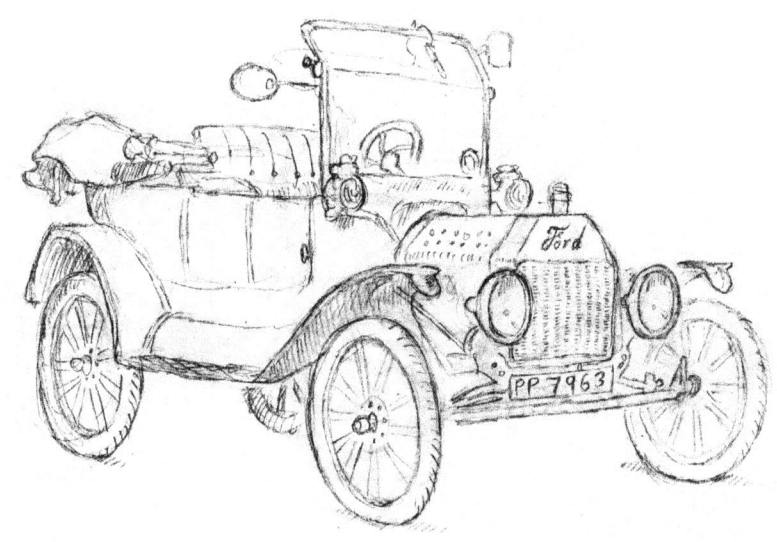

Ford Model T, 1916

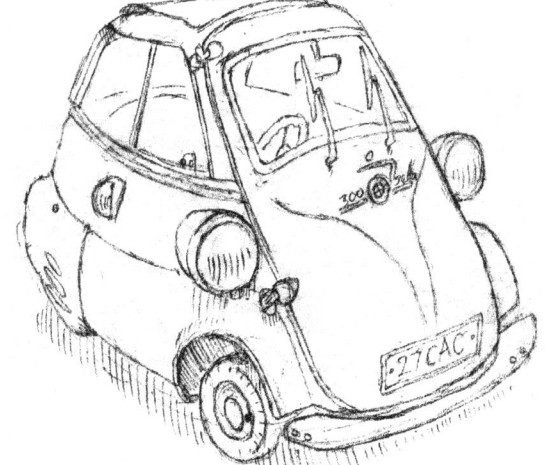

BMW Isetta 300, 1961

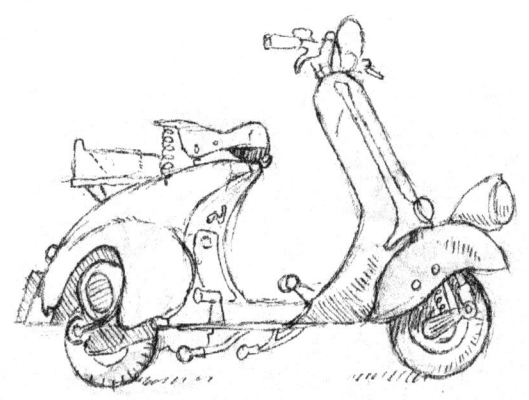

Vespa 125 Scooter, 1948

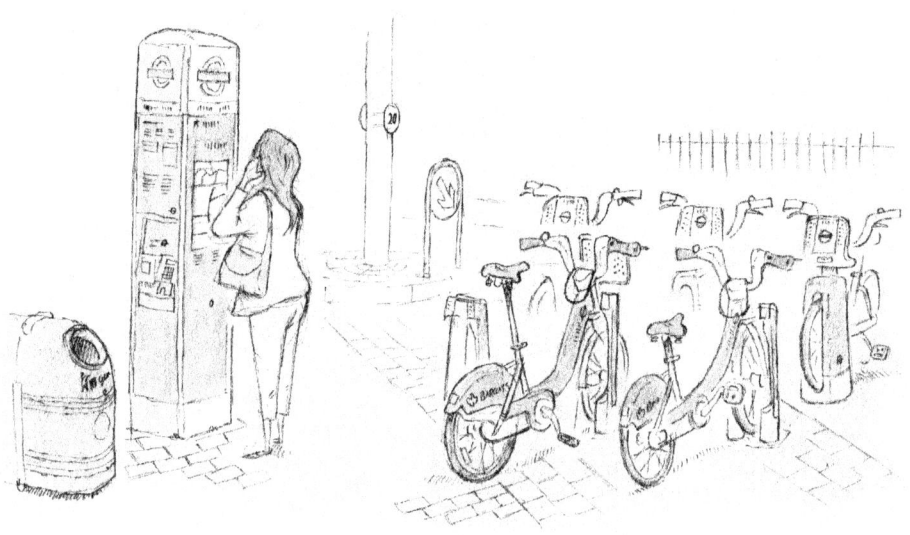

Boris Bikes on Exhibition Road

The Royal Albert Hall

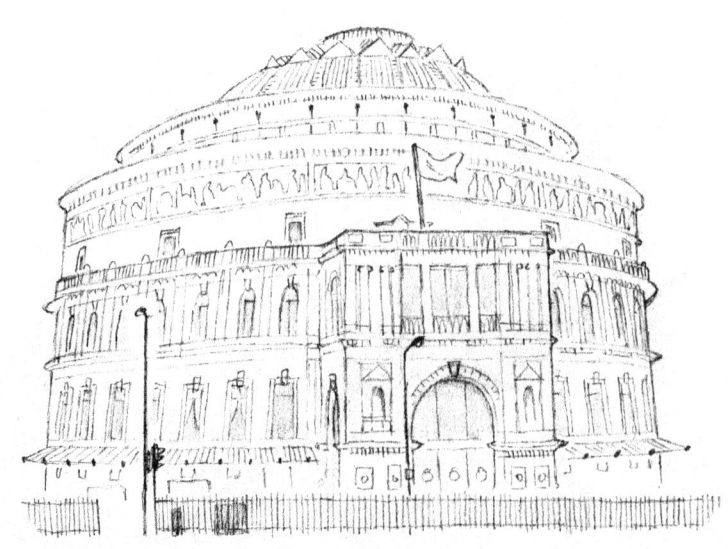

The Victoria & Albert Museum

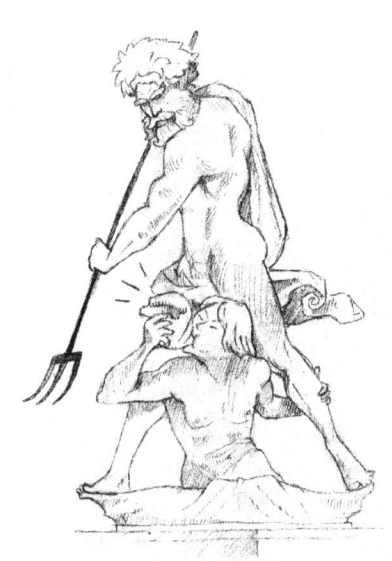

Neptune and Triton 1622-3,
Giovanni Lorenzo Bernini

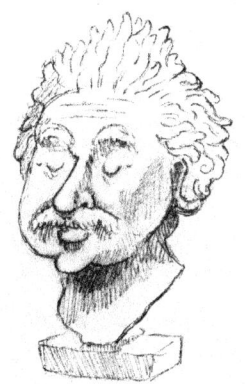

Albert Einstein 1933,
Jacob Epstein

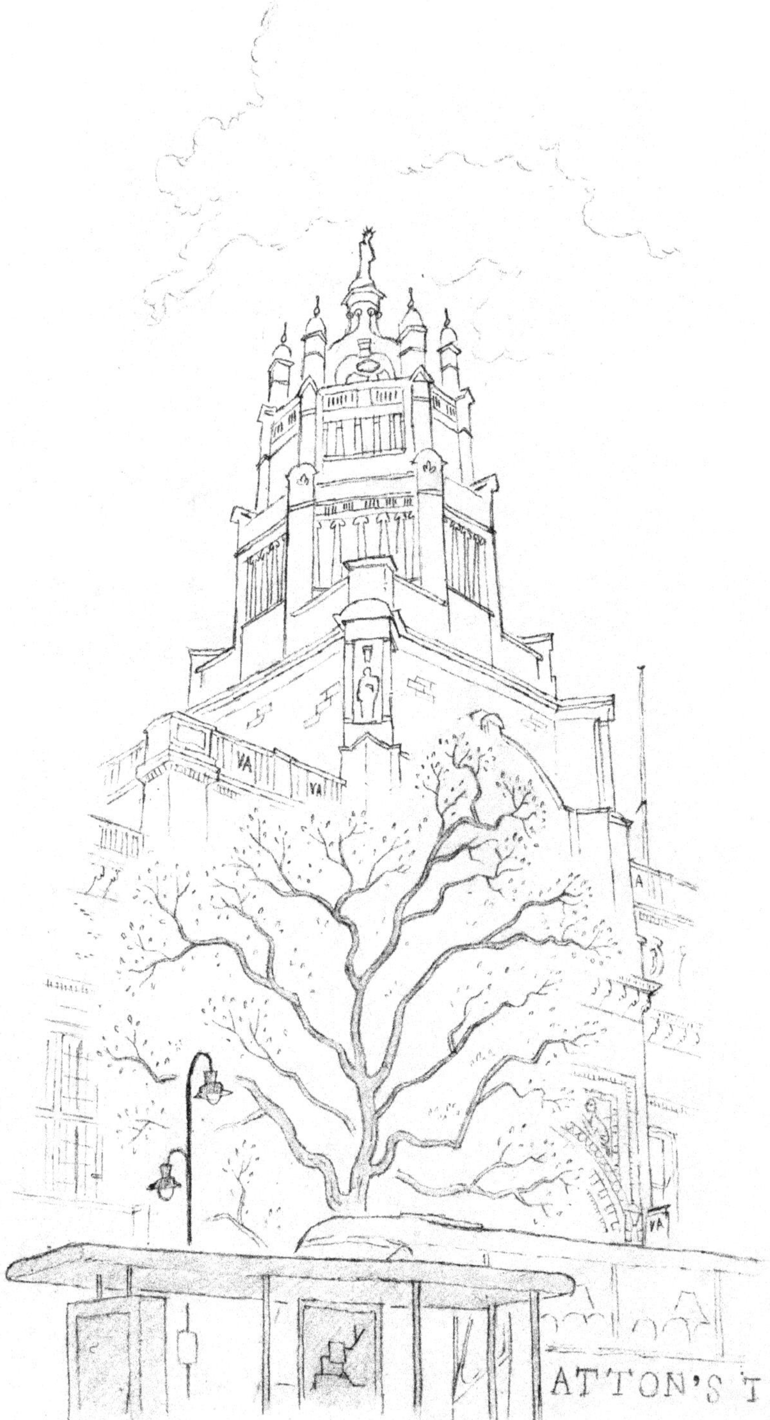

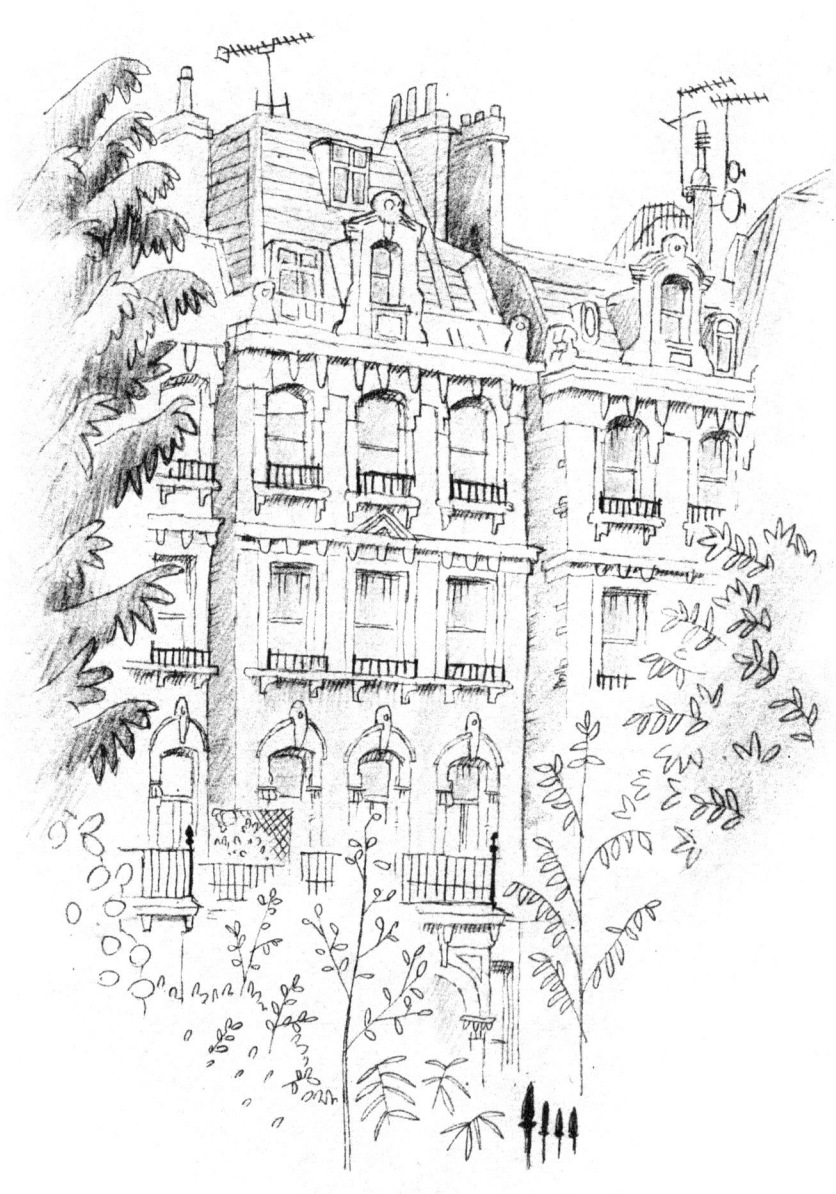

Redcliffe Square Gardens

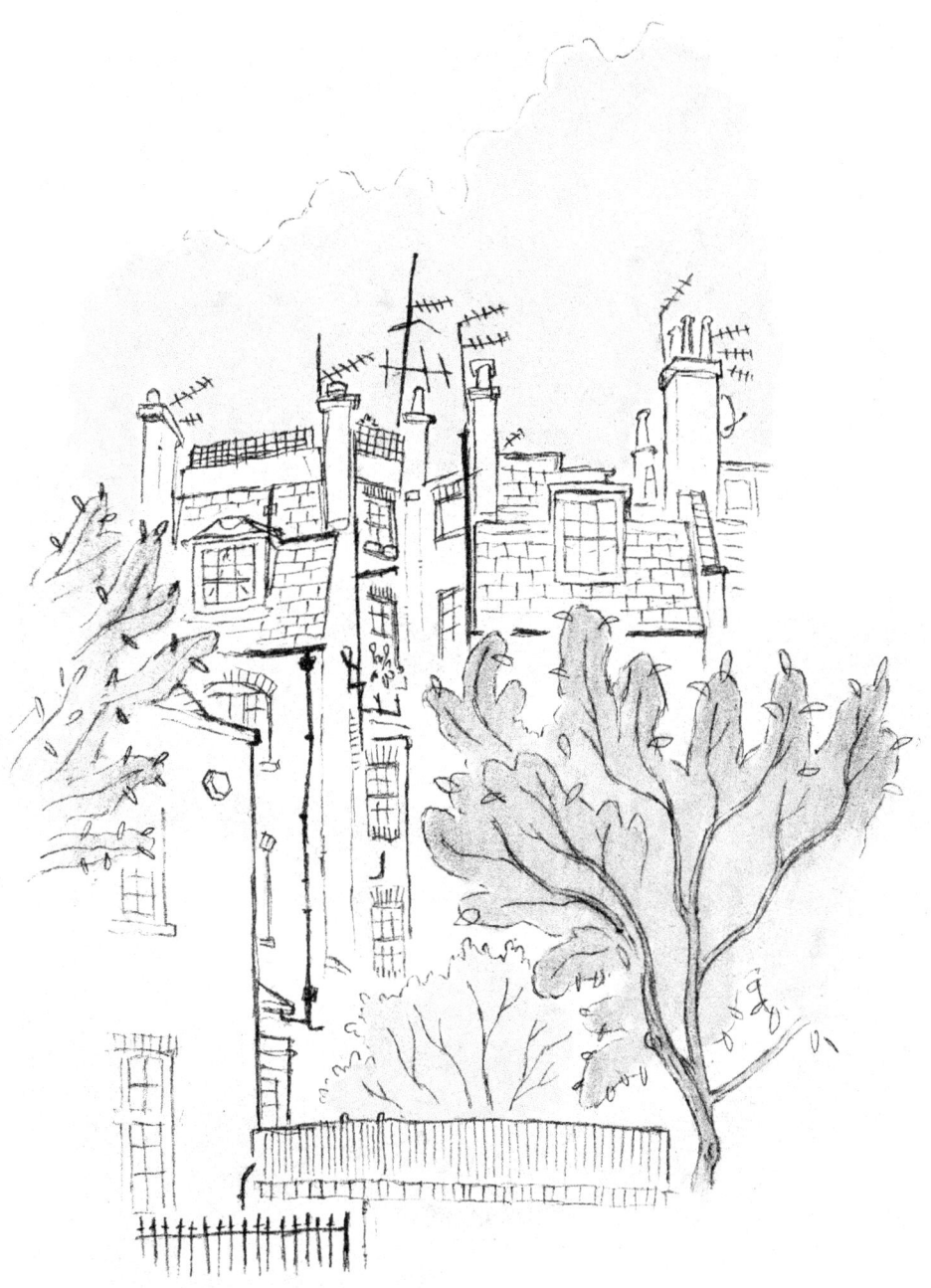

Houses on Elystan Place

If you ever find yourself near Sloane Square and fancy refreshments with a good view, be sure to check out the Peter Jones Cafe. Unfortunately I'm not being paid to say this. The view from the top floor looks north and you can see all the way across to the Natural History Museum and the Royal Albert Hall. You may even bump into Liza Minnelli having a coffee.

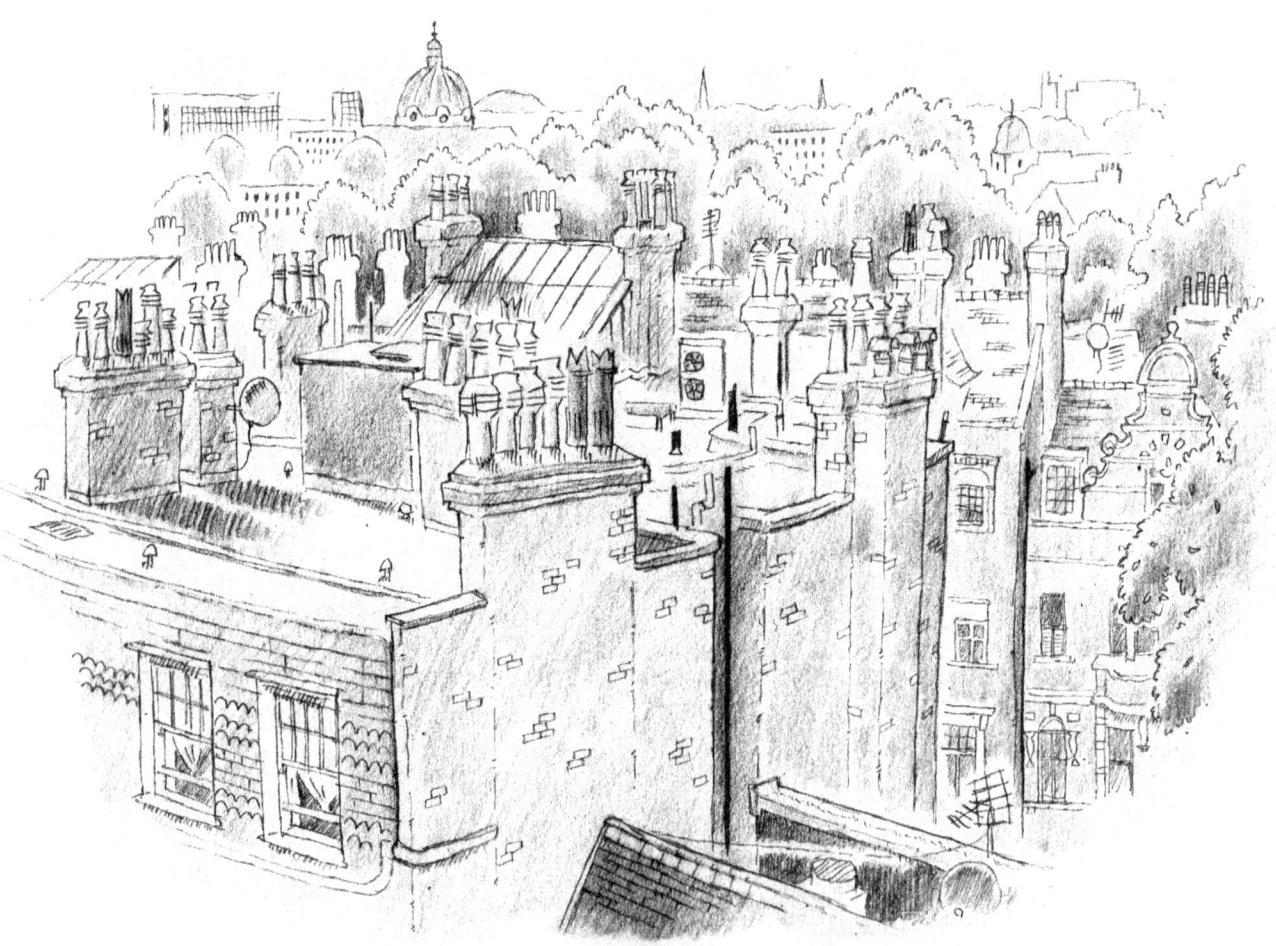

View north west from Peter Jones cafe

Man selling headphones at Portobello road market

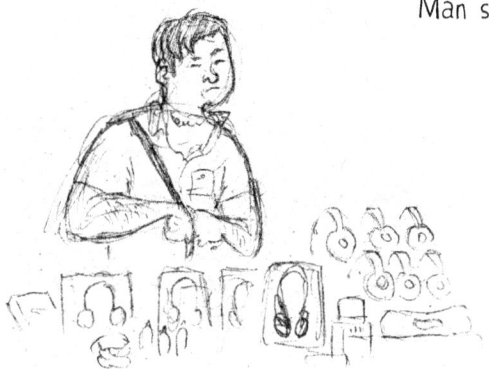

Peter Jones at Sloane Square

This building, completed in 1936, was one
of the earliest in Britain to use the curtain
wall architectural technique. With the outer
wall being non-structural, this means you can
take more creative liberties with its
shape, such as the wave design
seen here.

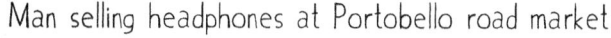

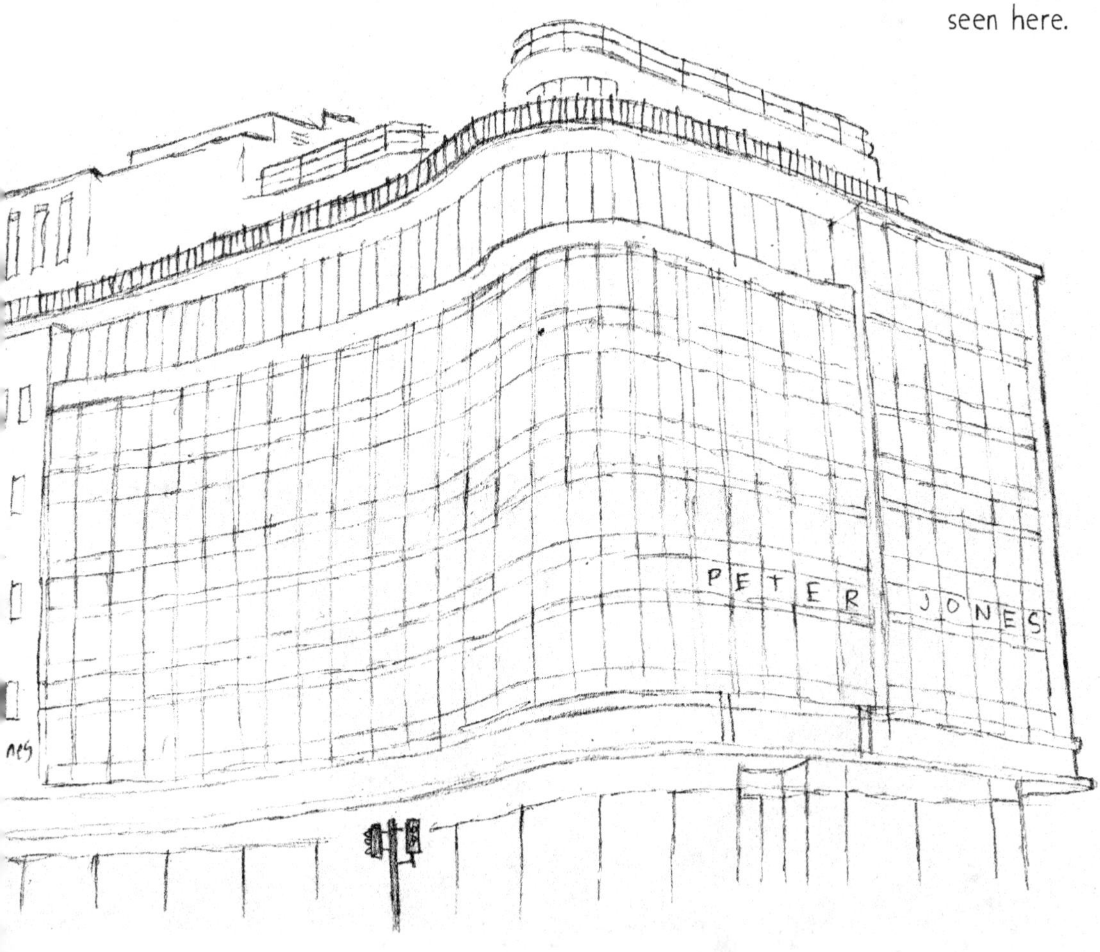

City of Westminster

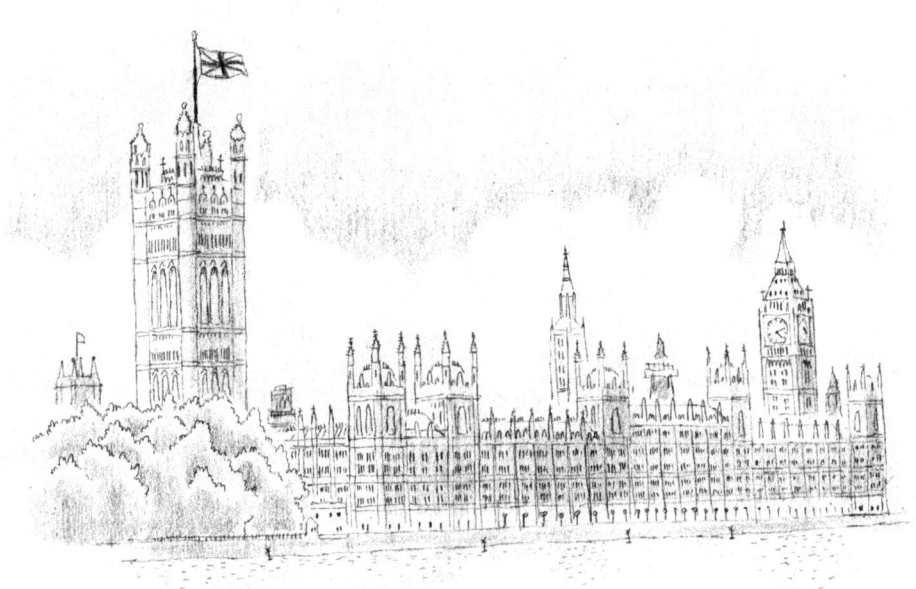

Palace of Westminster

Parliament Square Statues

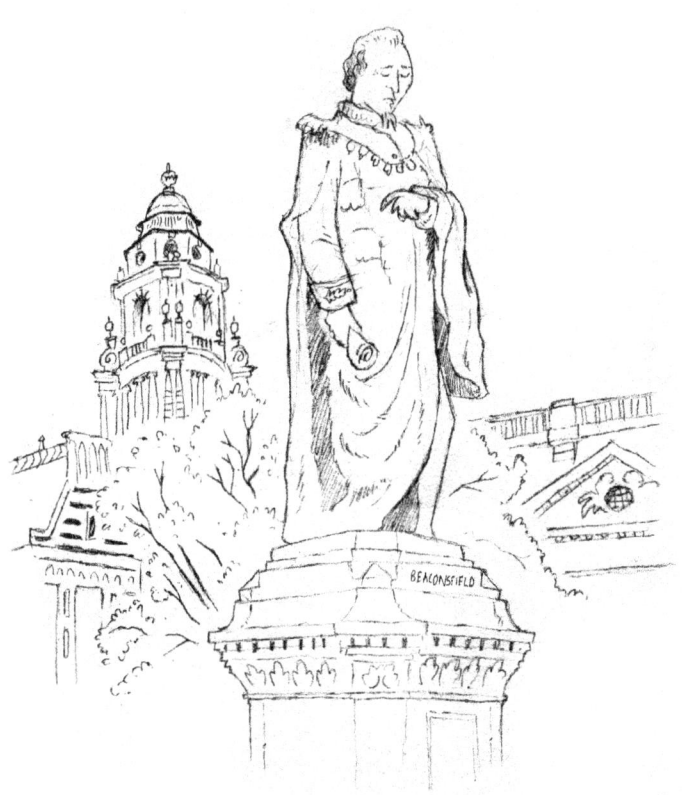

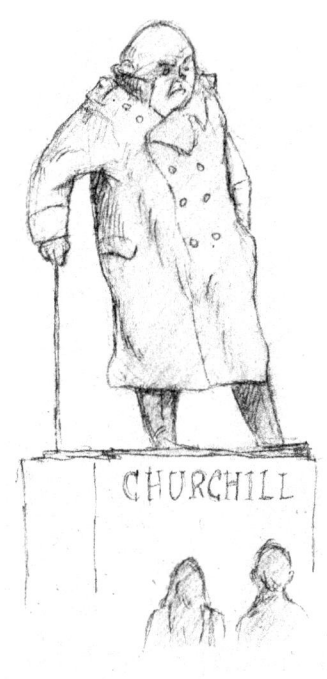

Benjamin Disraeli, 1st Earl of Beaconsfield

Sir Winston Churchill,
Politician

No Sketching Allowed!

After securing tickets to see Prime Ministers questions from my local MP, myself and a fellow artist went along in the hope of sketching inside the house of commons. Unfortunately we were told on entry that along with photography, no sketching was allowed. It felt like an opportunity missed, to draw something people are very familiar with but rarely get to see. All those MPs going "Yaah, Boo" though childish, would have been great to draw. I guess the parliament channel will just have to do :(

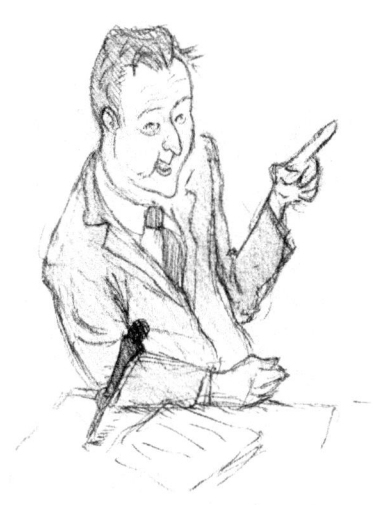

View from St James
Church garden,
Piccadilly

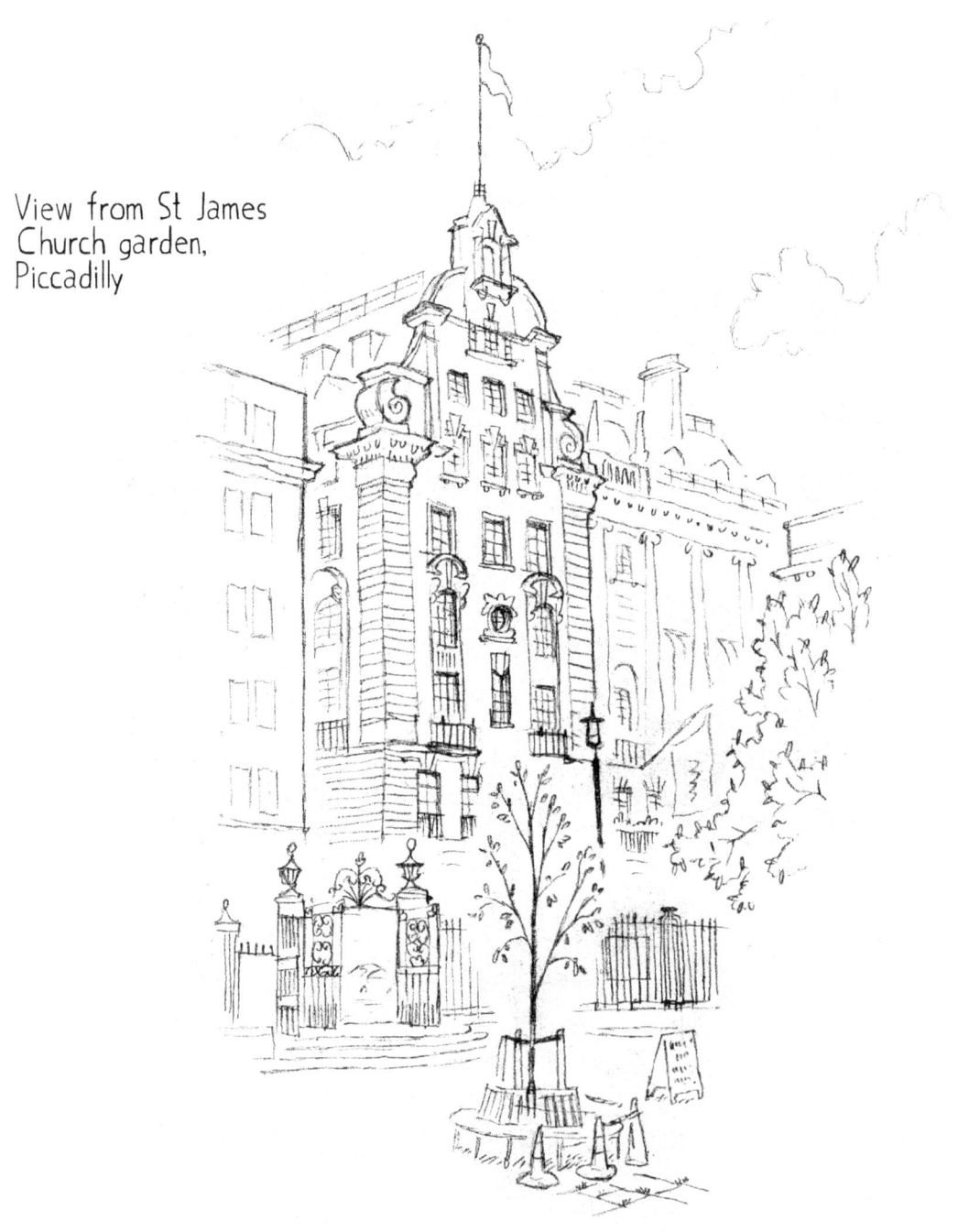

Opposite:
Inside Westminster
Cathedral

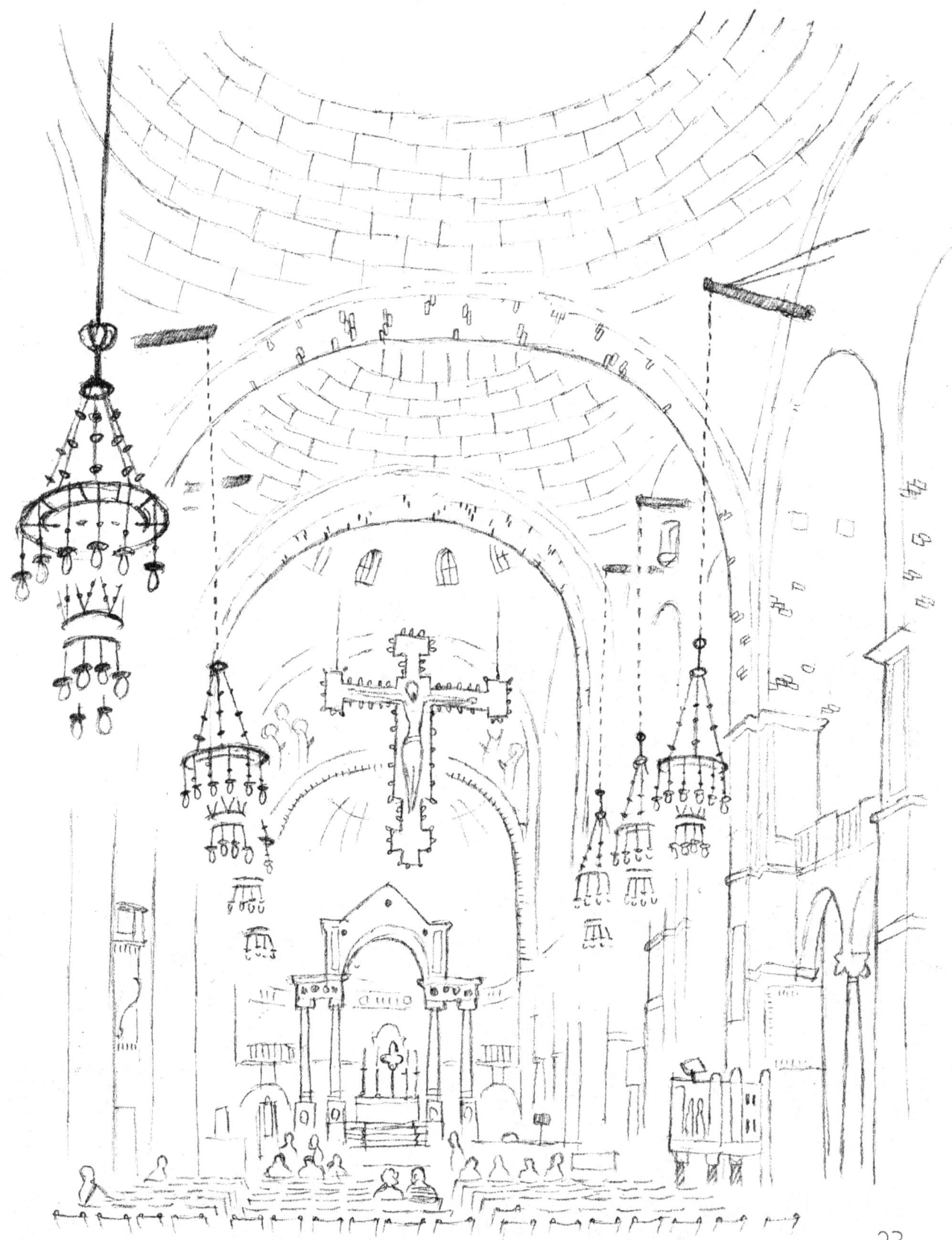

23

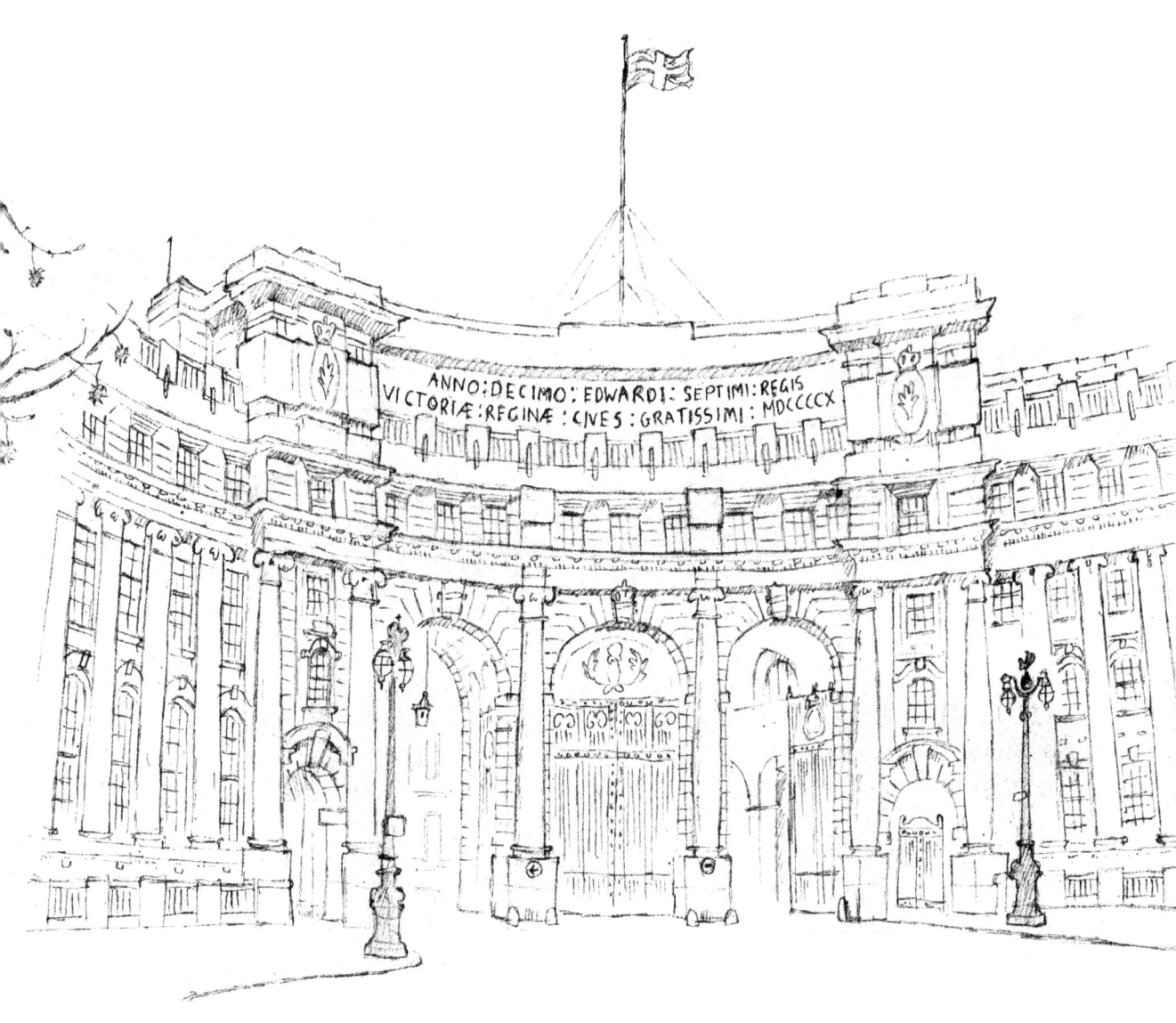

ANNO : DECIMO : EDWARDI : SEPTIMI : REGIS
VICTORIÆ : REGINÆ : CIVES : GRATISSIMI : MDCCCCX

Admiralty Arch, The Mall

Duke of York Column, St James

Finished in 1834 and standing at 42m, this is a monument to Prince Frederick the Duke of York, the second son of king George III. Originally the observation platform at the top was open to the public but unfortunately this closed some years after opening. You can see the slits up the sides that allow light into the spiral staircase inside. London's other famous observation tower, the Monument in the City of London, can still be staggered up though. With only 311 steps!

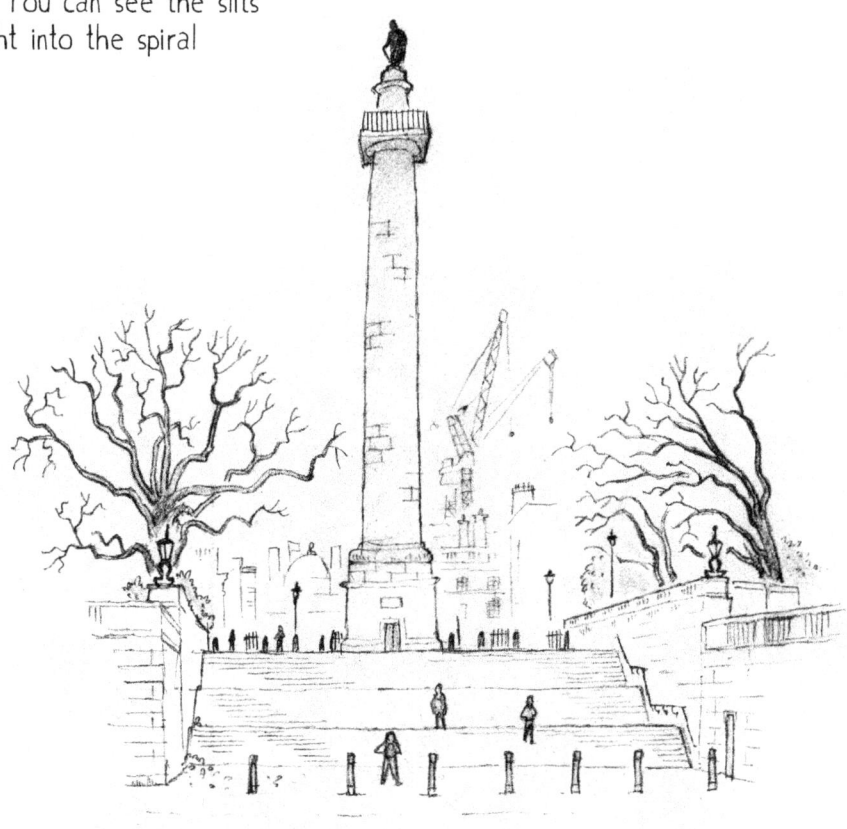

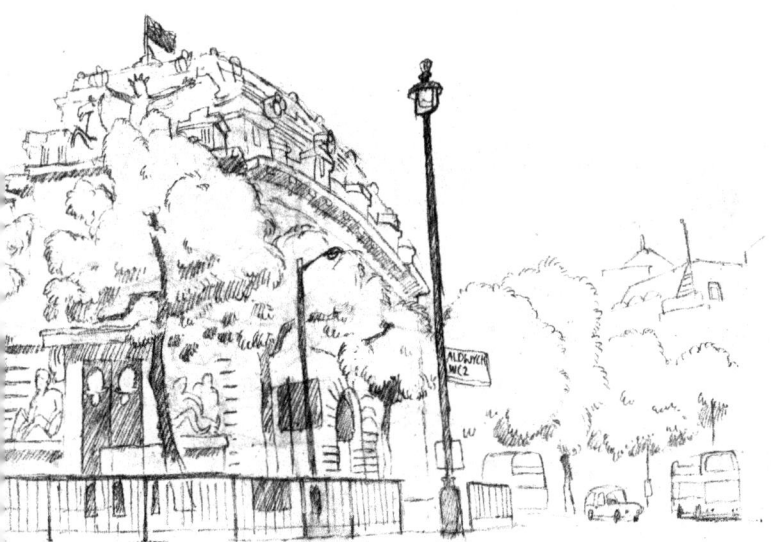

Australian High Commission, Strand

Opened in 1918 Australia House has been occupied by the Australian commission ever since. It is the longest continuously occupied foreign mission in London and apparently often handles more voters than any Australian poll station during Australian elections.

London Zoo

Nestled at the top of Regents Park, this is the oldest scientific zoo in the world. Created in 1828 as a collection for scientific studies, it was then opened to the public in 1847. I can't believe I completely forgot to sketch the Gorilla :(

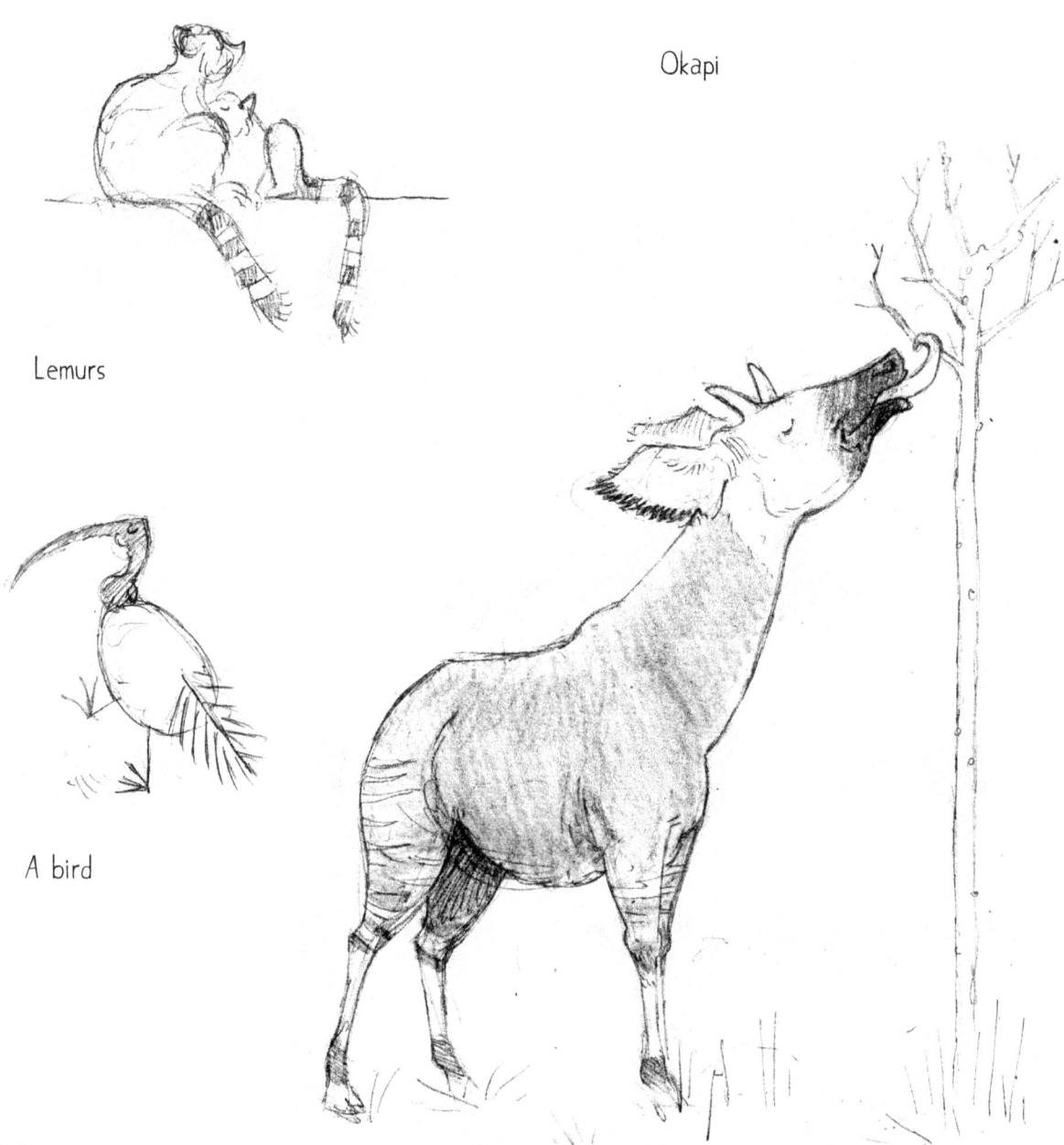

Okapi

Lemurs

A bird

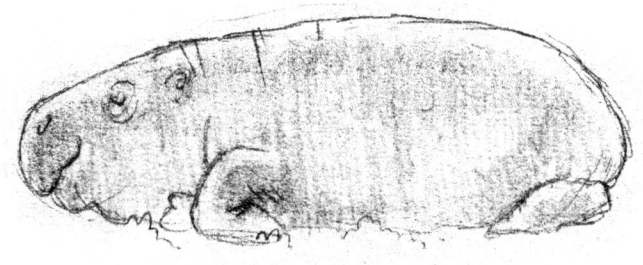

Pygmy Hippopotamus

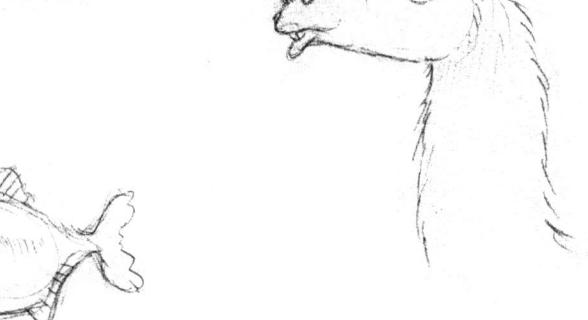

Piranha   Lama

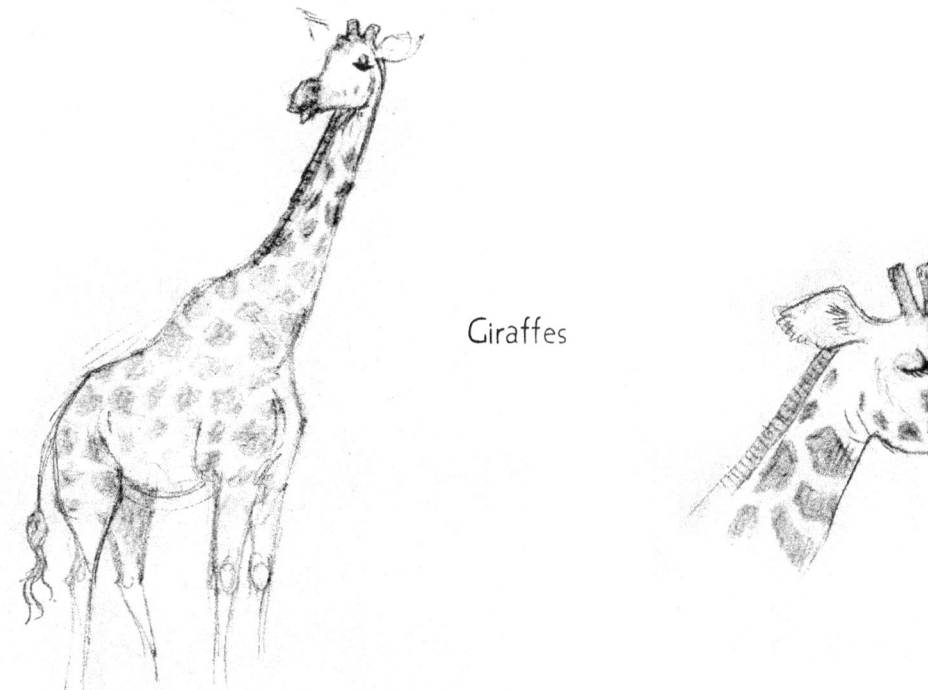

Giraffes

A little tip, if you want to draw the Giraffes for free, you can peak through the bars by walking along the Outer Circle which cuts right through the zoo. Sneaky! ;)

27

Chinatown

Standing here at the end of Gerrard Street to draw this Chinese Gate, my nose certainly soaked up the exotic smells. It just so happens there is a very good Japanese restaurant right around the corner called Tokyo Diner, as well as some great Korean food to be found nearby. As for Chinese there are plenty of options left right and centre If you are on a tight budget try Wong Kei just make sure you take cash. If you feel particularly adventurous, go for some duck tongue!

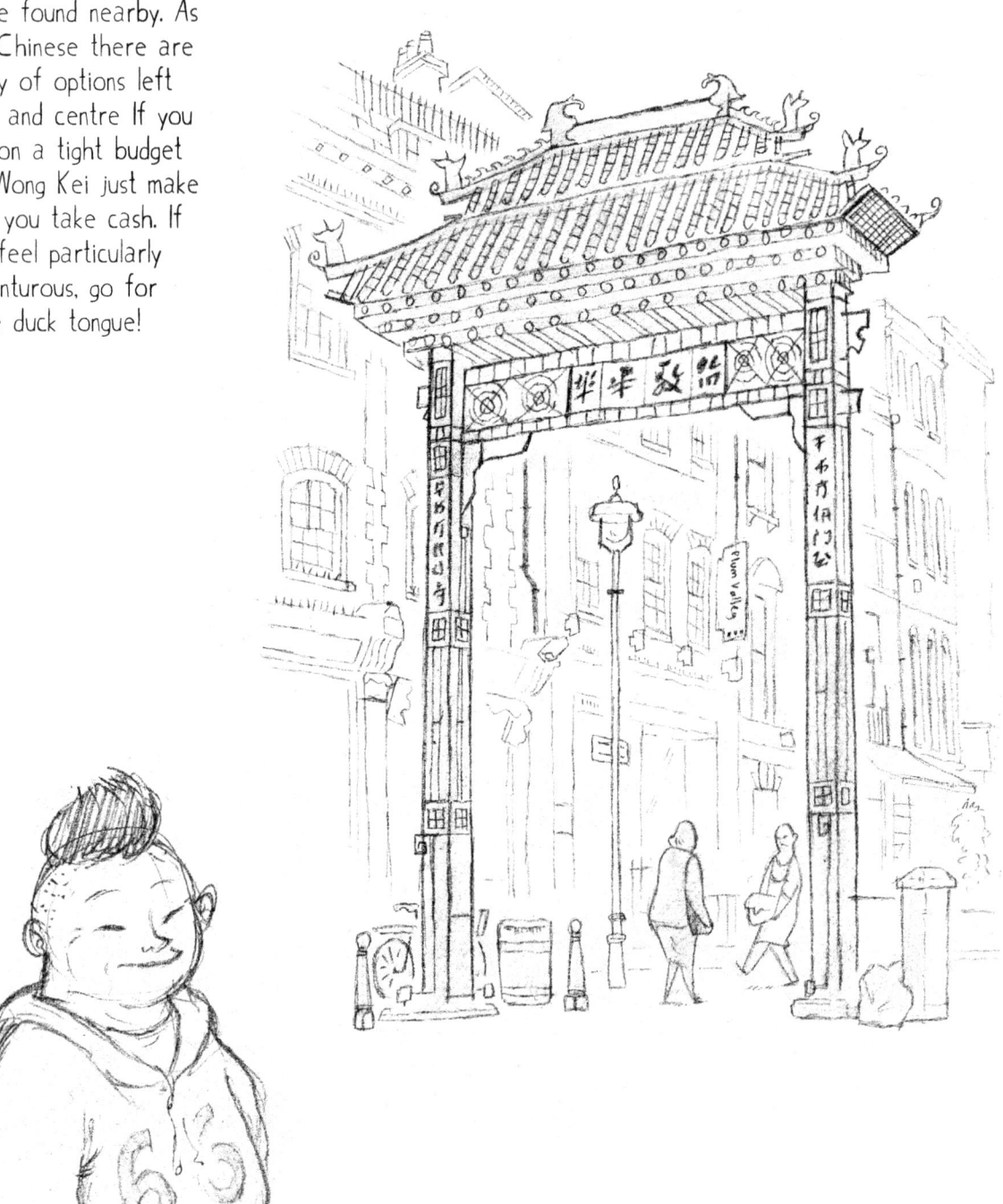

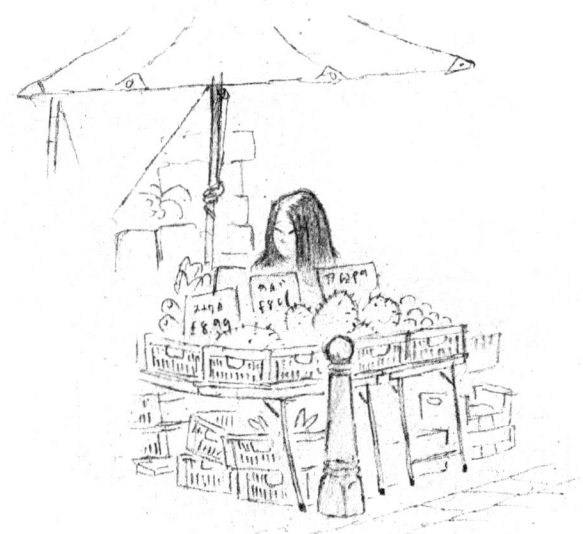

Chinese Grocery Stall

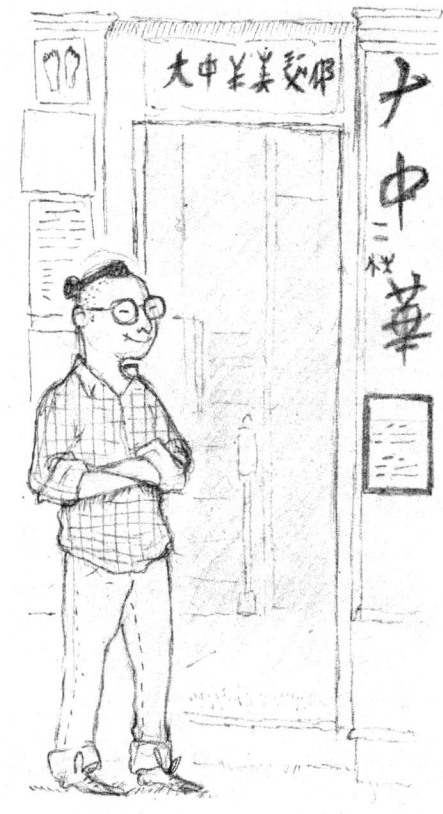

Man & Mary's Team Hair &
Beauty, Gerrard street Chinatown

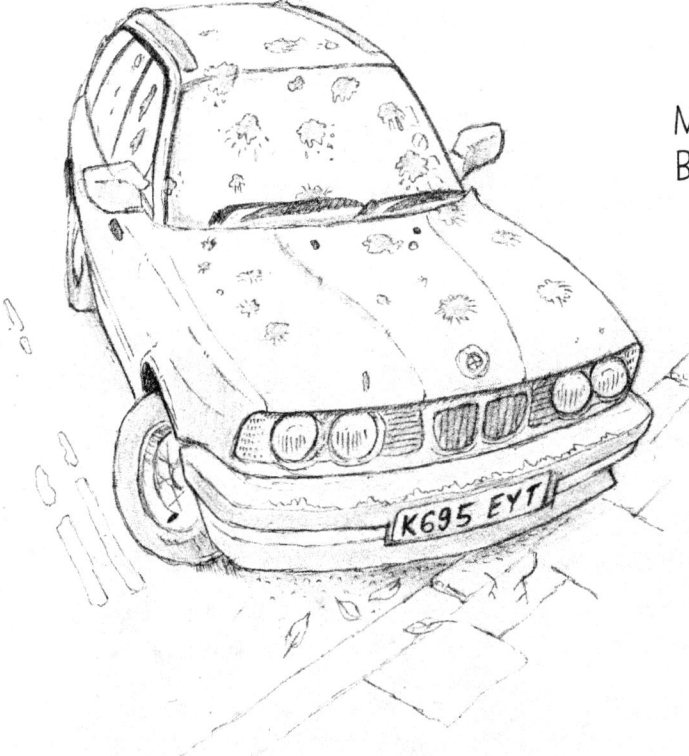

This car by Soho Square was turning heads but for all the wrong reasons. Those splodges on the windscreen were green coloured bird droppings. A bit of public art maybe? Two weeks later it had been replaced by a van, complete with more green droppings.

The Gay Hussar Restaurant, Greek Street

A Hungarian restaurant next to Soho square, famous for it's left wing customers such as Michael Foot & Barbara Castle.

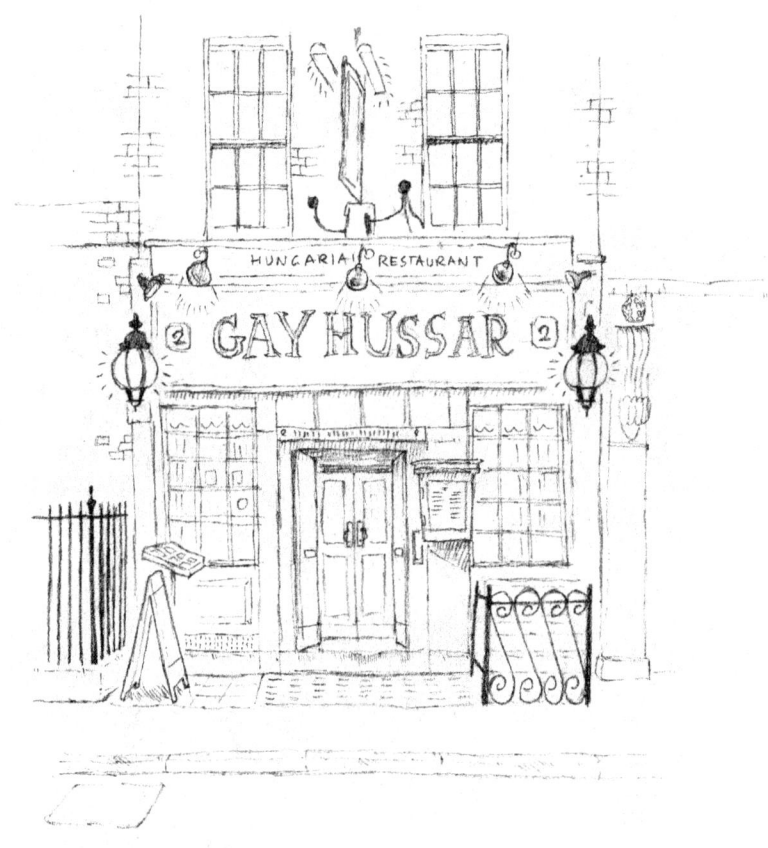

Shifty looking lady in Soho Square. A spy perhaps?

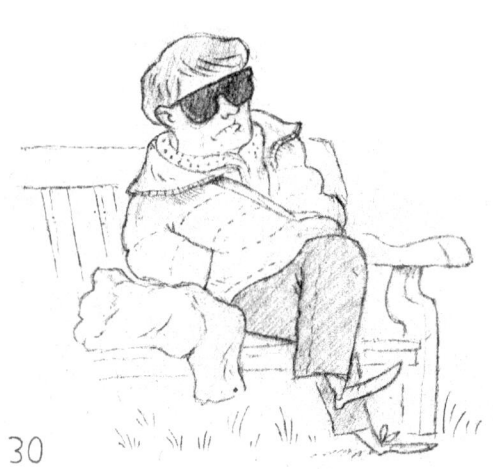

St James's Park

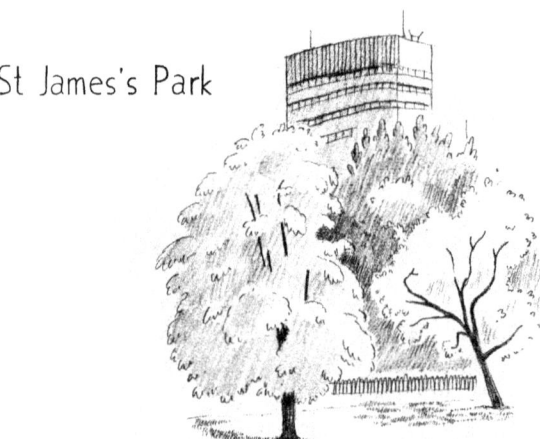

En Plein air Sketching

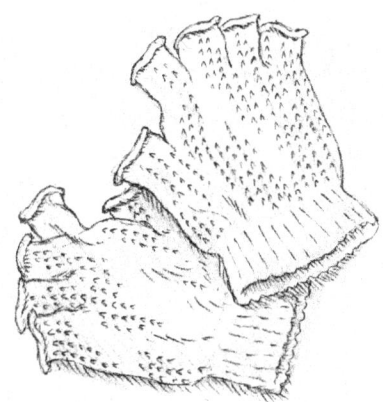

Fingerless Gloves

Fingerless gloves, essential for the sketcher in winter.

All the drawings in this book were made in front of the subject (save for the London map). I used to prefer taking photos and doing the work in the comfort of a warm home but not any more. Making myself sketch outside and taking on the elements not only helps the concentration but can also add extra character into your work. The awkward stance when trying to support a large book and prevent the pages flapping about in the wind puts a certain constraint on your hand movements. This can lead to an unsteady and more interesting line.

As well as preventing me from being too neat, bad weather also prevents me from taking too long over a picture. Quickness in drawing is a great way to improve as you are forced to push against the urge to be accurate. Although I am not the quickest sketcher by any means, it's good to put some time constraint on your work.

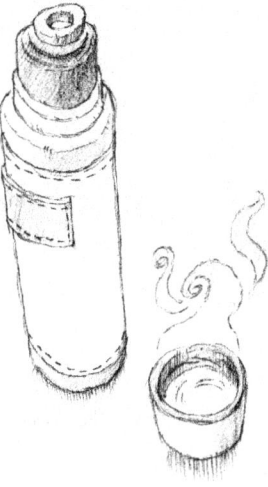

Flask of Coffee

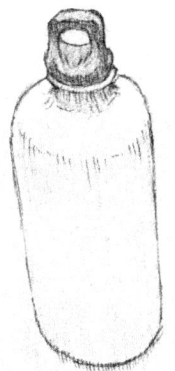

Water Bottle

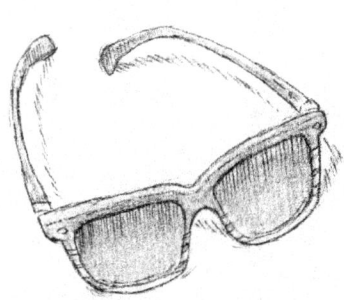

Sunnies

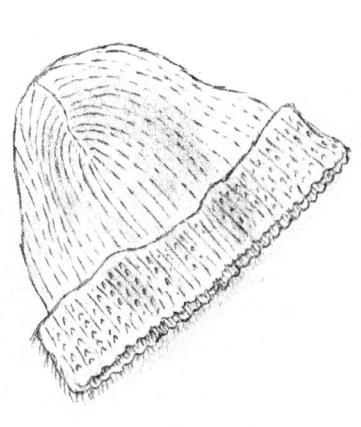

Woolly Hat

On The Tube

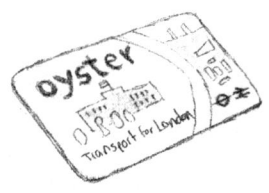

Being such a
multicultural city, the
great thing about sketching
people on the underground is
the endless variety. Each carriage
has people from different religions, cultures,
countries, all ages and fashion tastes. However
you often don't have much time between
stops, for either yourself or the person you're
drawing. This often leads to a quick scribble of
the head before the body disappears out the
door.

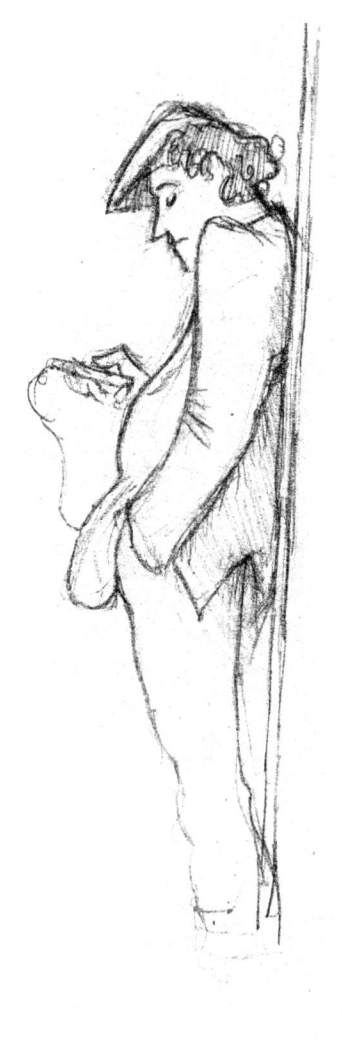

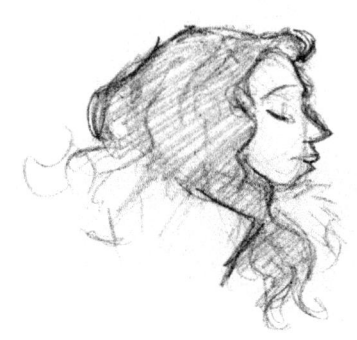

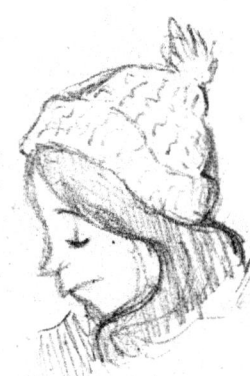

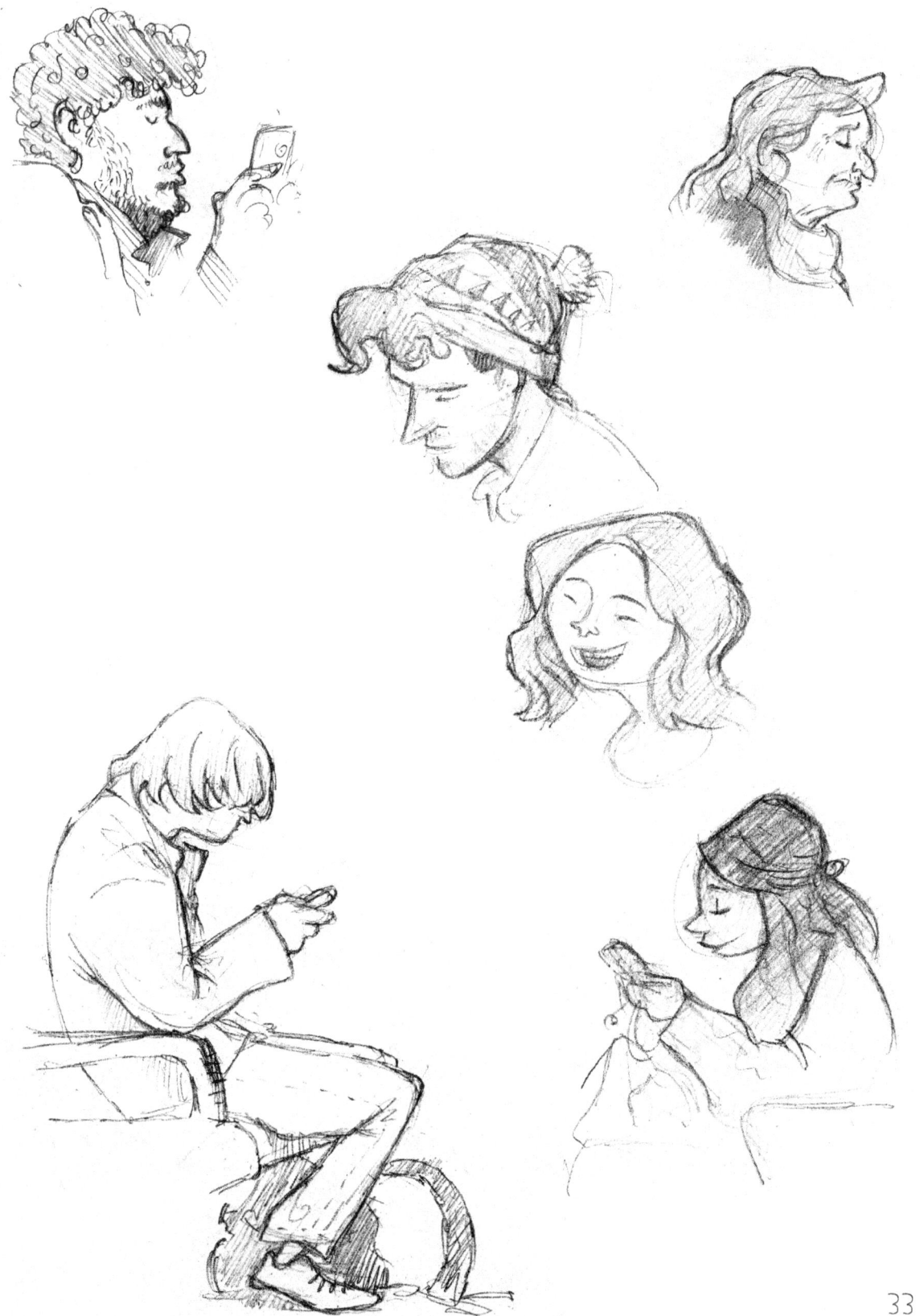

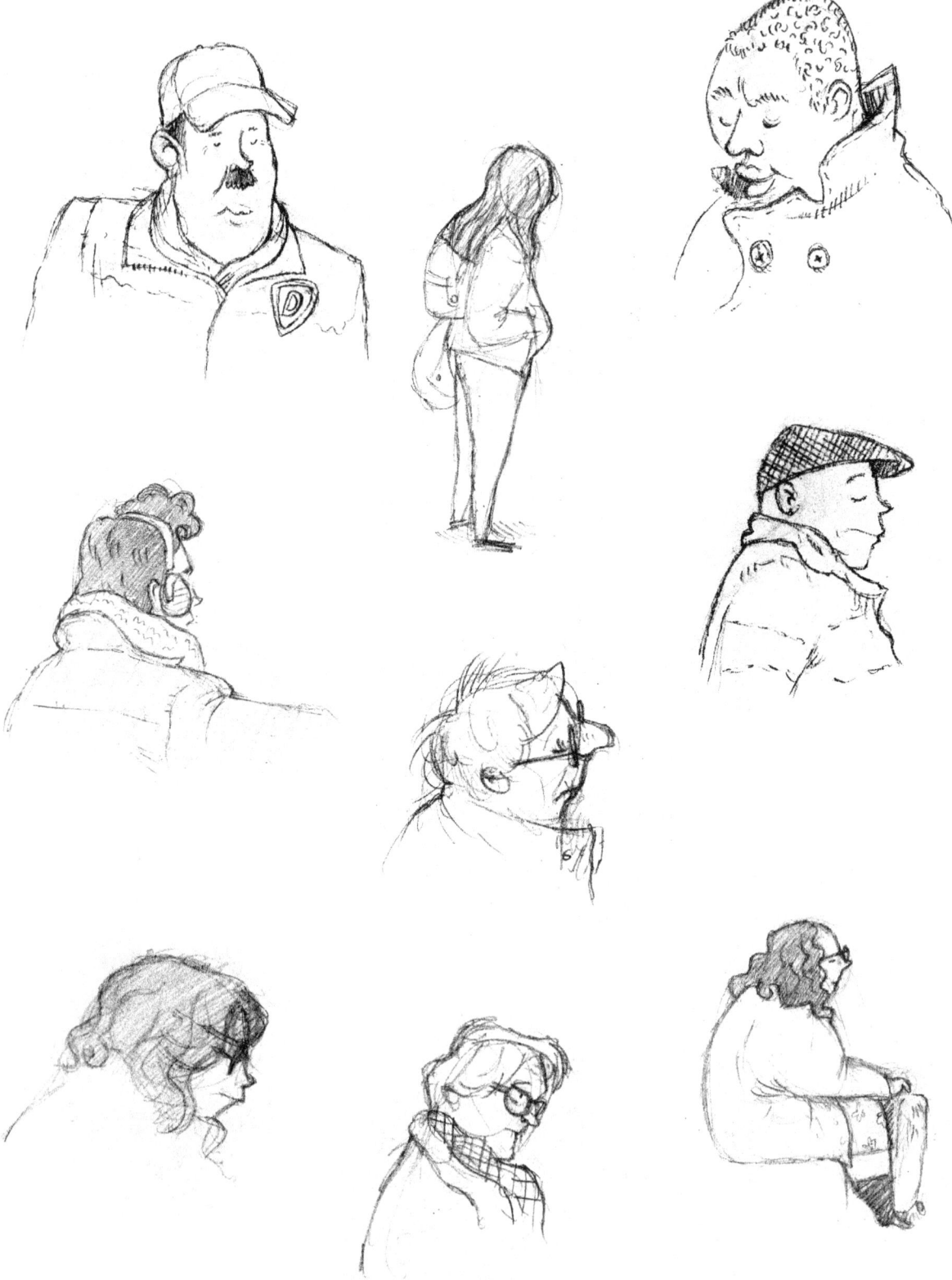

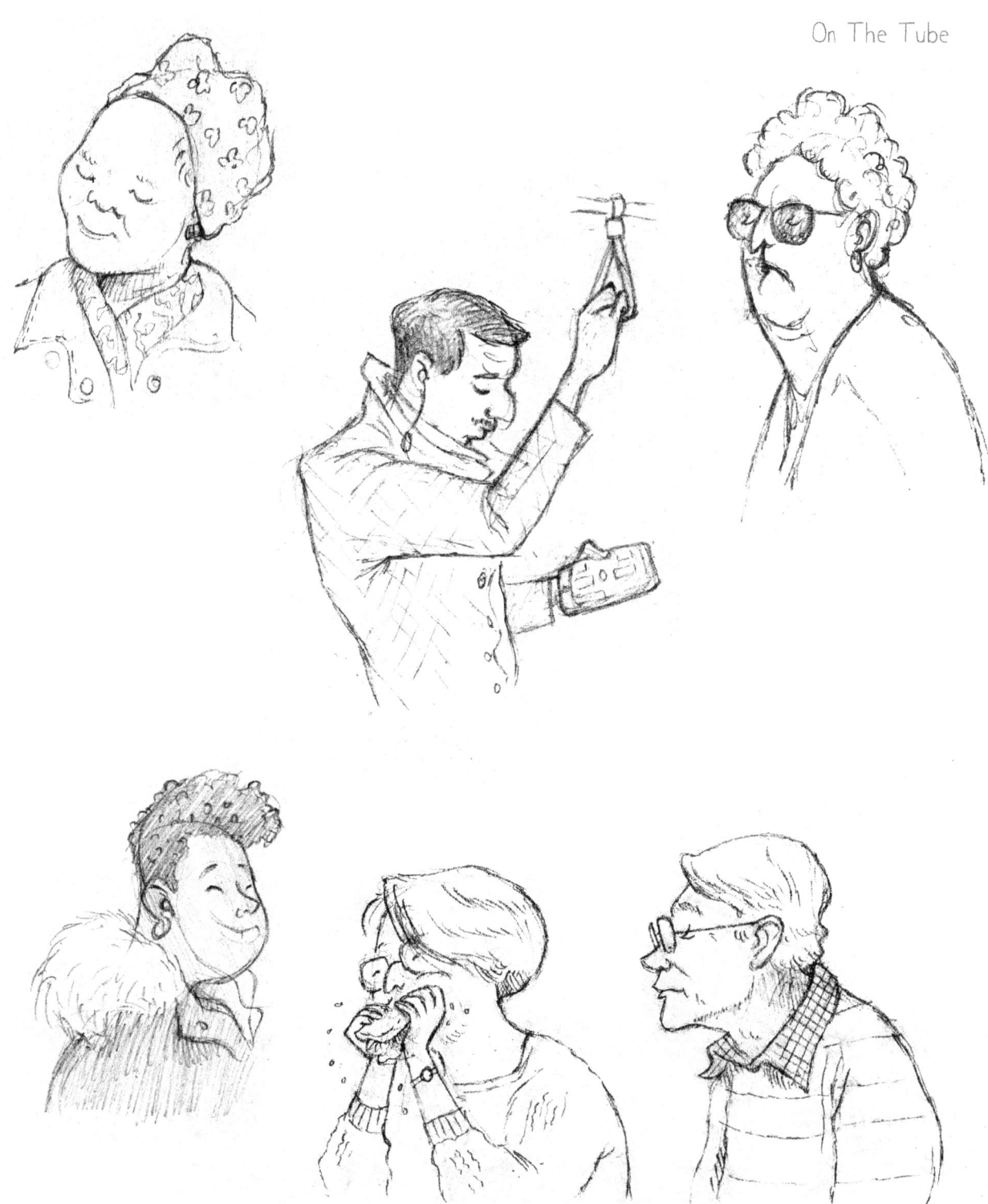

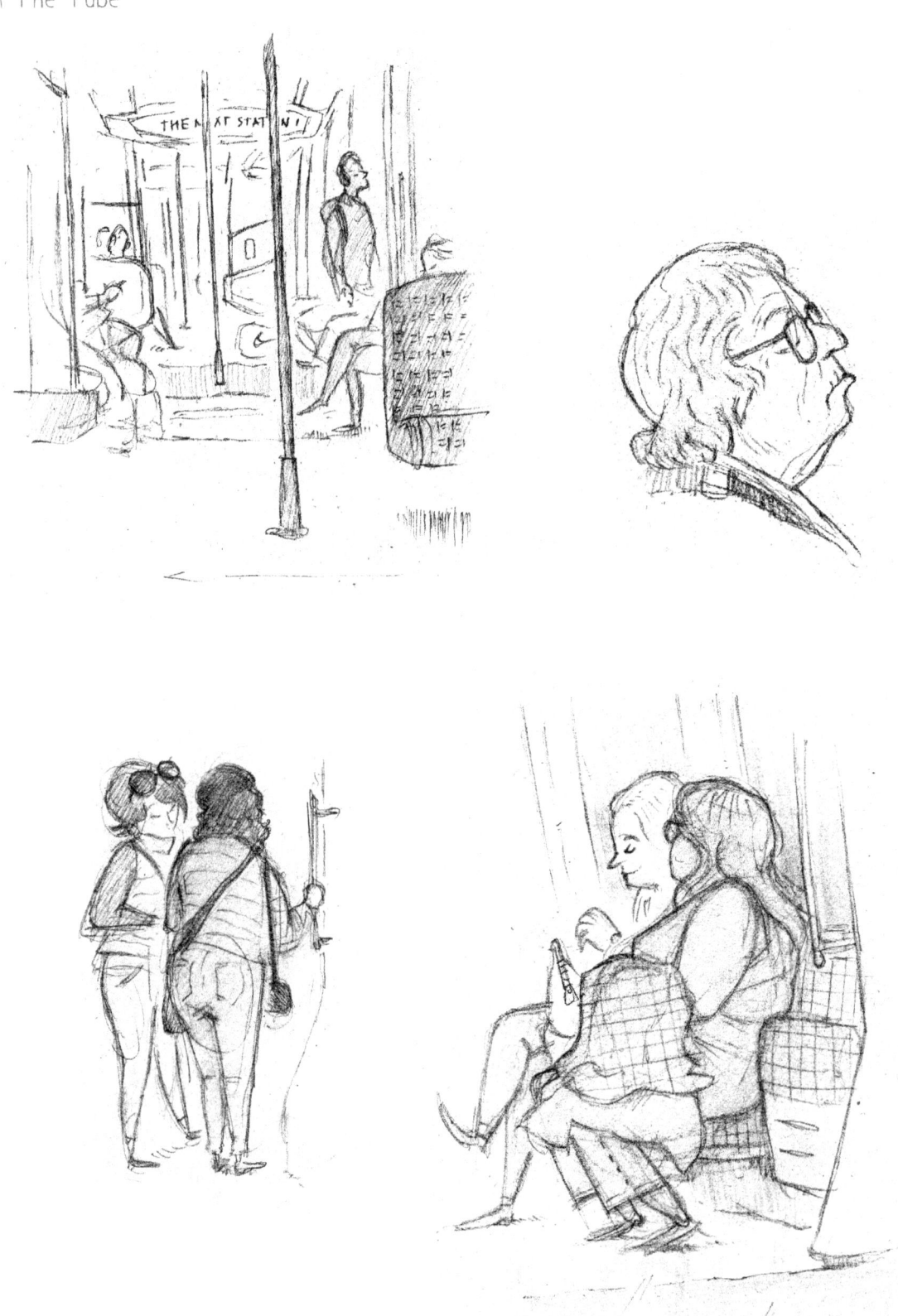

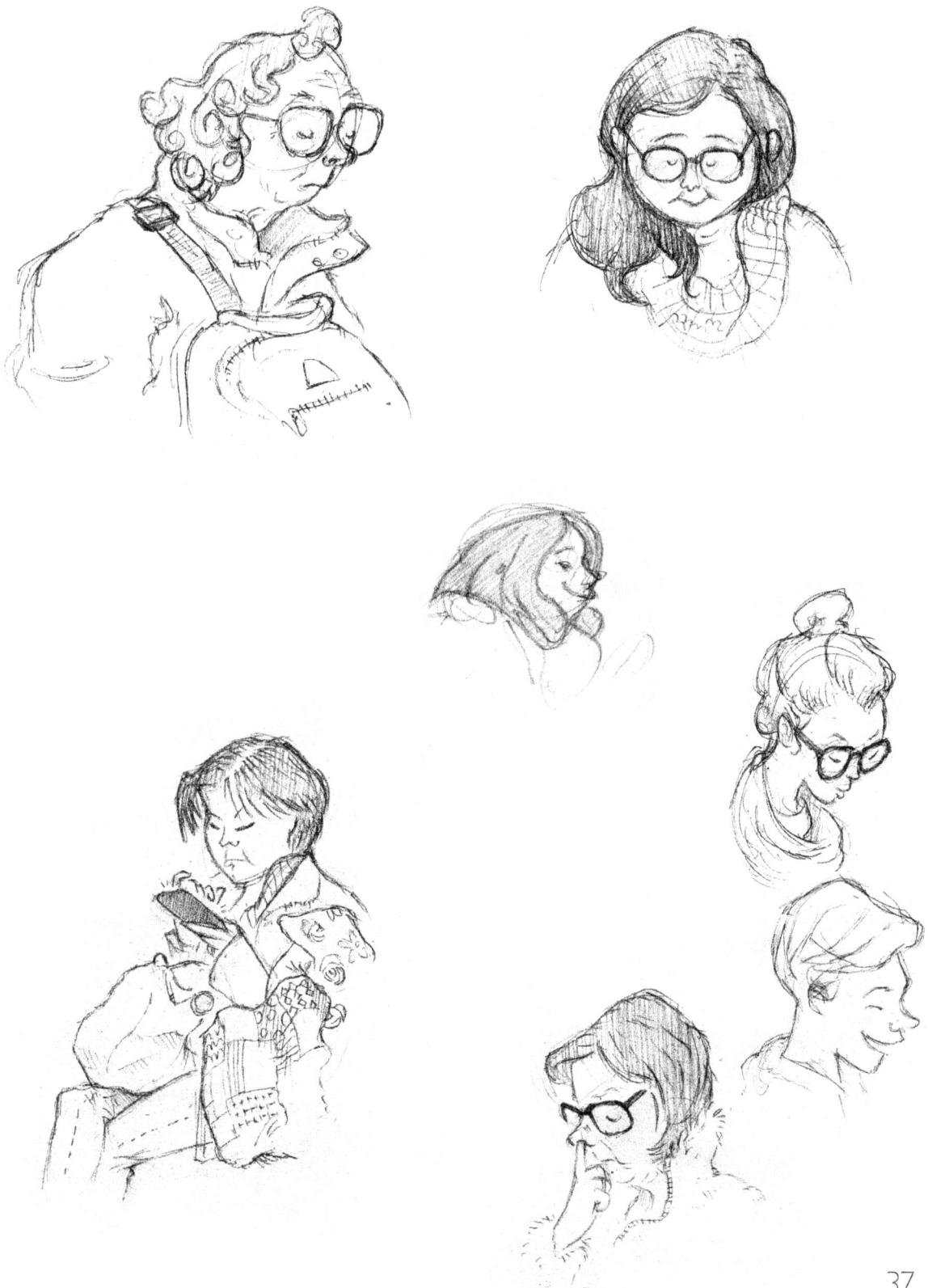

I have always taken great pleasure looking at artists rough sketches. You get to see the process and the decision making laid bare on the paper. When you know it is a brief piece of work you also get a looseness which allows, or can encourage you to make more fluid movements.

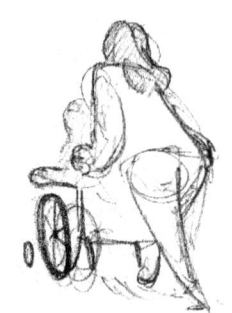

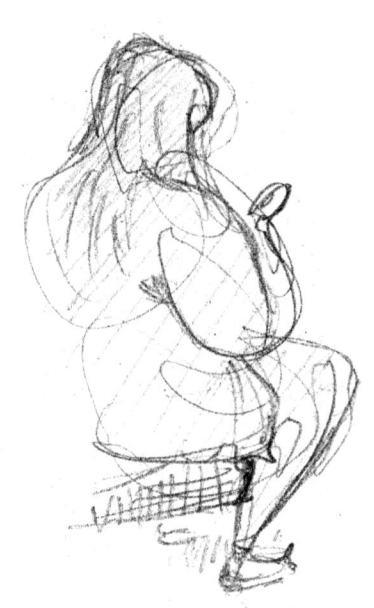

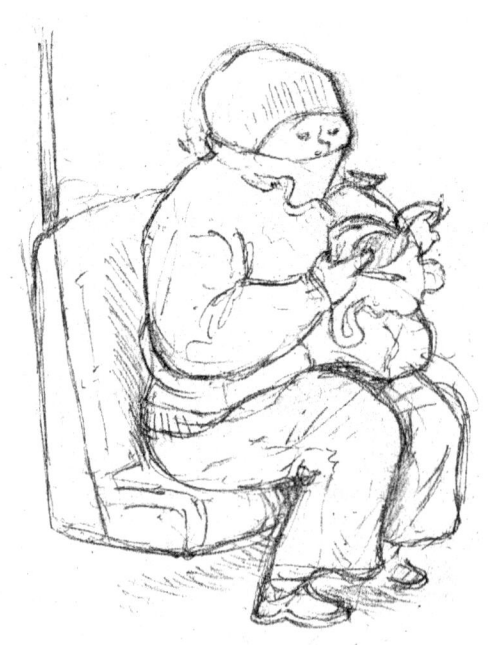

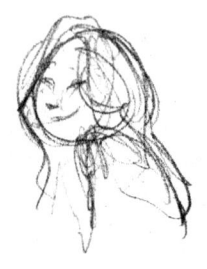

Camden

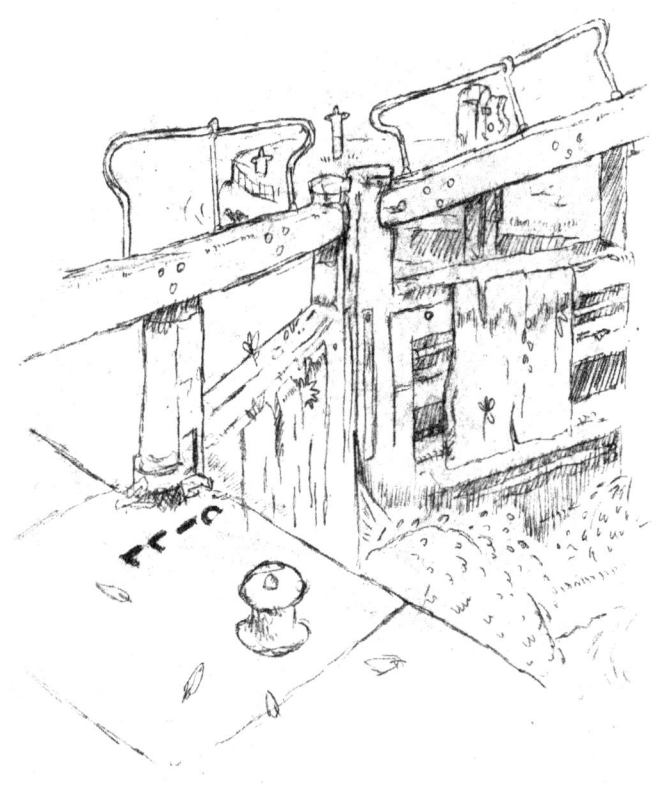

Camden Lock

Lincoln's Inn Fields

The largest public square in London includes tennis courts and some very big trees. Surrounding the square are many historic buildings including the Sir John Soane's Museum and the Royal College of Surgeons. In the latter can be found the Hunterian Museum containing many jars with specimens of varying gruesomeness. Just off the square you can also discover The Old Curiosity Shop of Charles Dickens fame, which may or may not have inspired him to write the novel of the same name.

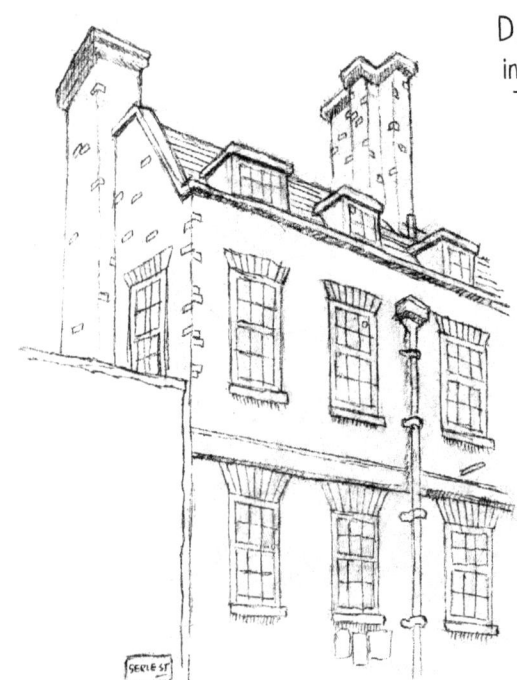

Trees

Drawing trees is an interesting challenge. To be able to represent the species of tree without giving too much detail away. Sometimes I think I should spend time sketching just trees. They are easy to take for granted but each species has a distinct shape and structure that needs to be understood to get their full character across.

Canadian Maple

Serle Street

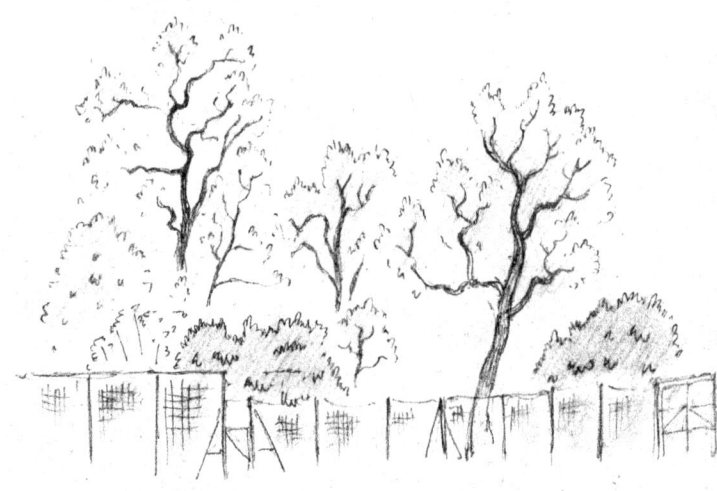

40

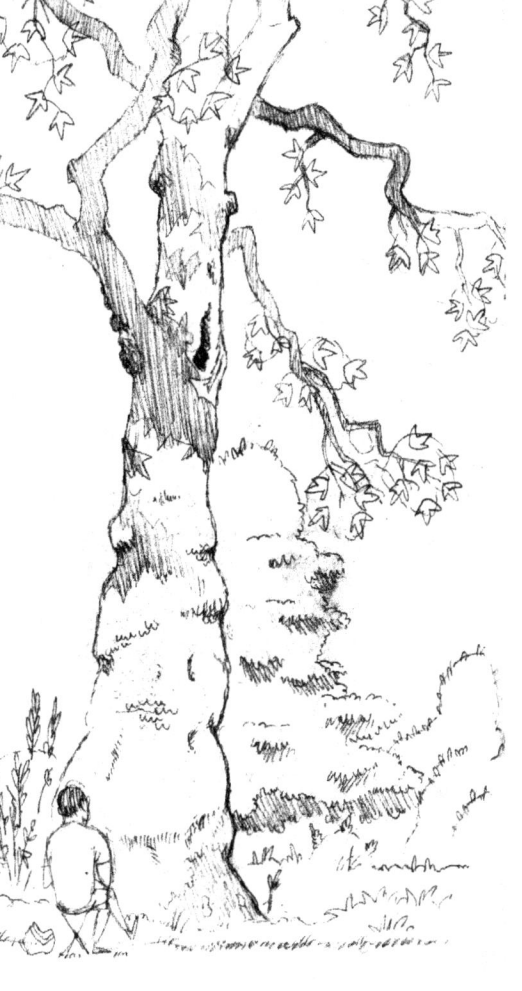

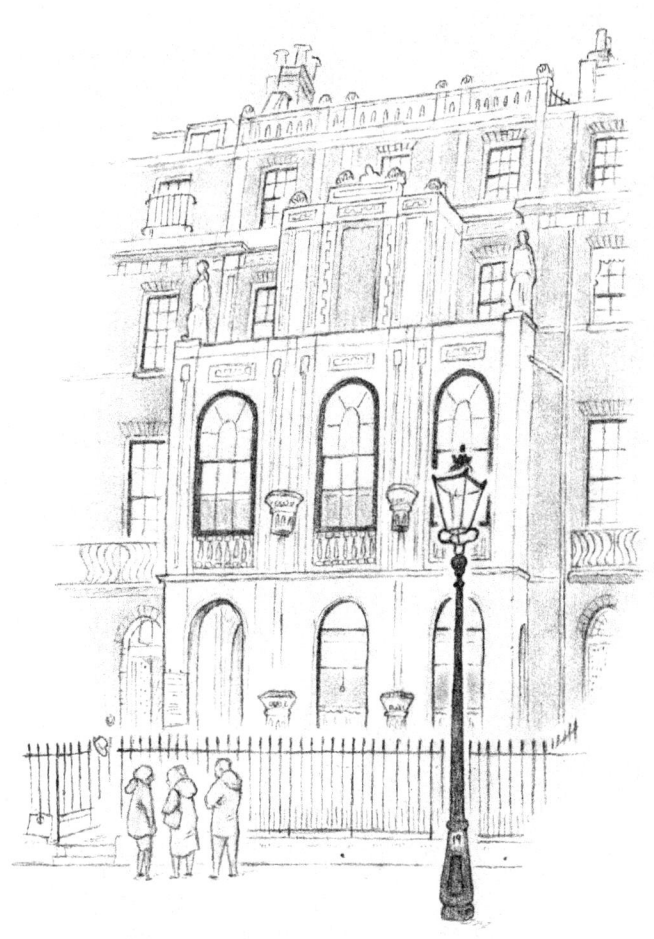

Sir John Soane's Museum

Another free museum, this one contains the lifetime collection of architect John Soane (1753 – 1837). Don't go in if you suffer from Catoptrophobia (a fear of mirrors).

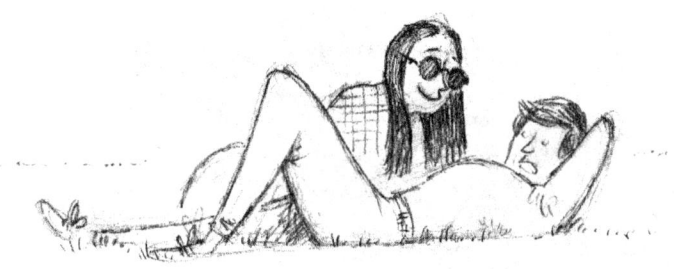

One corner of
Victoria House.

Bloomsbury Square

One of London's earliest garden squares, Bloomsbury's was originally laid out in the 1660s. The most impressive building currently surrounding the square is the imposing Victoria House to the east.

I often found myself sitting in this square on my way to a life drawing class in Holborn. Life drawing incidentally is a great way to improve drawing people, probably the toughest of subjects to tackle. It can help you learn to capture a persons pose or gesture and inturn describe a story or scene.

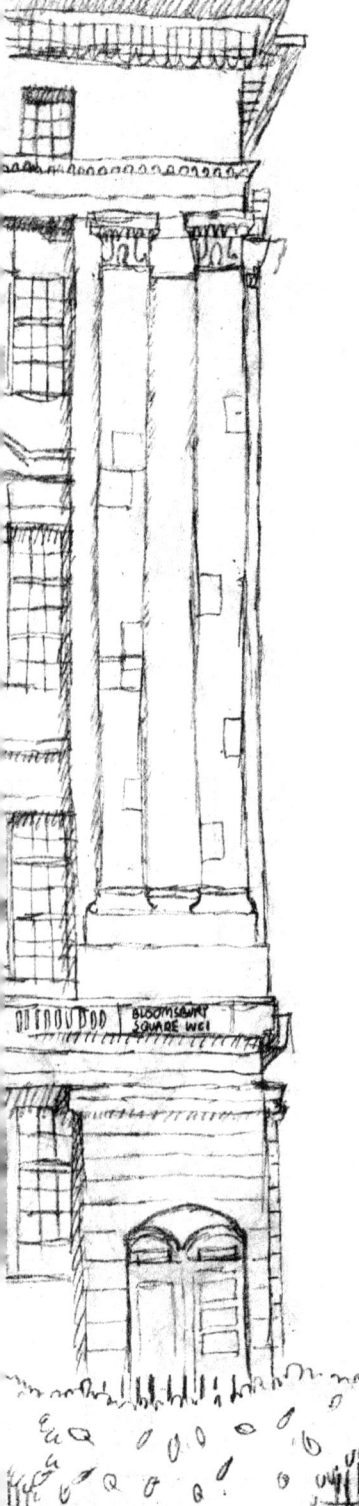

Housing on the west side of the square.

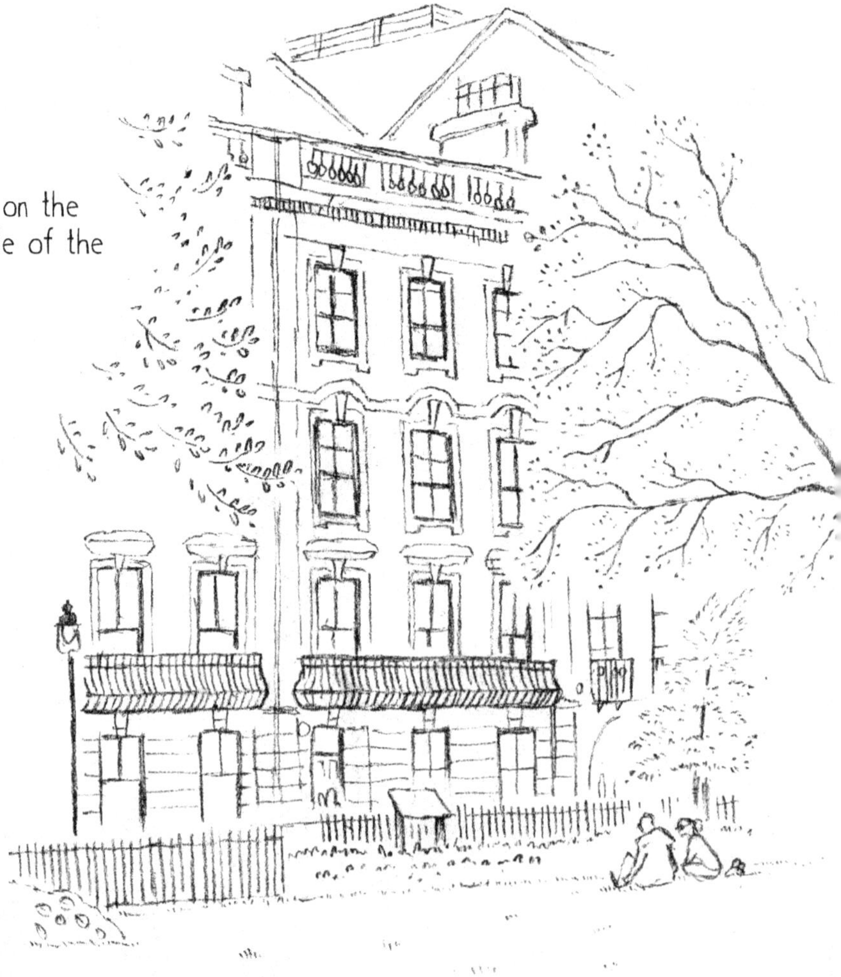

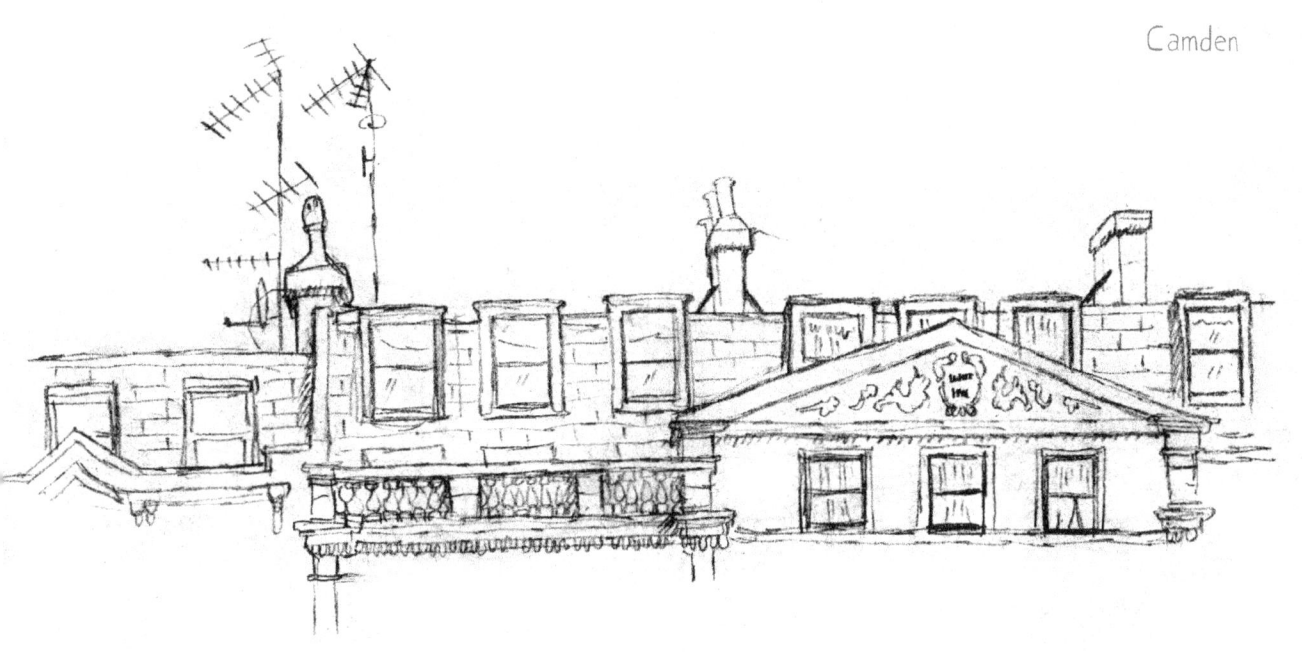

I love drawing rooftops and many in London have a unique charm.
I think it's the mixture of romantic styles and repetition of
features that make them so enjoyable to sketch. The heavy
concentration of windows, chimneys and television aerials
add a great deal of character to a small space. There
is also something very romantic about rooftops with
views. I'd imagine it would be a great place for an
artist to live.

Pigeons in
tree

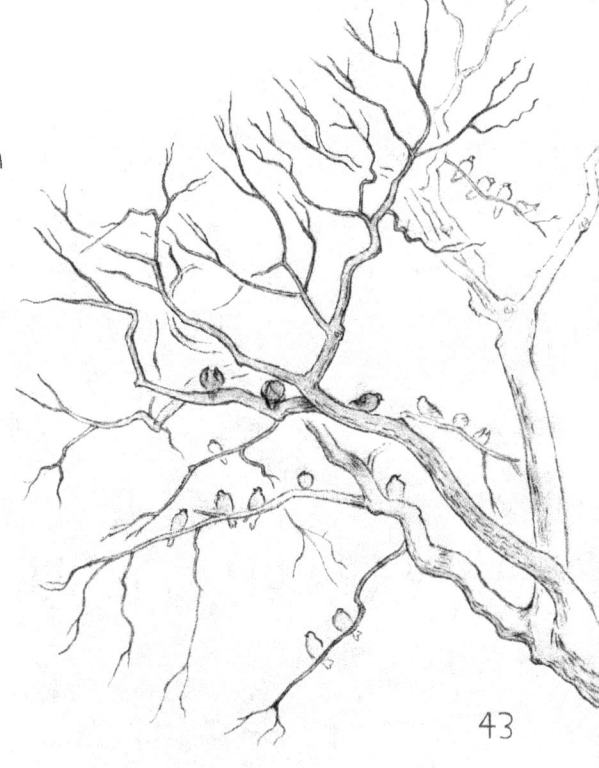

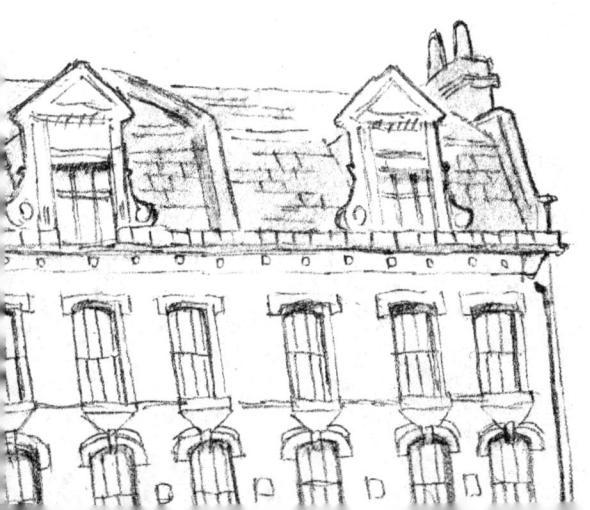

Brunswick Centre

A grade II listed structure designed by Patrick Hodgkinson and constructed between 1961-72. It combines 560 flats with shops, cafés, restaurants and a cinema.

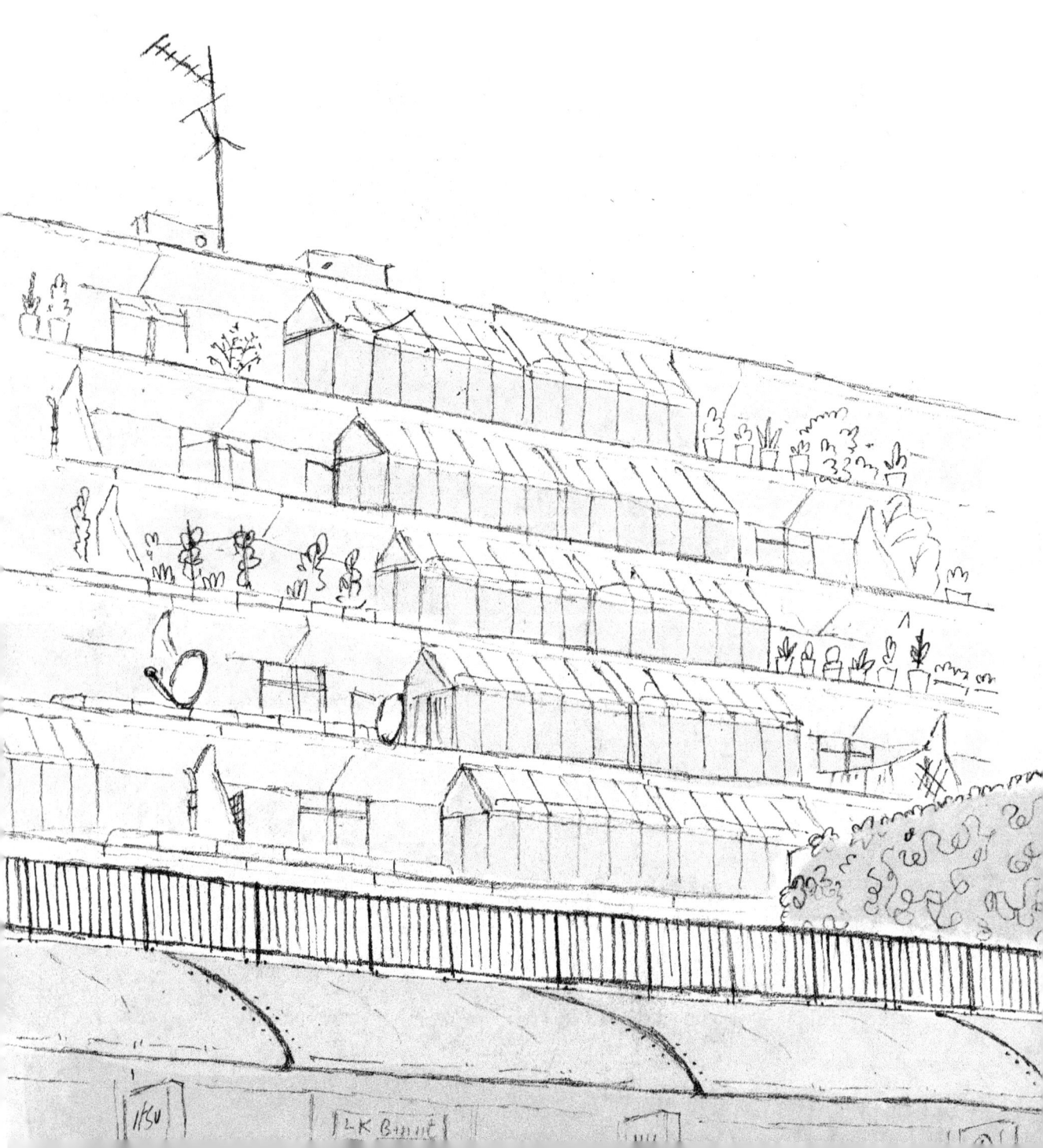

Shoppers at the Brunswick Centre

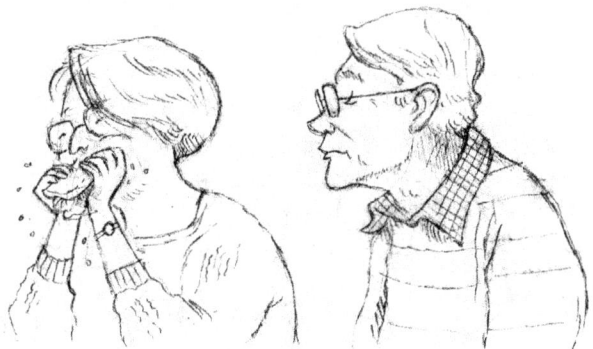

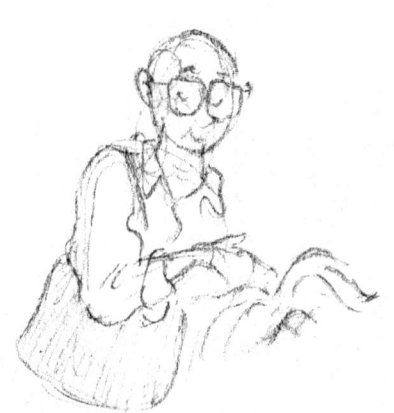

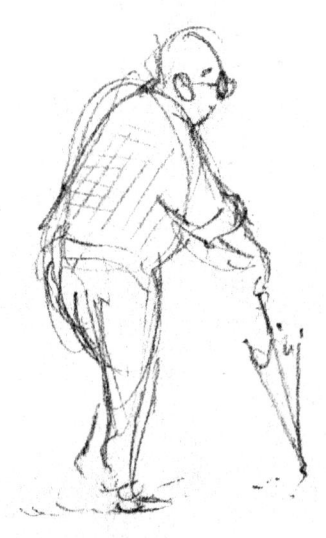

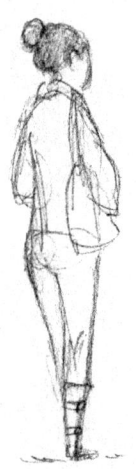

Highgate Cemetery

Opened in 1839 along with six other new city cemeteries in an effort to solve London's grave space crisis as its population expanded. Highgate now houses 53.000 graves containing more than 170,000 people. That's quite a person to grave ratio.
Amongst the many notable people laid to rest here are Dickens' wife, parents and brother, Jeremy Beadle and Ralph Milliband. What a mix. Also the writer Douglas Adams rests here with a small pot of pens next to his grave stone (see below).

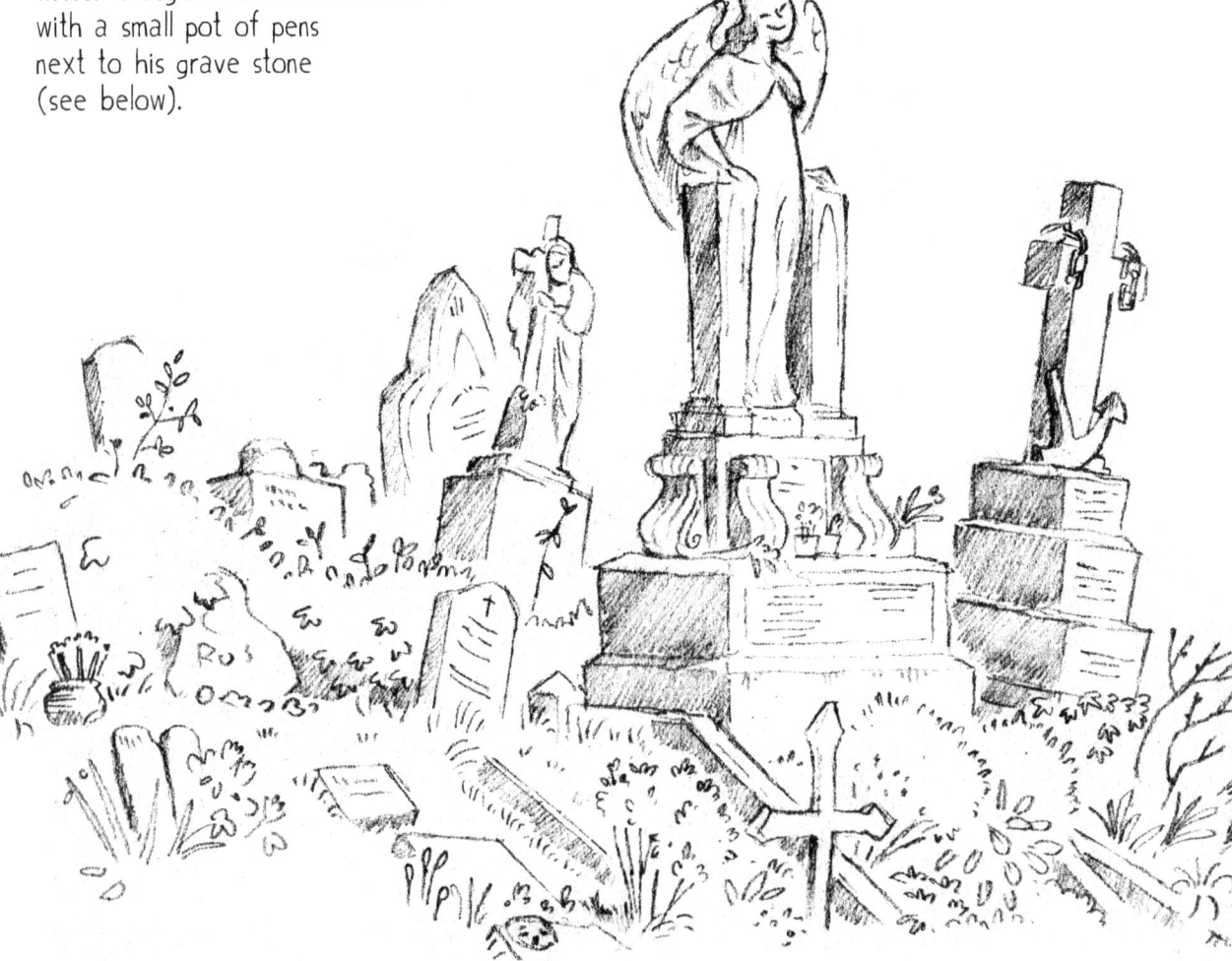

Evelyn Muriel Dray M.B.E. (1889 - 1926) & Family

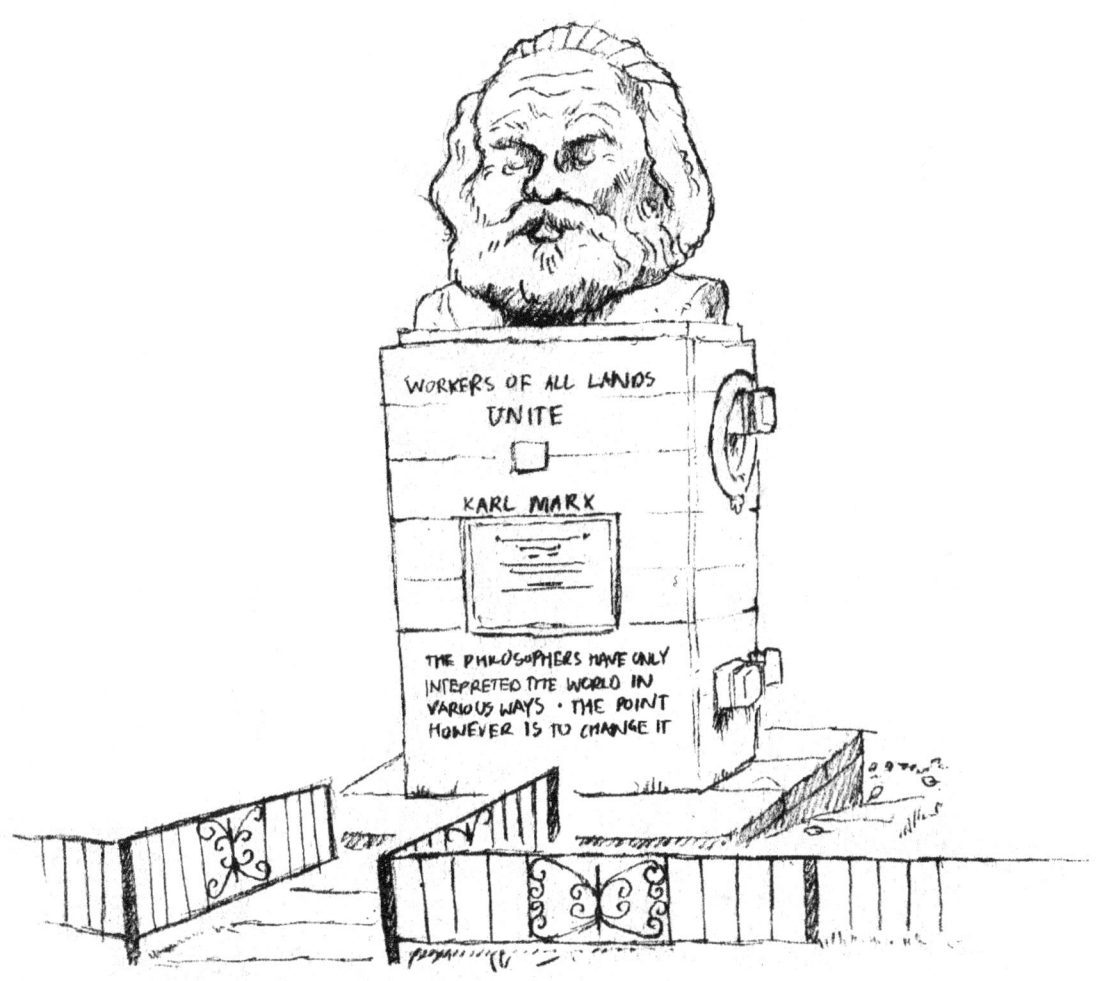

Karl Heinrich Marx, 1818 – 1883

The father of modern communism moved to London in 1849 where he was to write the book 'Das Kapital'.

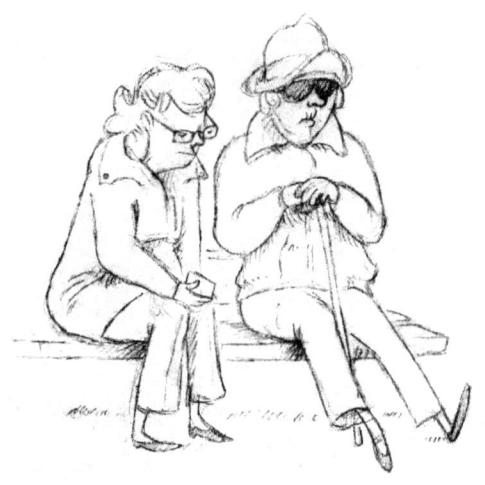

Ladies relaxing on a bench at the top of Primrose Hill.

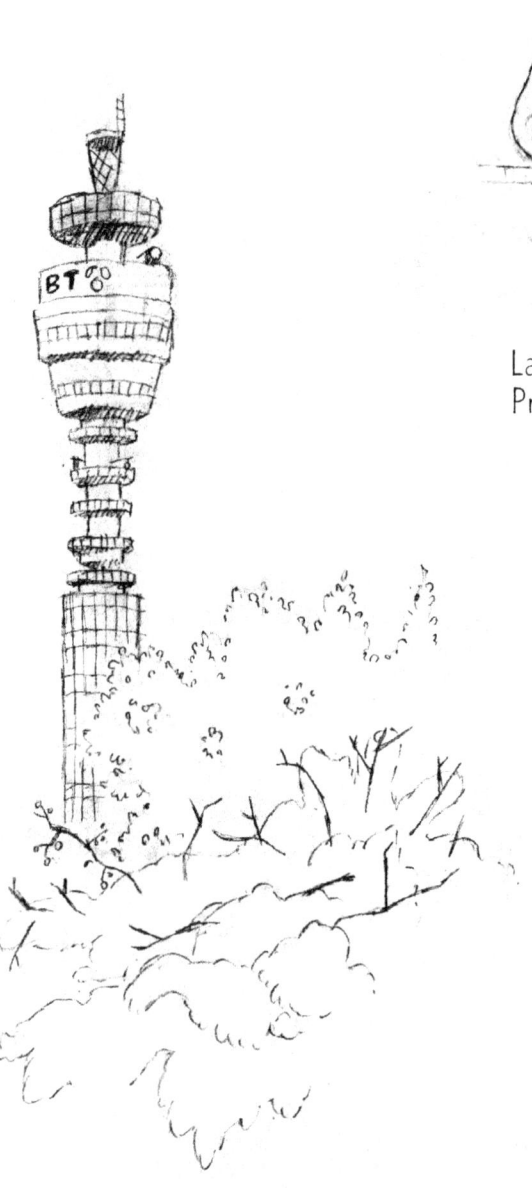

BT Tower, 177m

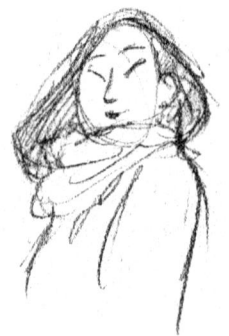

Medium

All the sketches in this book were created using the humble pencil and most of them with a simple HB. Nothing particularly arty about that. There is something very suited to the task of sketching with a pencil. It in no way imposes any thoughts of finality as you draw, encouraging you to loosen up. Of course you can sketch with ink or paint, (you can sketch with anything you like really) but a more permanent medium can sometimes engender a lack of freedom. The pencil invokes images of scribbled ideas, drafting designs, my grandfather calculating on a scrap of paper or my father with one tucked behind his ear. There is also something gratifying about a pencil lasting such a long time. In fact I don't think I have ever really finished one. I remember discovering incredibly short, almost unusable pencils lying around my grandparents house as a child. Mine always seem to go missing before they get to that stage.

When it comes to sharpening I prefer to use a knife rather than a pencil sharpener. I don't suppose it makes much difference to the work, although you can see more of the lead. I think it's more about the sculpted shape of the wood that appeals to me.

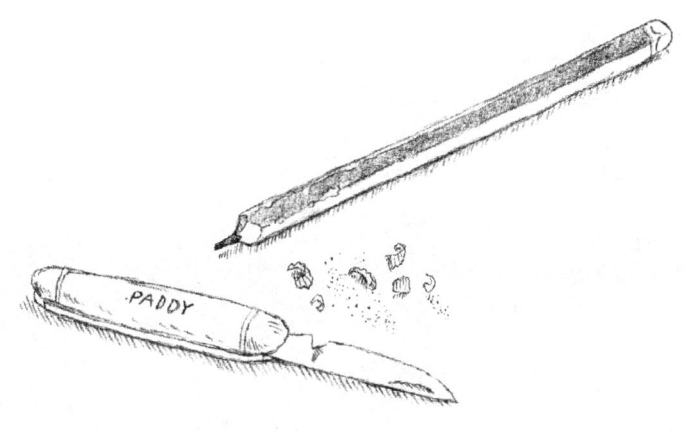

49

Sketching With Others

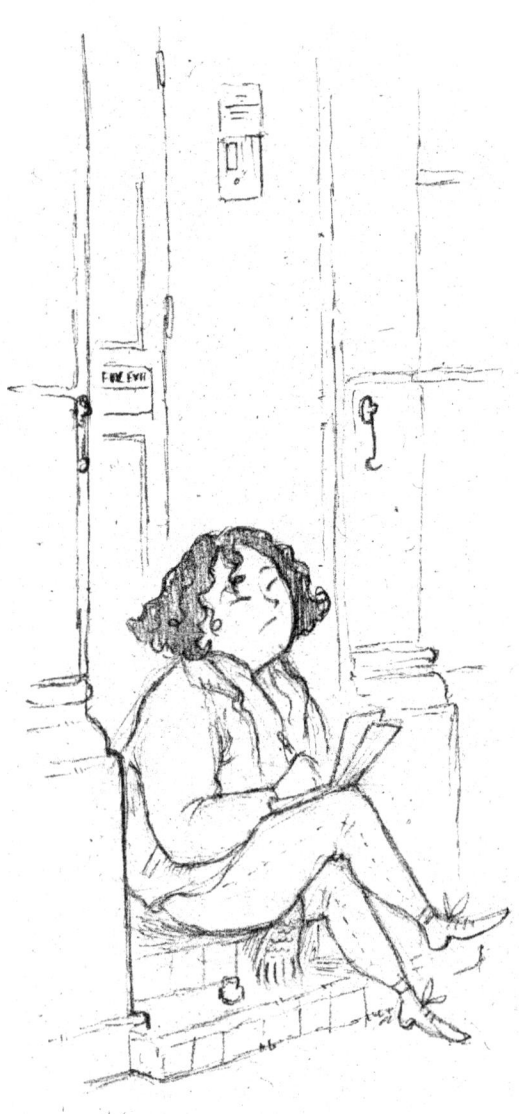

Sketching is often thought of as a solitary activity, much like painting or writing. Indeed as with other artistic practices, the concentration needed to get the most out of your work does not always make conversation easy. Especially not for those of us who struggle with multi-tasking like myself.

So it was fantastic to discover there are plenty of groups in London that meet up to sketch together. Sketching attracts people from all walks of life, not just those with a background or profession in art. It's a great way to meet others with the same outlook on life and explore a new environment, (or rediscover a familiar one). You always look at your surroundings with a fresher, more inquisitive eye when searching for something to sketch. Then at the end of the day people get together to share their work over a drink.

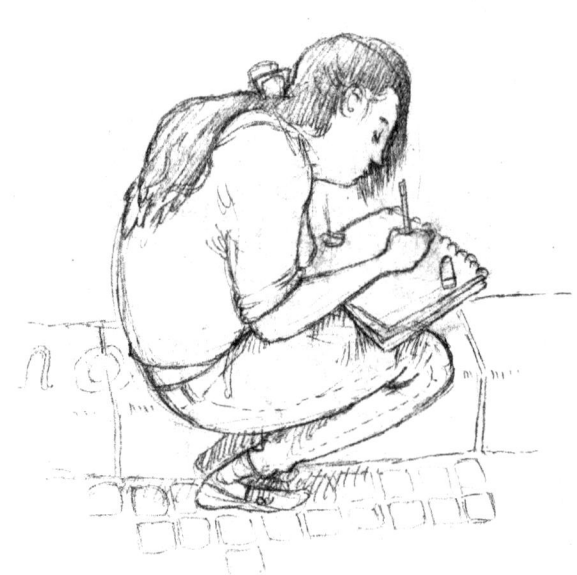

Islington

The Royal Agricultural Hall
(now the Business Design Centre)

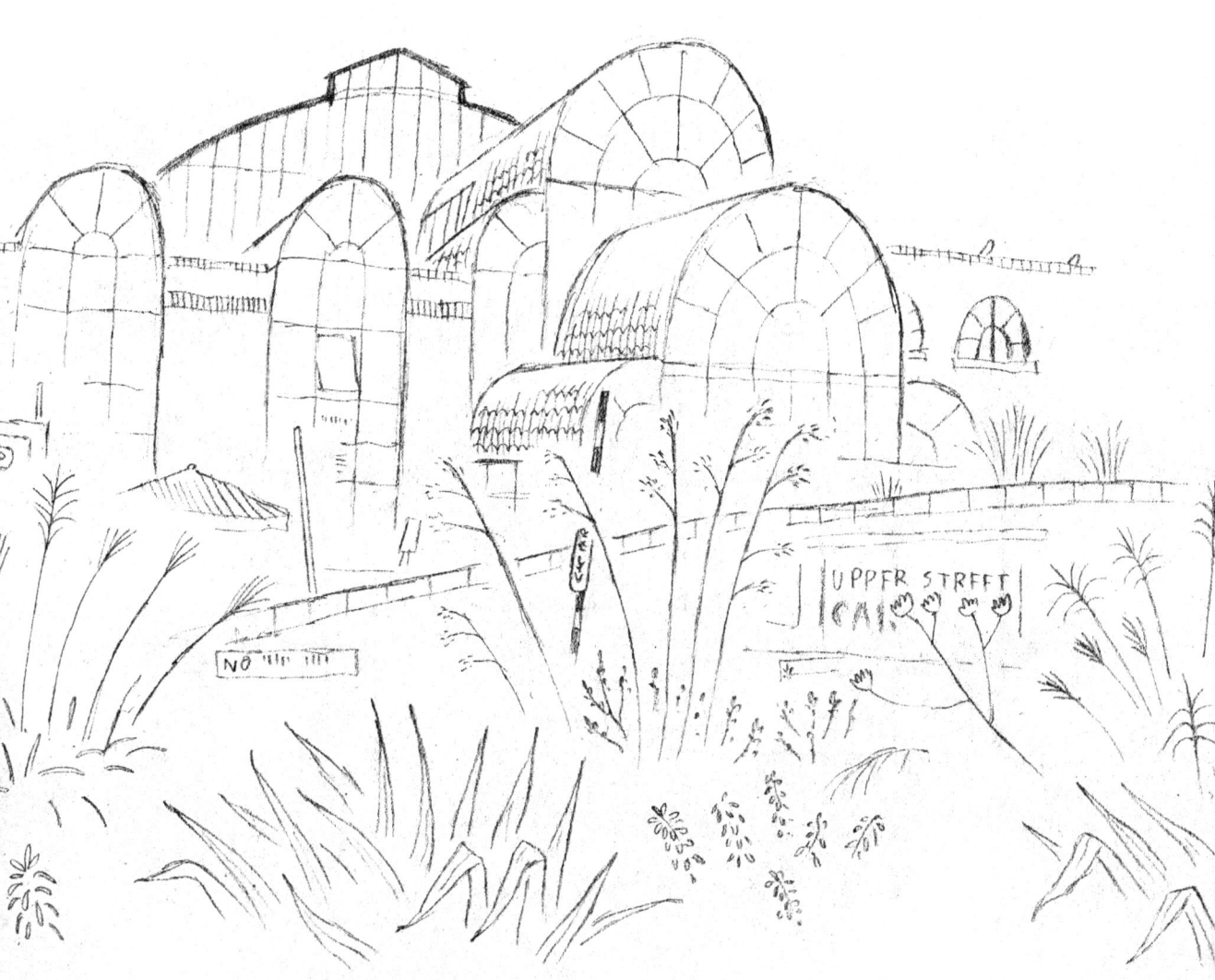

Kings Place

Opened in 2008, this modern, wavy building
hosts businesses and public art exhibitions,
lectures and concerts.

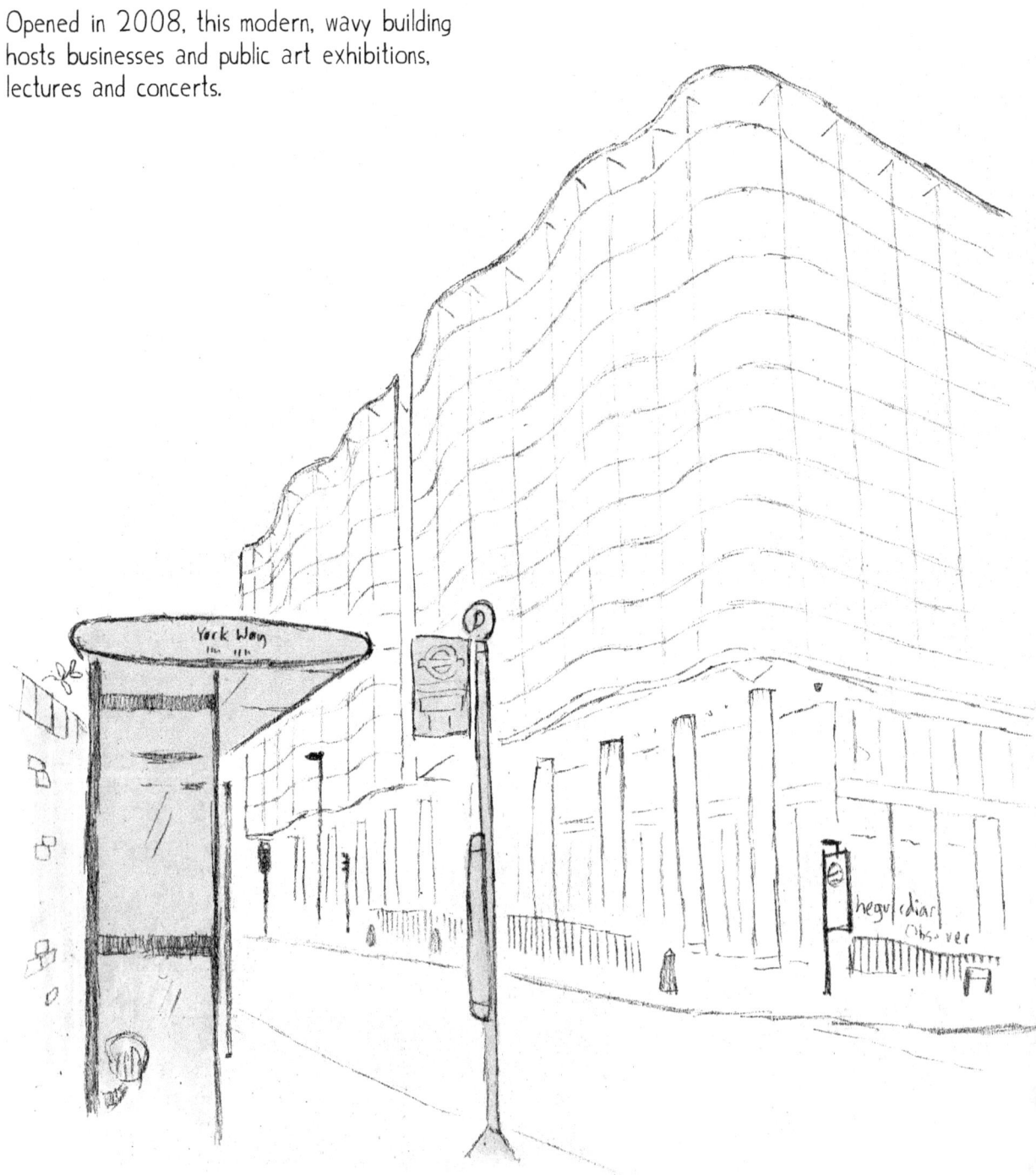

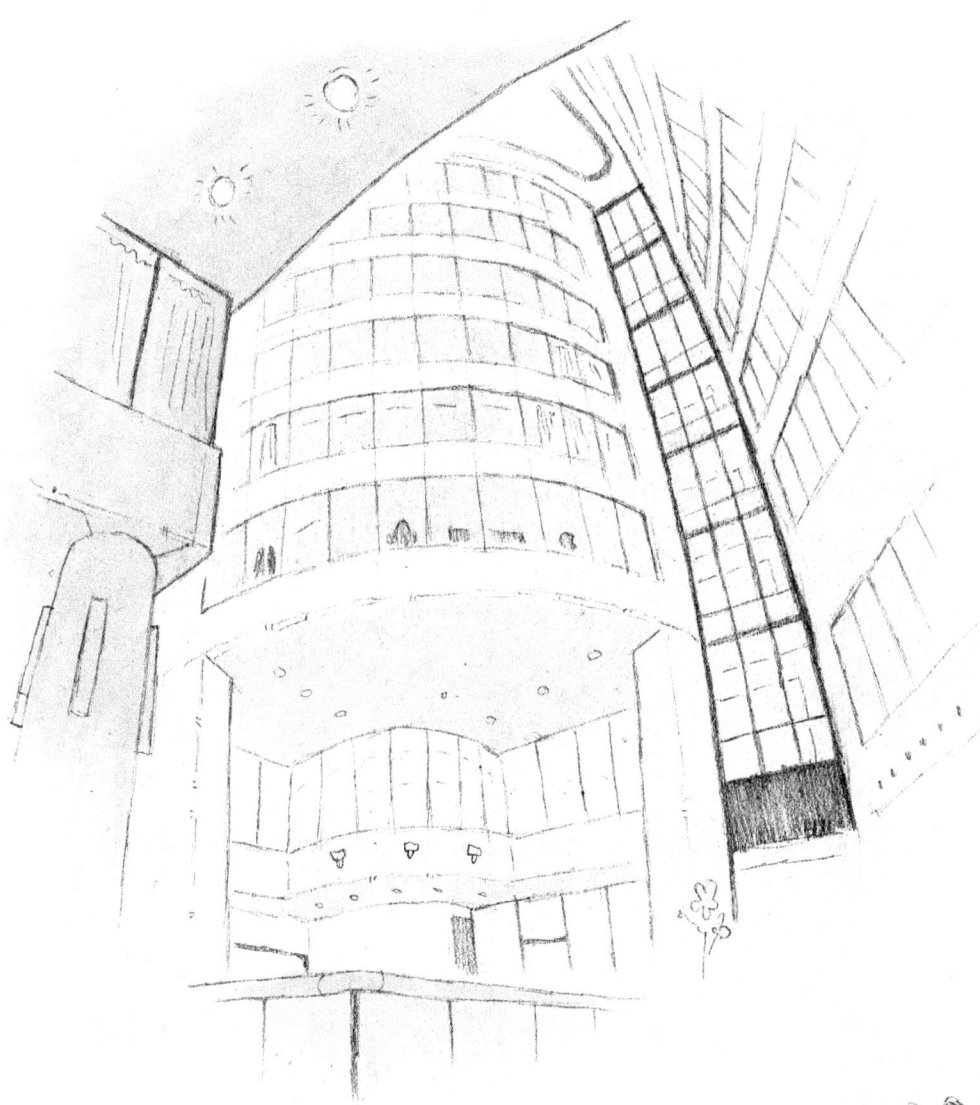

Inside Kings Place the central space is open plan looking up towards the off ices and down to the art galleries below. With a cafe, bar and plenty of comfy sofas this is a great place to have a midday meet, for business or pleasure.

The Angel Building

Opened in late 2010, this redeveloped
office space by Allford Hall Monaghan
Morris has been nominated for design
& architecture awards including the
Sterling prise for architecture short-list
2011.

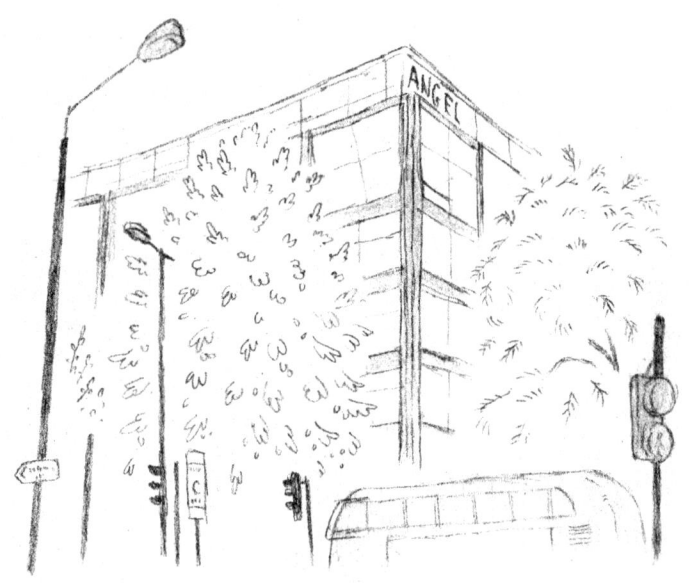

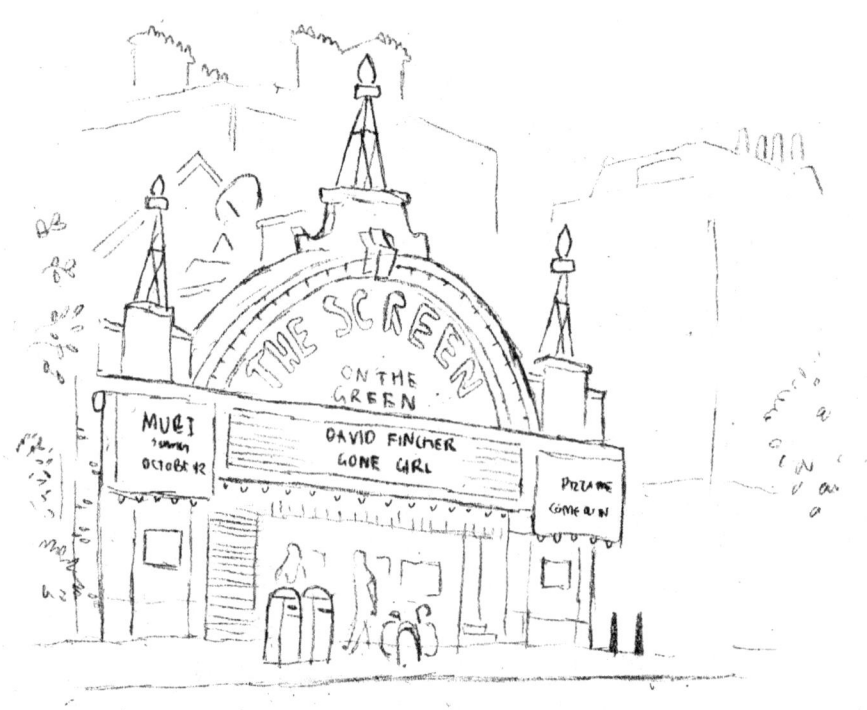

The Screen on The Green cinema, 83 Upper Street

Opened under another name in 1913, this is one of the oldest continuously
running cinemas in the country. It also has stature in the music world, hosting the
first public performance of the sex pistols to include Sid Vicious in 1977.

City of London

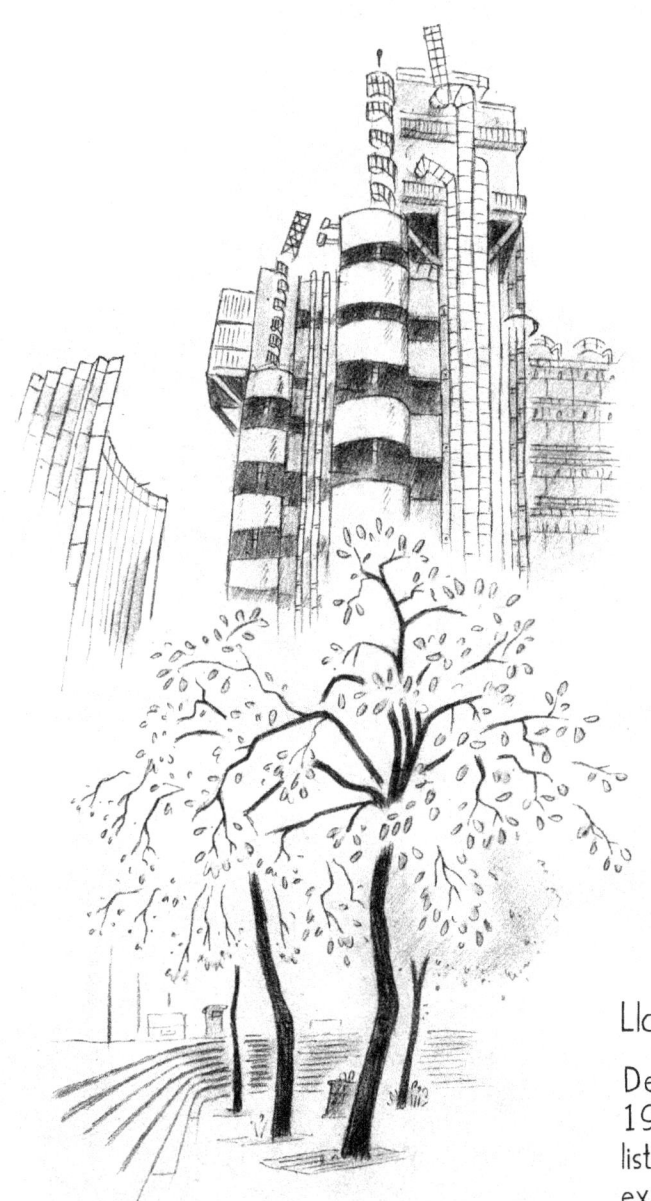

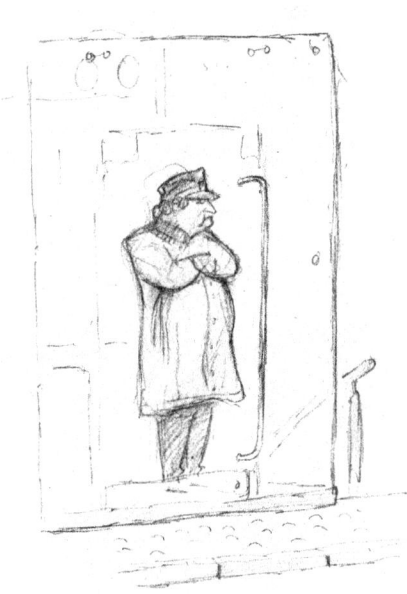

Lift man at Lloyd's

Lloyd's Building

Designed by Richard Rogers and opened in 1986, it stands at 95m and in 2011 was listed as a grade 1 building. It's notable as an example of Bowellism architecture, with the buildings services on the outside.

Sir Christopher Wren's Churches

After the great fire of London in 1666 there were 87 city churches that needed rebuilding. The architect Sir Christopher Wren was given the job to redesign 51 of these. These can be found within walking distance of each other, so if you like small churches the City of London is the place to go.

St Mary-le-Bow

Est. late 11th Century, rebuilt 1673

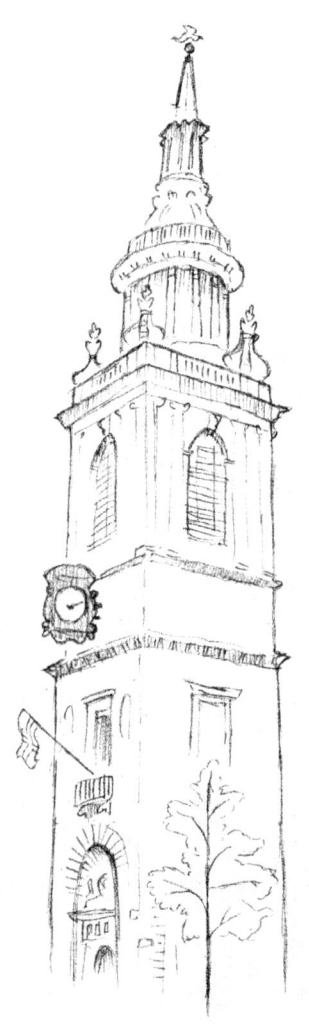

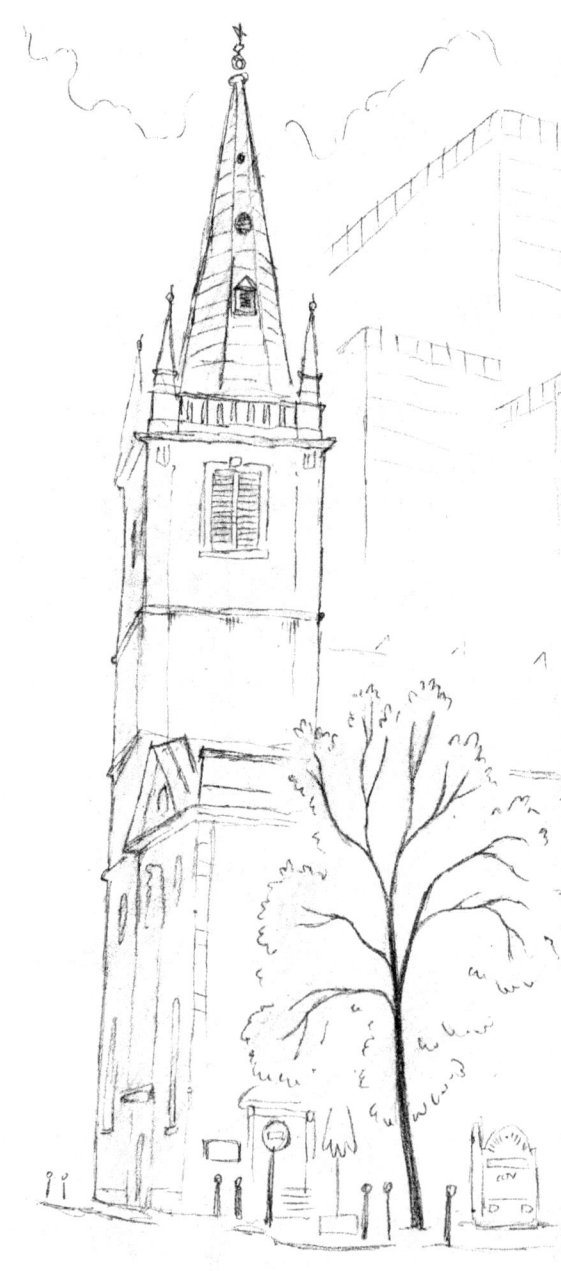

St Margaret Pattens
Est. 1067, rebuilt 1687

St Edmund, King & Martyr
Est. around 900, rebuilt 1679

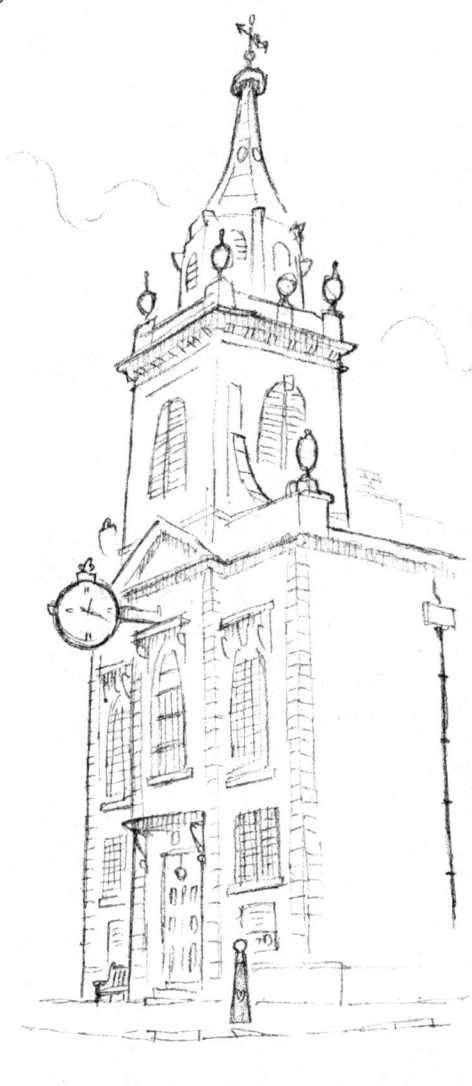

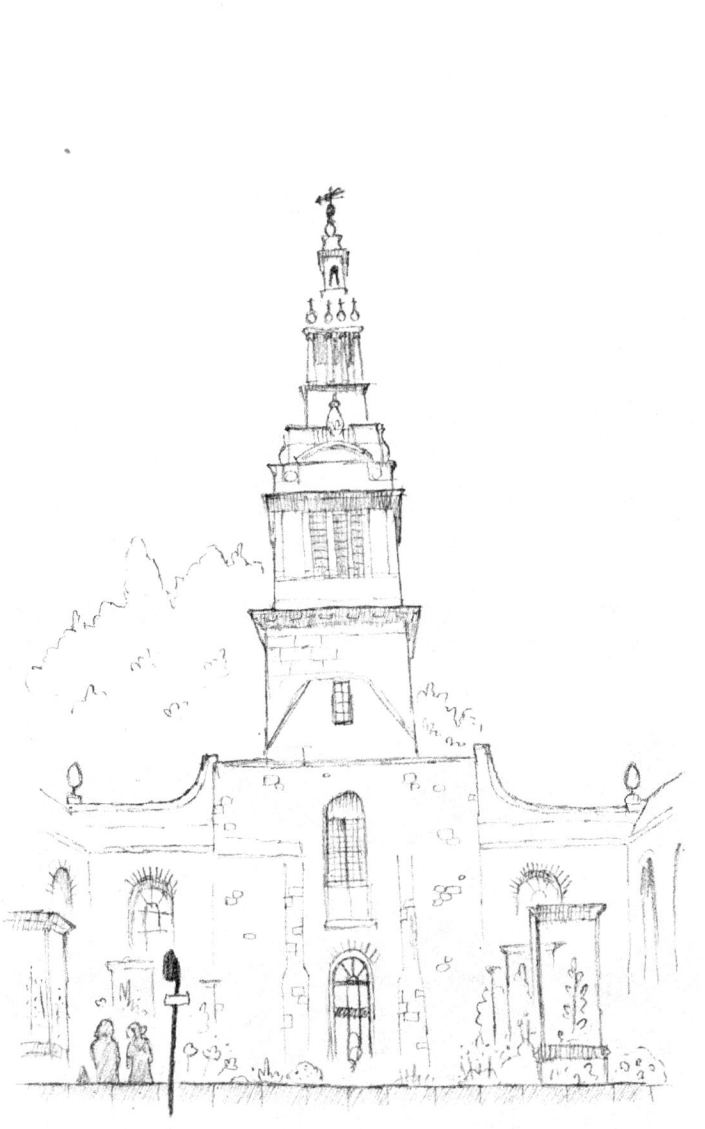

Christ Church Greyfriars
Est. 1225, rebuilt 1704

St Magnus the Martyr,
Rebuilt 1687

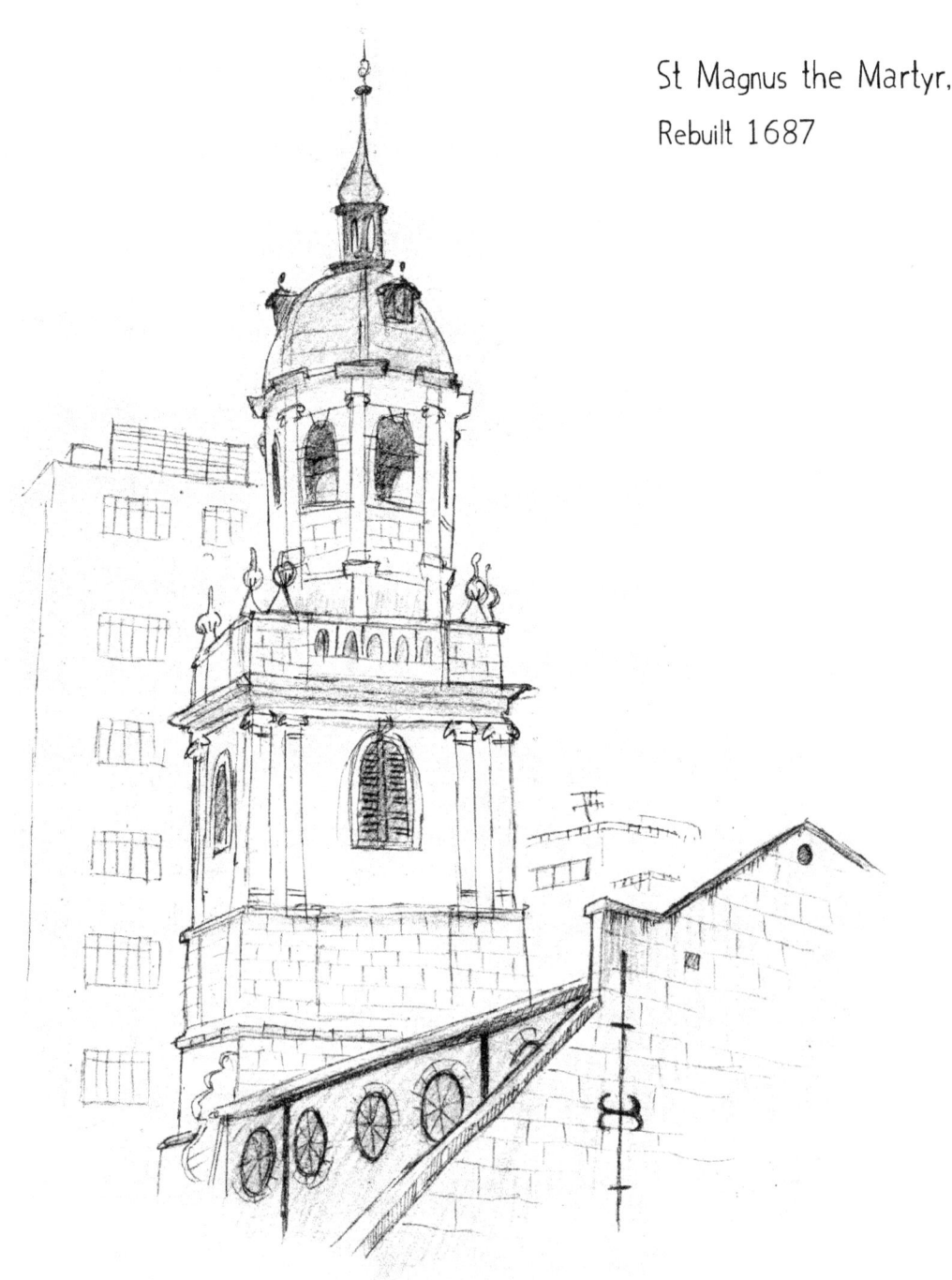

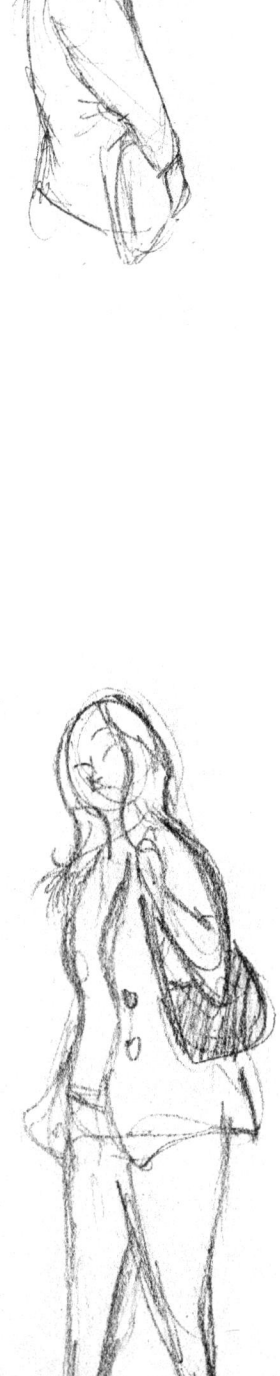

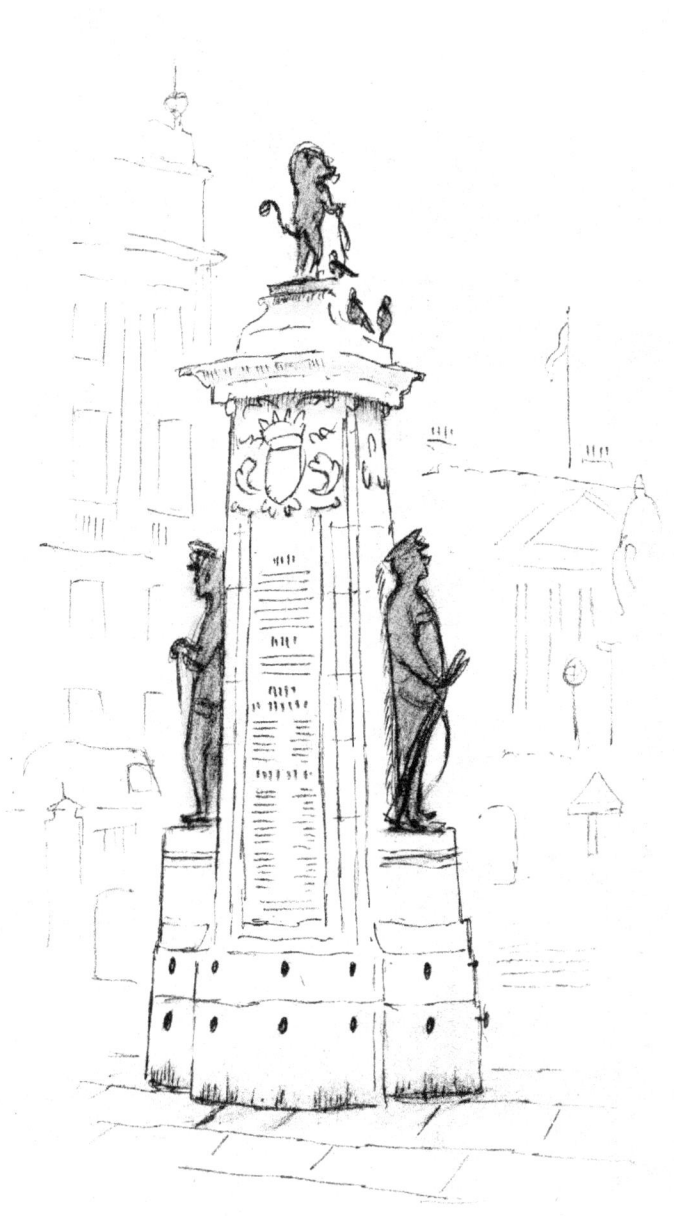

War Memorial to London Troops, London Exchange

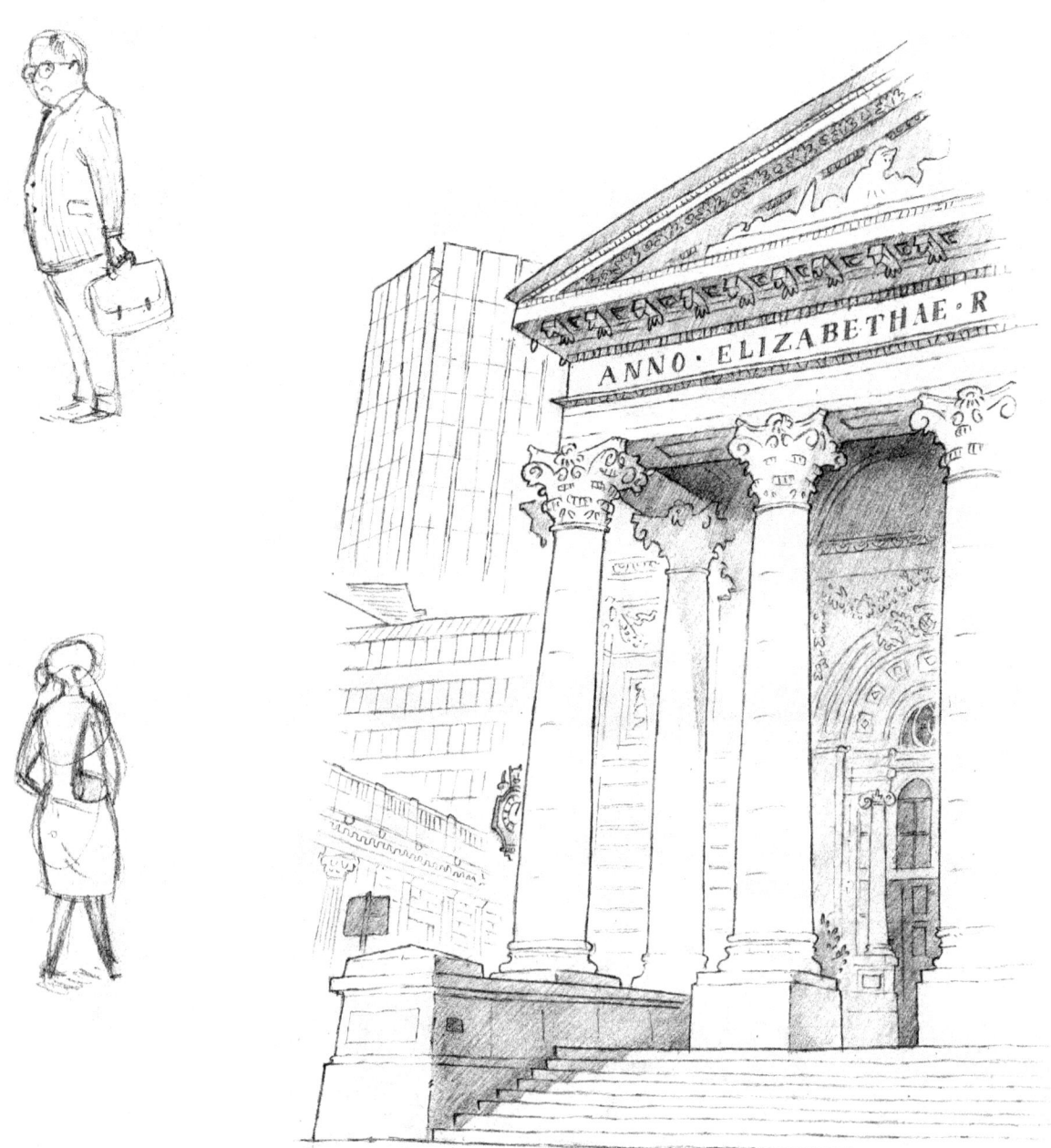

Royal Exchange

Originally opened in 1571 by Queen Elizabeth I before being destroyed by fire in 1666 and again in 1838, this was to serve as a centre for commerce in the city. Trading ceased at the outbreak of the Second World War and since its refurbishment in 2001, it now houses luxury shops.

Leadenhall Building, (under construction)

Nicknamed the Cheese-grater, this Richard Rodgers designed building stands at 225m with 48 floors. Completed in 2014.

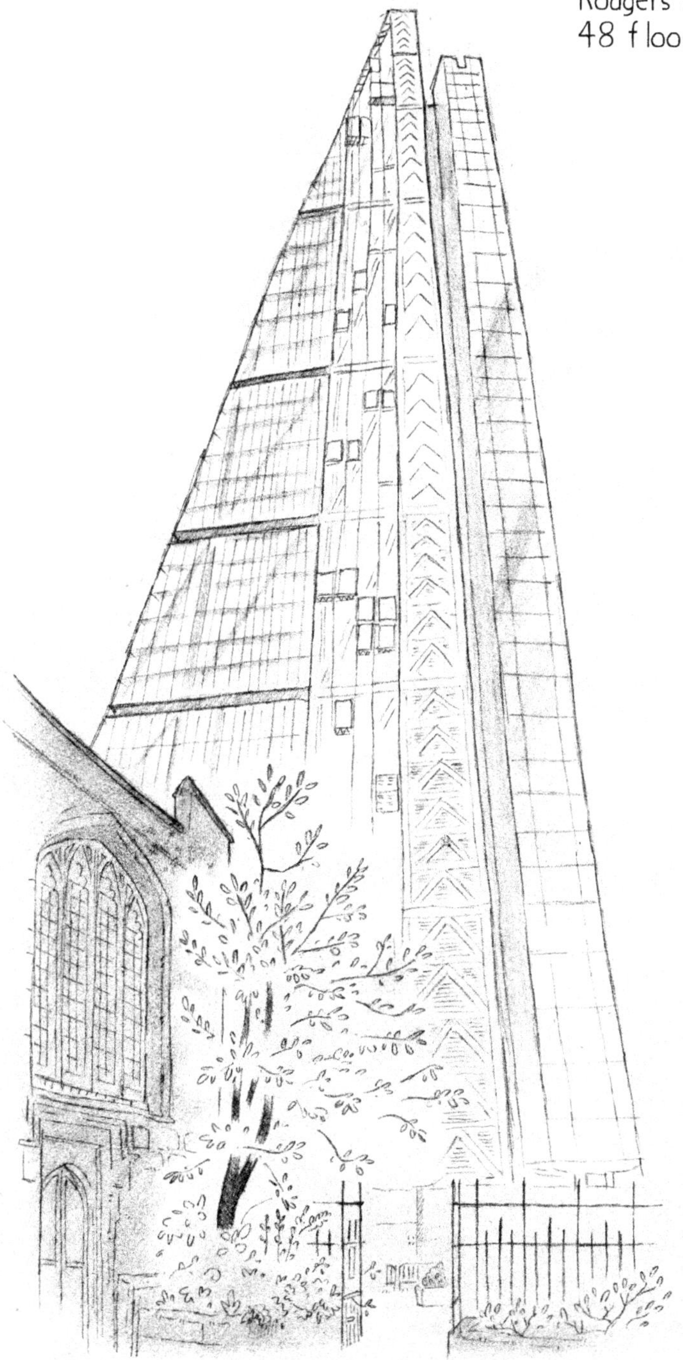

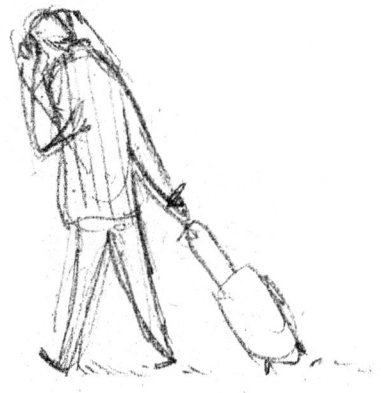

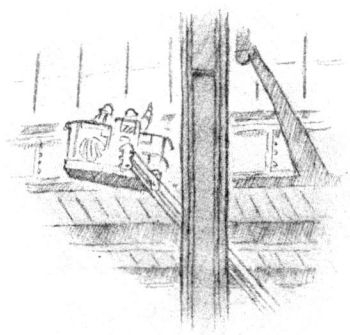

Builders on the Leadenhall building. 17 January 2014

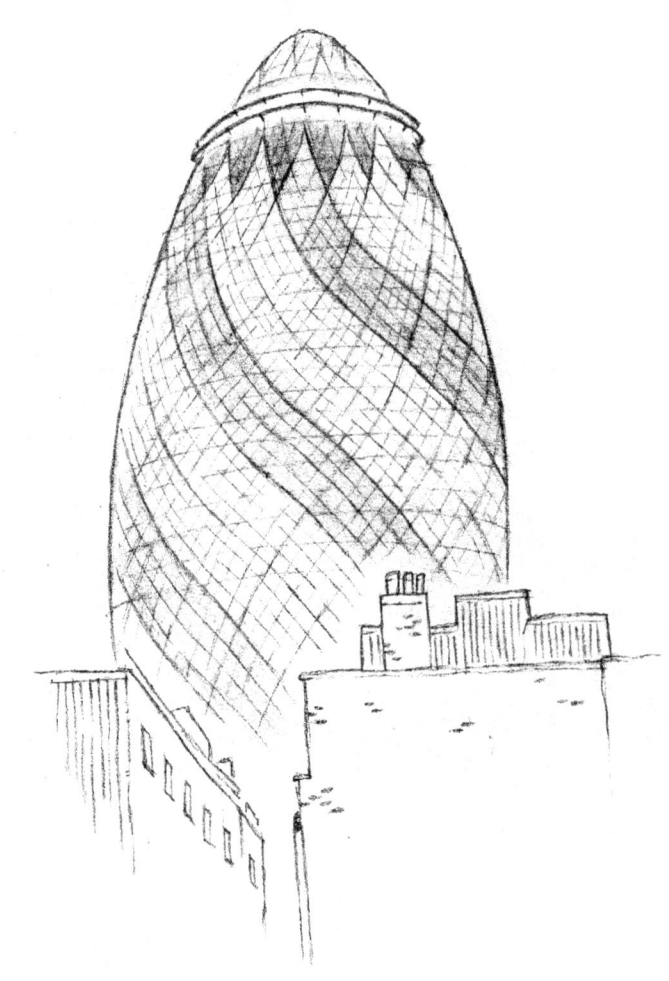

30 St Mary Axe (The Cherkin), 180m with 41
floors. Designed by Norman Foster and opened in
2004.

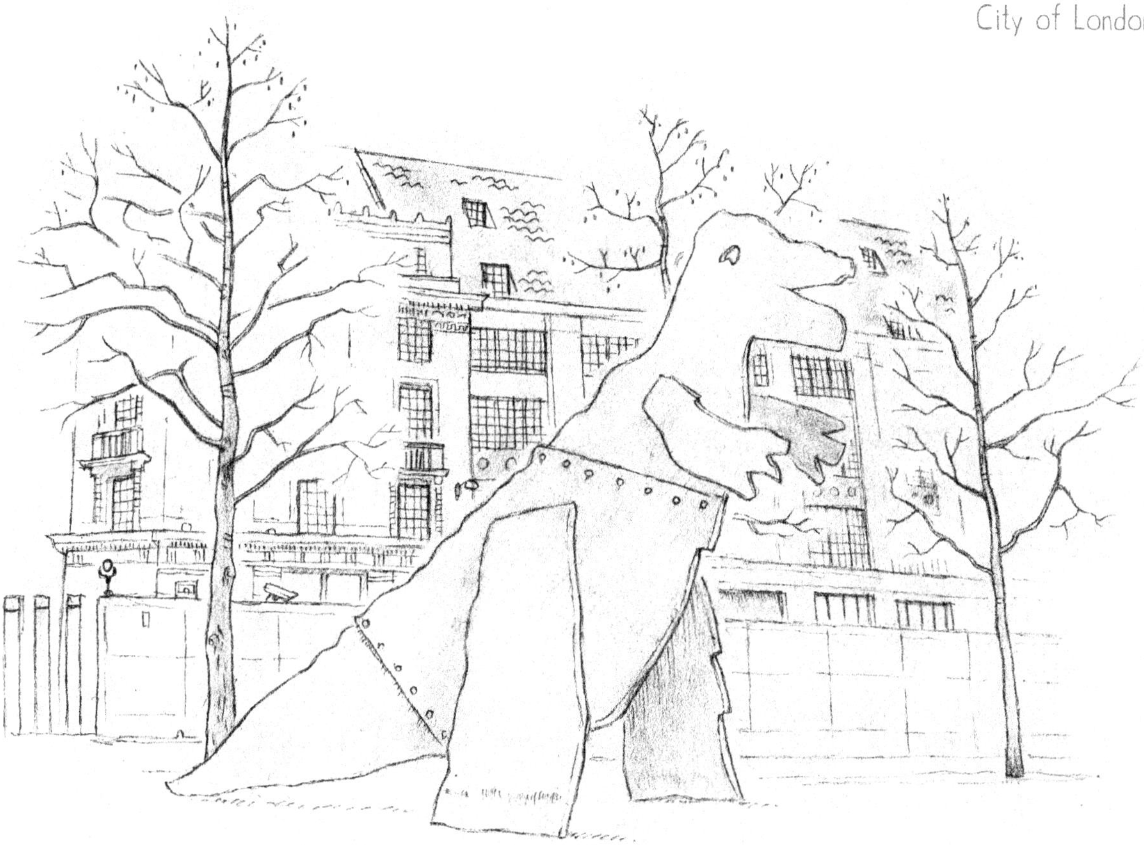

A metal Tyrannosaurus in front of the Inturnational Chamber of Shipping, next to the Gherkin.
This is one dinosaur in the Chapman brothers sculpture 'The Good, The Bad and The Ugly'.
I guess this one's the bad guy. These were part of the 2013 annual 'Sculpture in the city'
held in the City of London's insurance district.

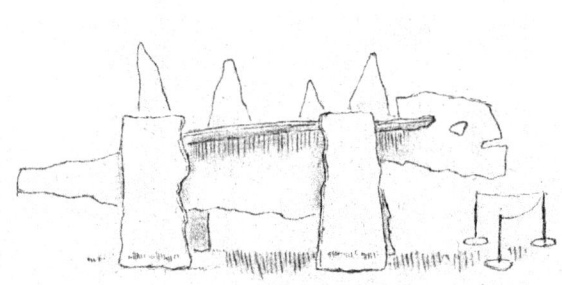
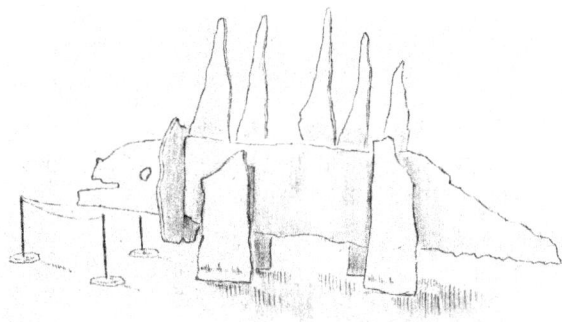

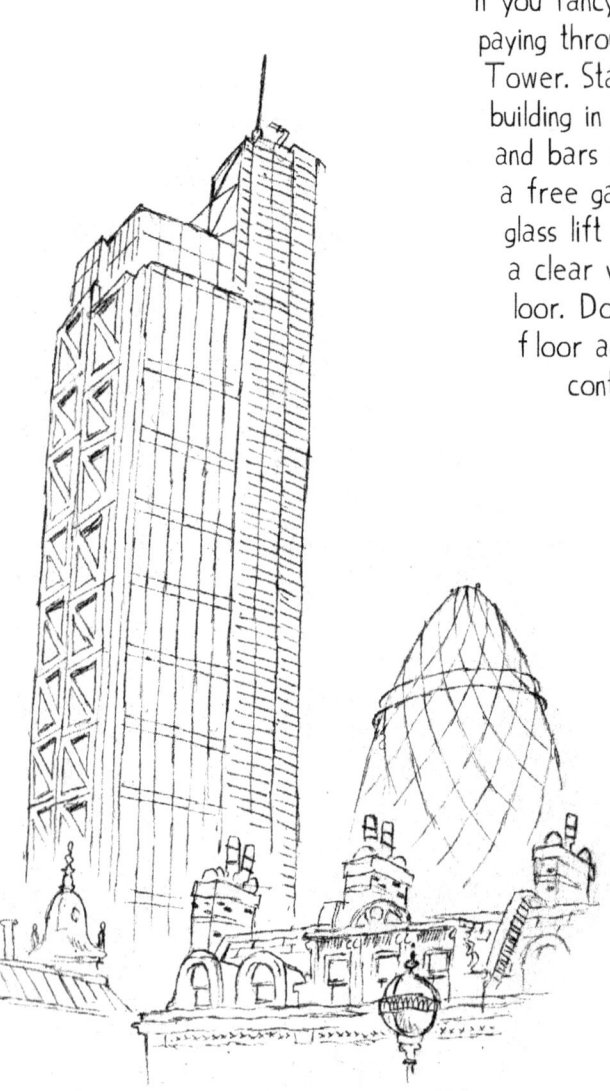

If you fancy an amazing aerial view of London without paying through your nose, try going up the Heron Tower. Standing at 230m, Its the third highest building in the UK. It has a couple of restaurants and bars at the top and you can just pop up for a free gander during the day. The ride up in the glass lift is pretty spectacular as well, giving you a clear view West as you rise up to the 40th f loor. Don't forget to check out the huge ground f loor aquarium visible from the pavement, it contains over 1200 fish! You can't get up close but can peer through the windows. They do serve a lot of sea-life in the restaurants but I'm sure it's just a coincidence.

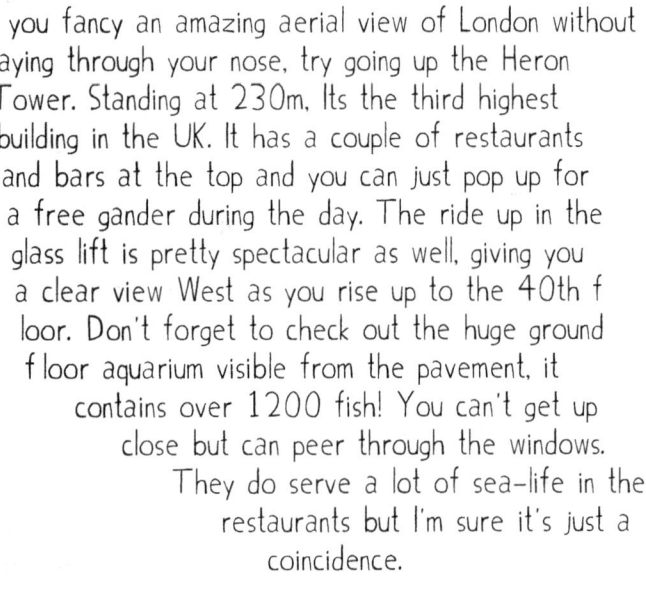

Heron tower and the Cherkin from Liverpool St Station

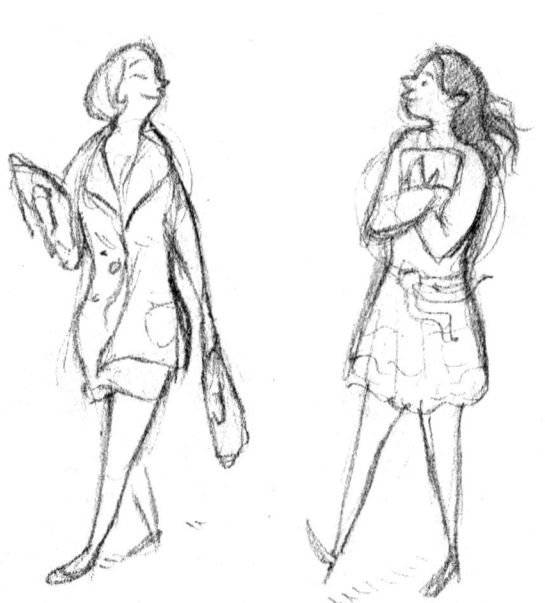

The Lauderdale Tower

Barbican Estate, 125m, residential. completed 1974

The Barbican Conservatory

Despite the fact that there are a few exotic looking palms here, it is not as warm as you might hope, at least not in mid January. Having lived in Cornwall I should know the presence of tropical plants is not always a guarantee of tropical temperatures :(

Portraits

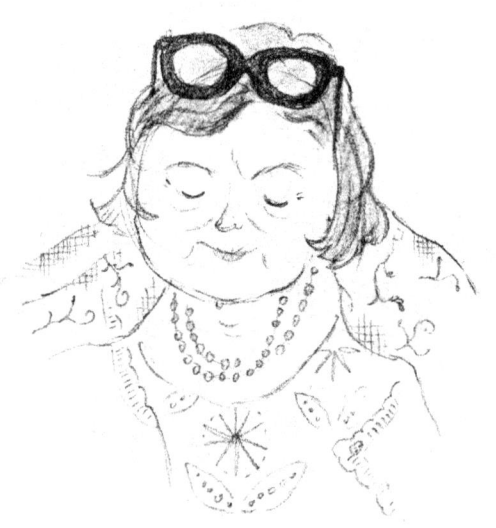
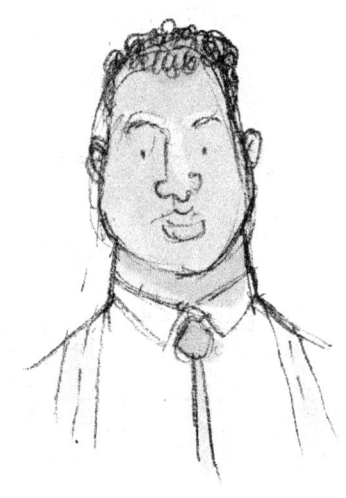

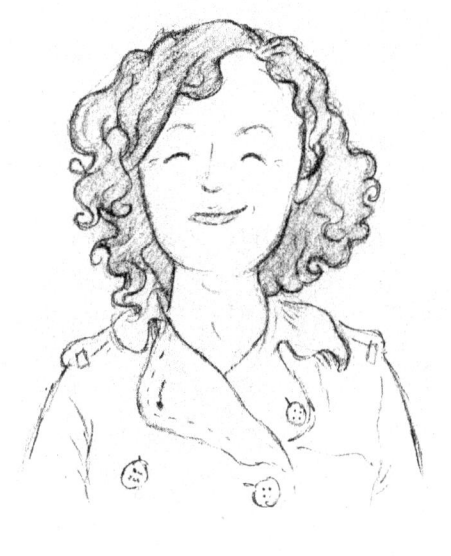

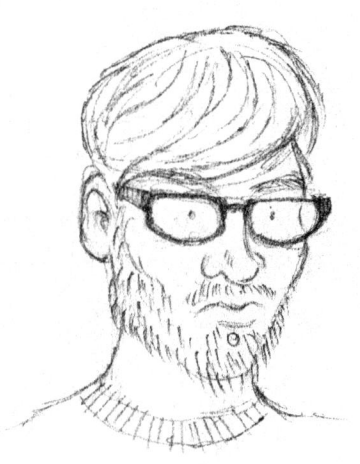

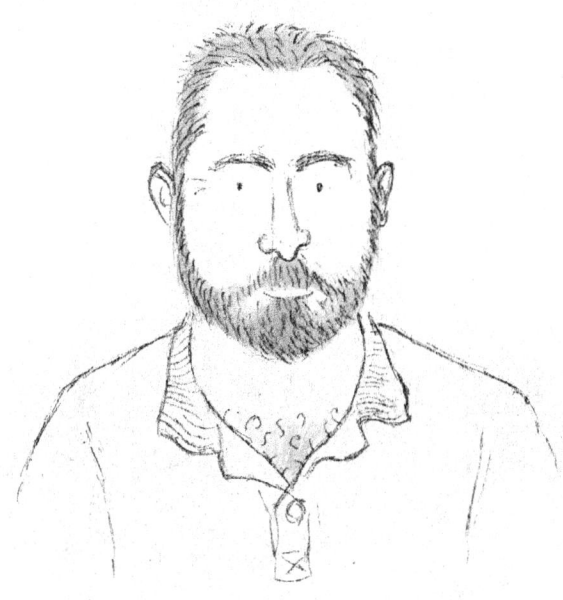

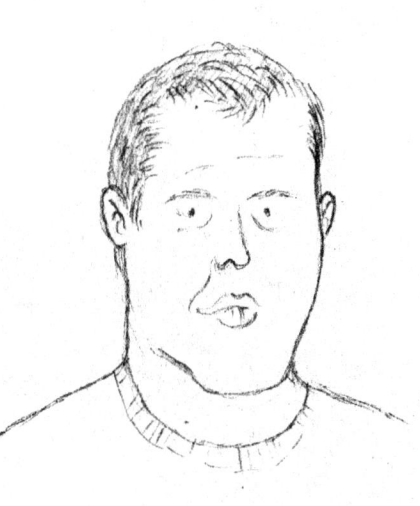

Hackney

The Geffrye Museum of the Home

A museum devoted to the English home and how it has changed over the centuries. It contains examples of rooms from 1600 to present day. When you make it to the end you might be able to spot furniture that reminds you of your grandparents, very comforting.

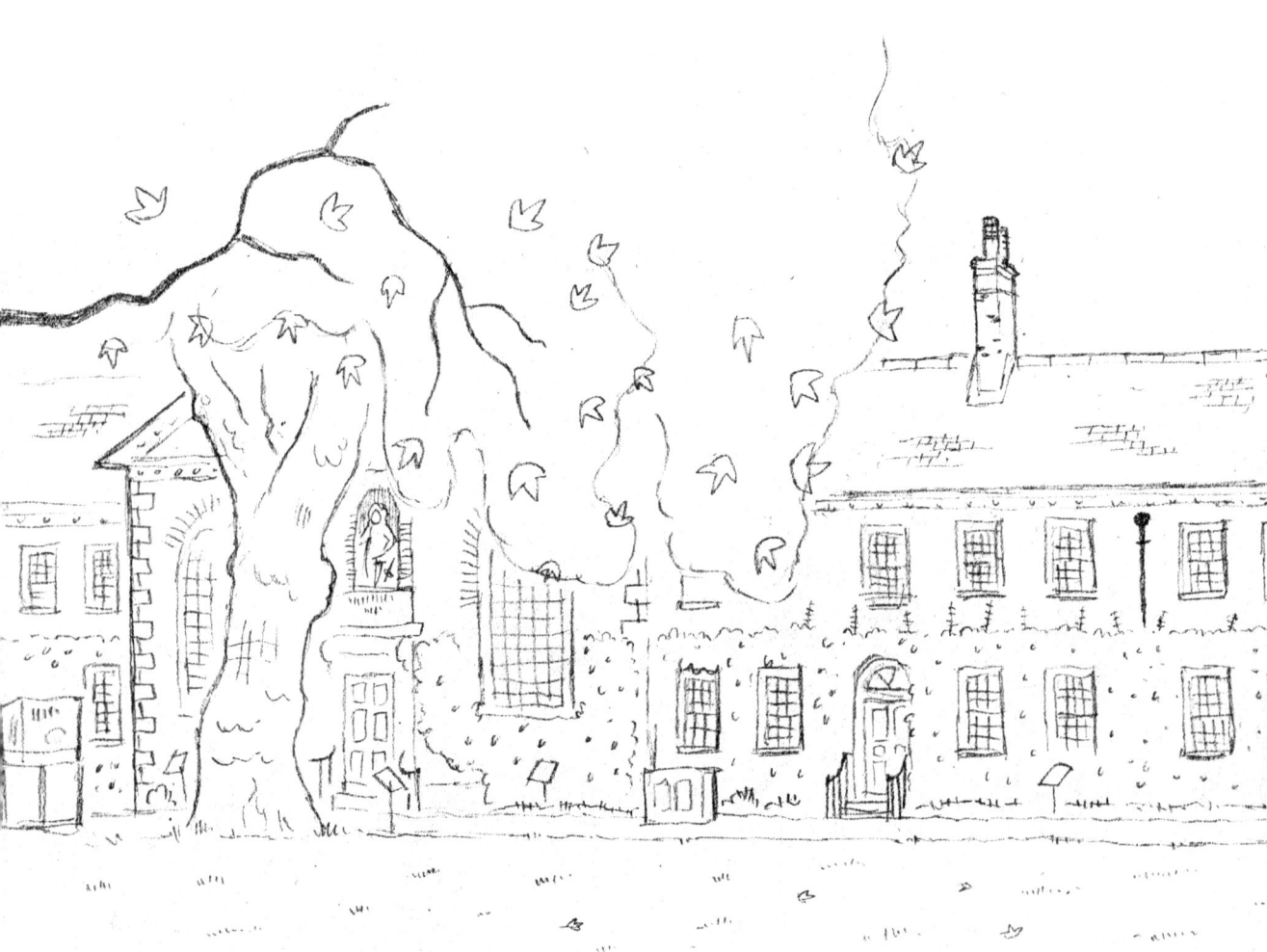

Edwardian Period Room
1900–1914

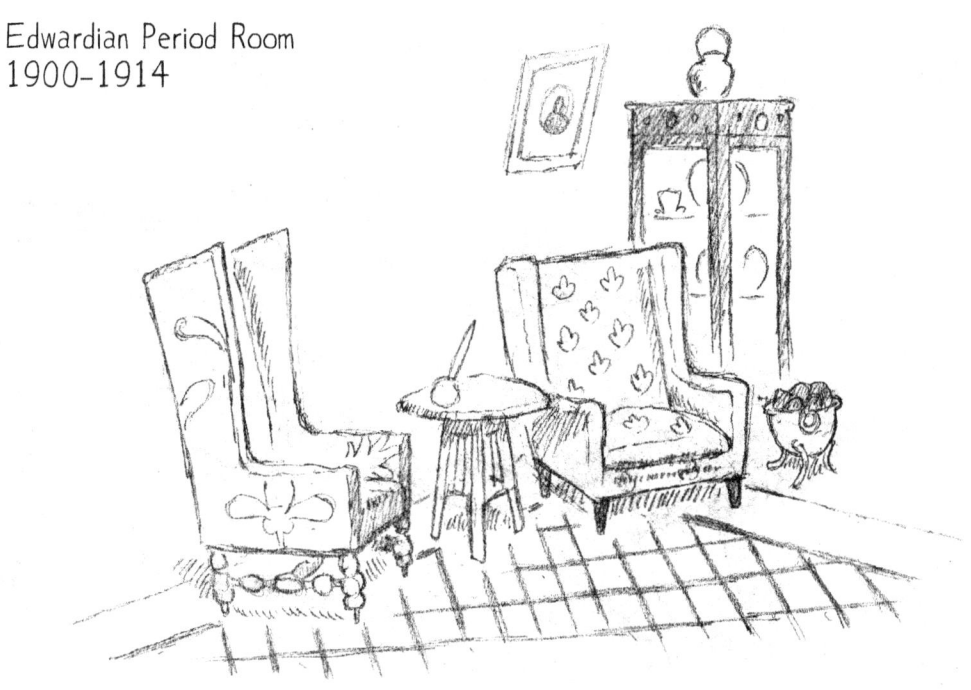

Drawing Room Chair
1870's

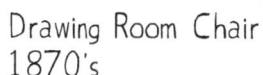

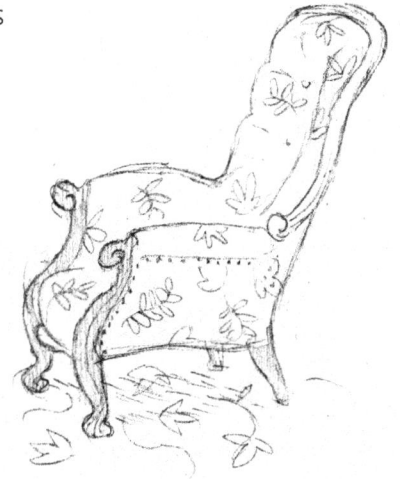

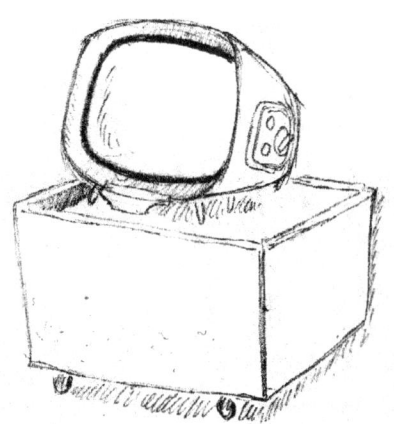

'Royal Star' Kolster–Brandes,
1957 Television 1955-65

Village Underground Centre

Created by furniture designer Auro Foxcroft as a solution to the lack of affordable studio space for artists in London. The eye-catching features on top of the main building are four disused tube carriages in which much creative work takes place. The renovated main building used to form part of a southern section on the Kingsland Viaduct.

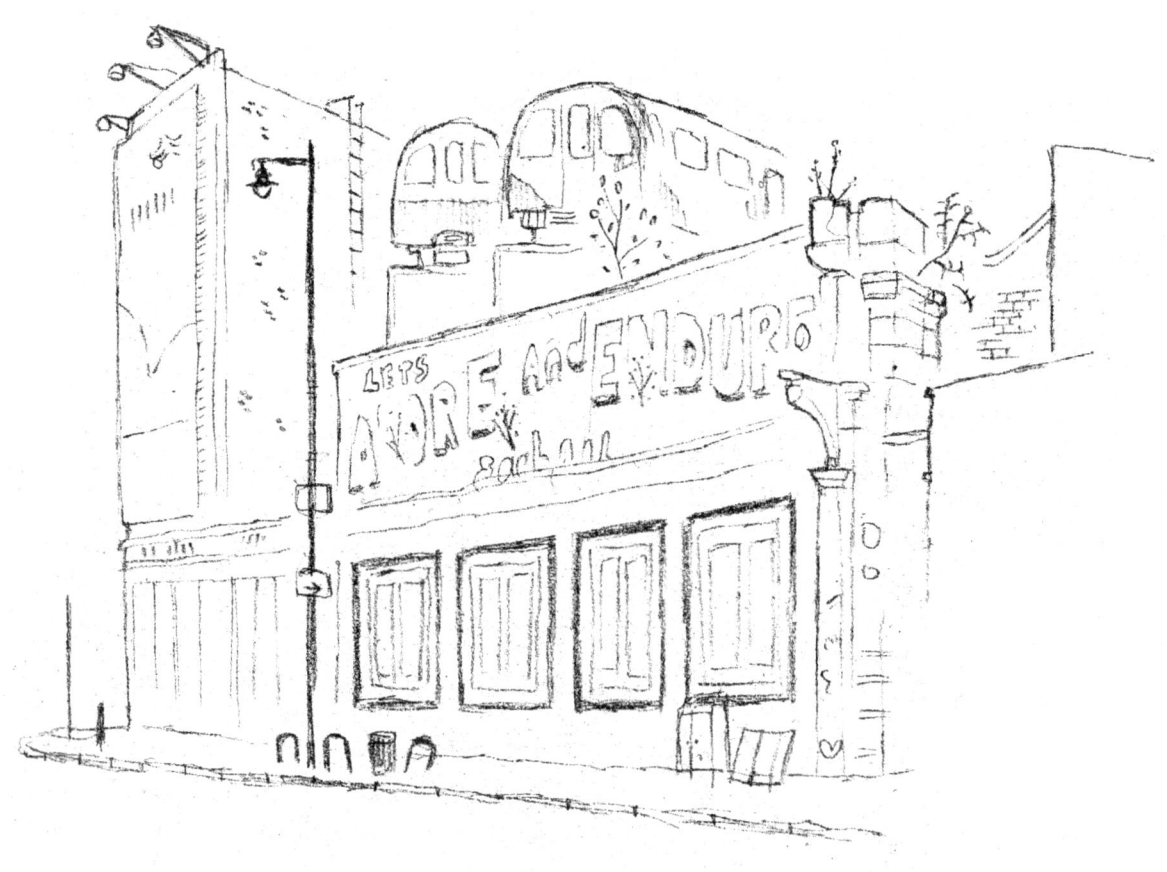

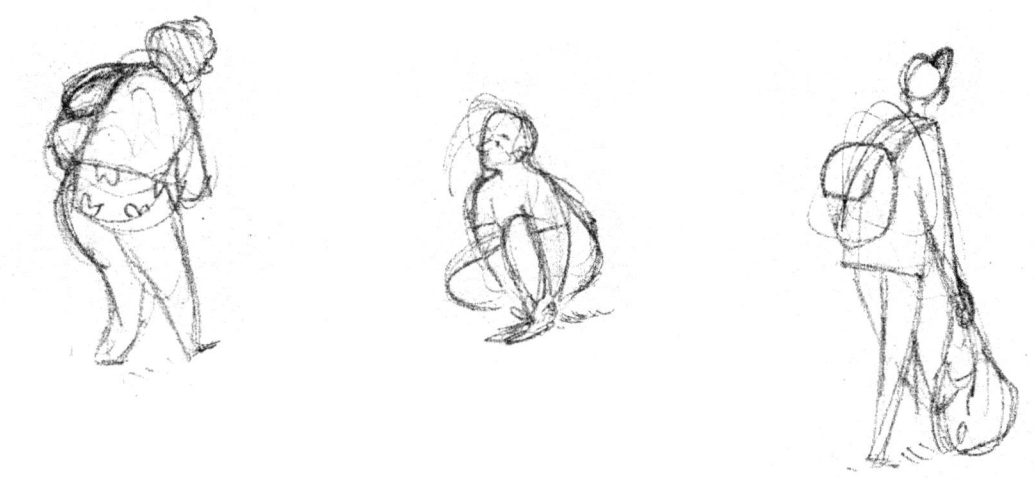

Central line over Shoreditch High-street

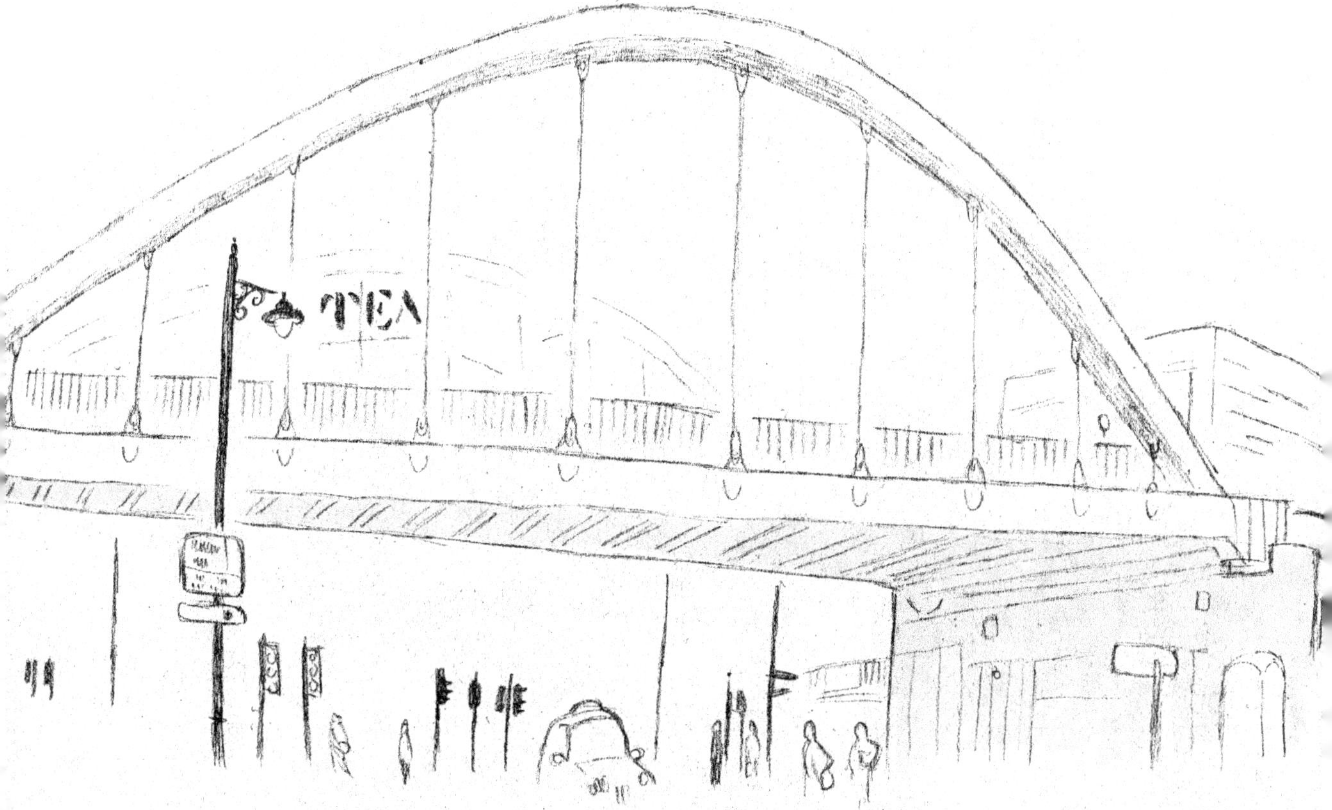

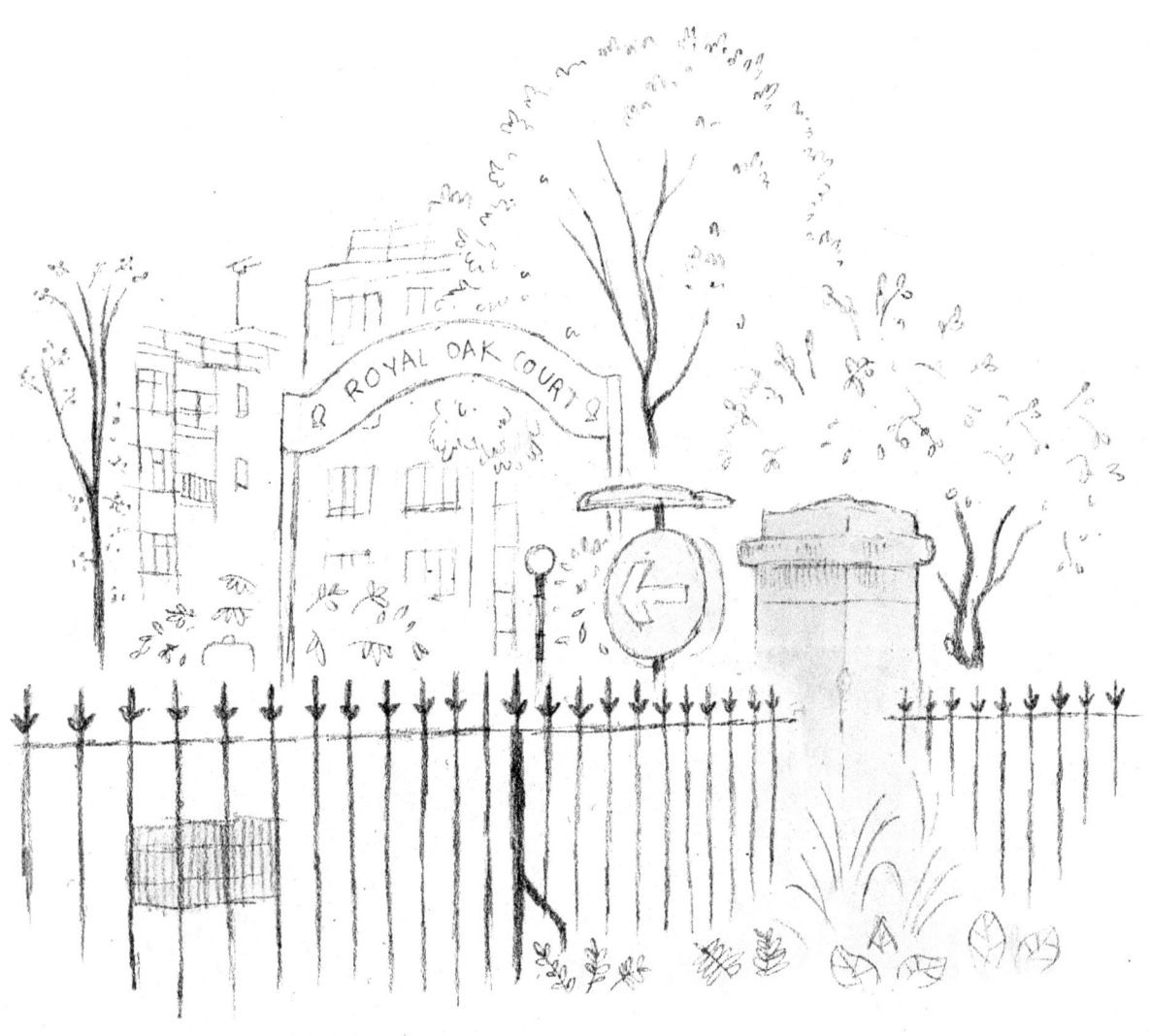

Royal Oak Court, Pifield Street

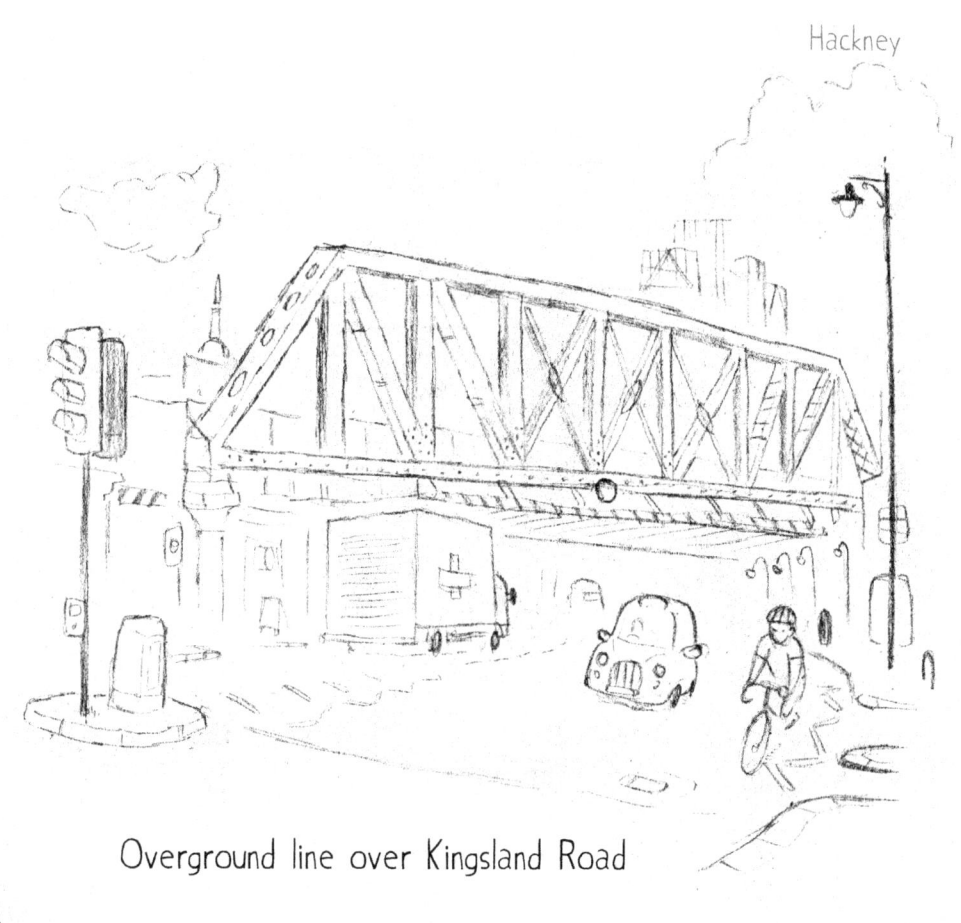

Overground line over Kingsland Road

The Old Blue Last Pub

Walking around south Hackney looking for something
eye-catching to draw I came across this interesting
looking pub. Little did I realise it had such a rich history.
Refurbished in 2004 and the venue for many famous
bands since, before 1876 on this site stood a previous
pub named 'The Last' and going further back it was the
site for a theatre reportedly frequented by Shakespeare.

Tower Hamlets

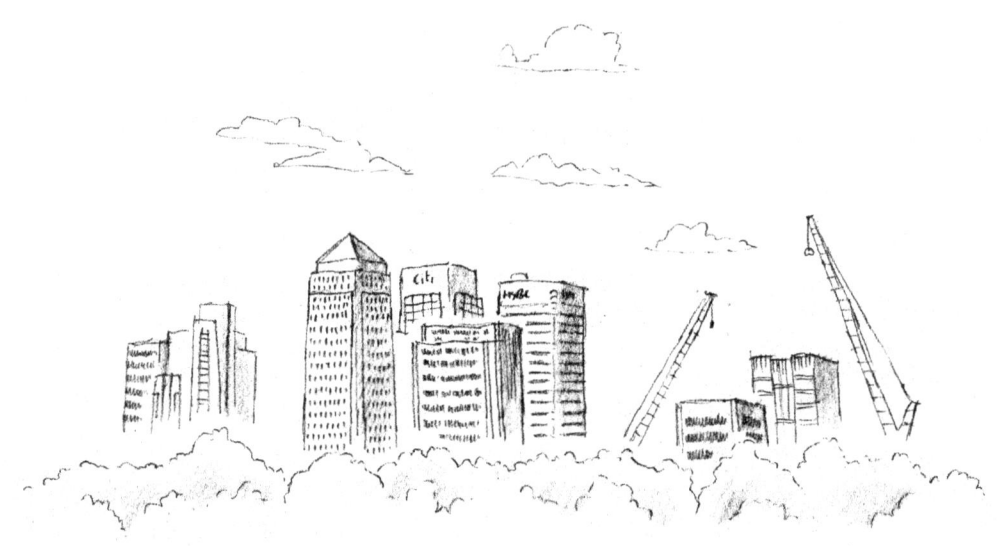

View of Canary Wharf from Greenwich

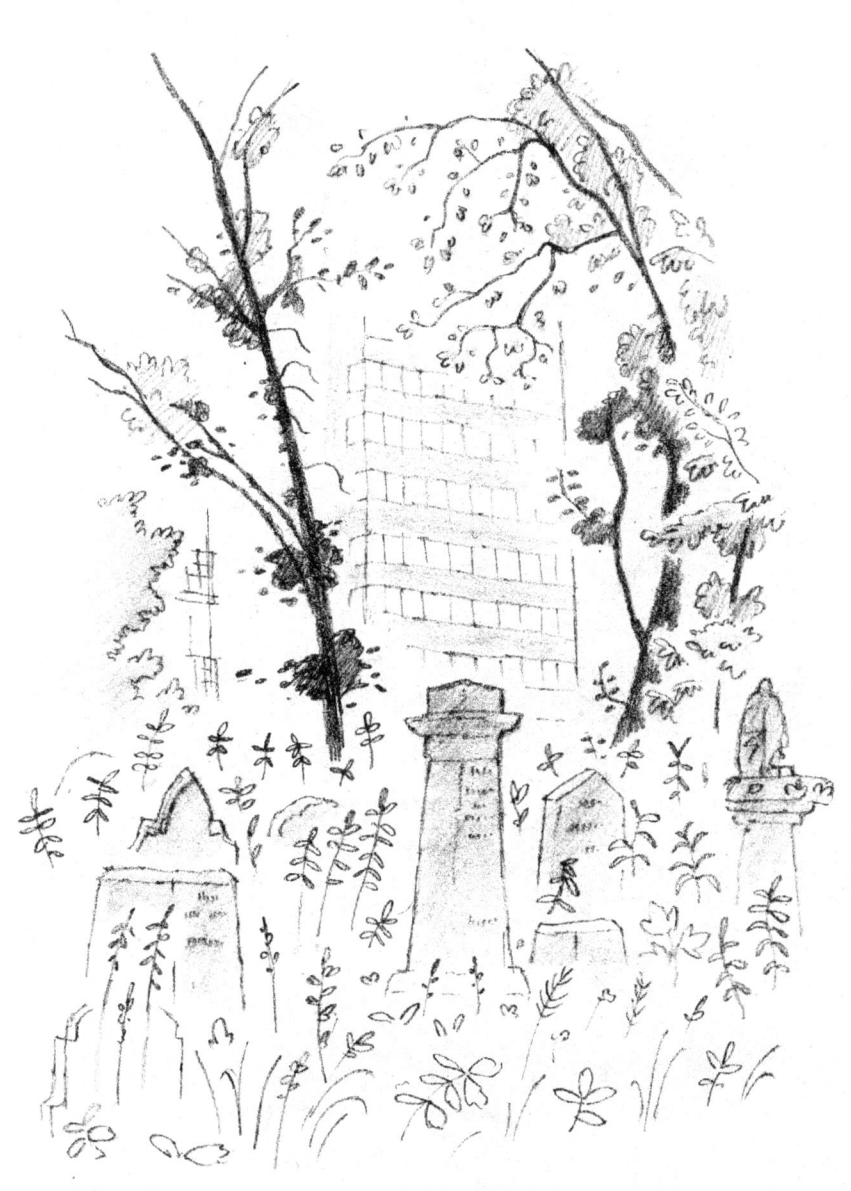

Tower Hamlets Cemetery

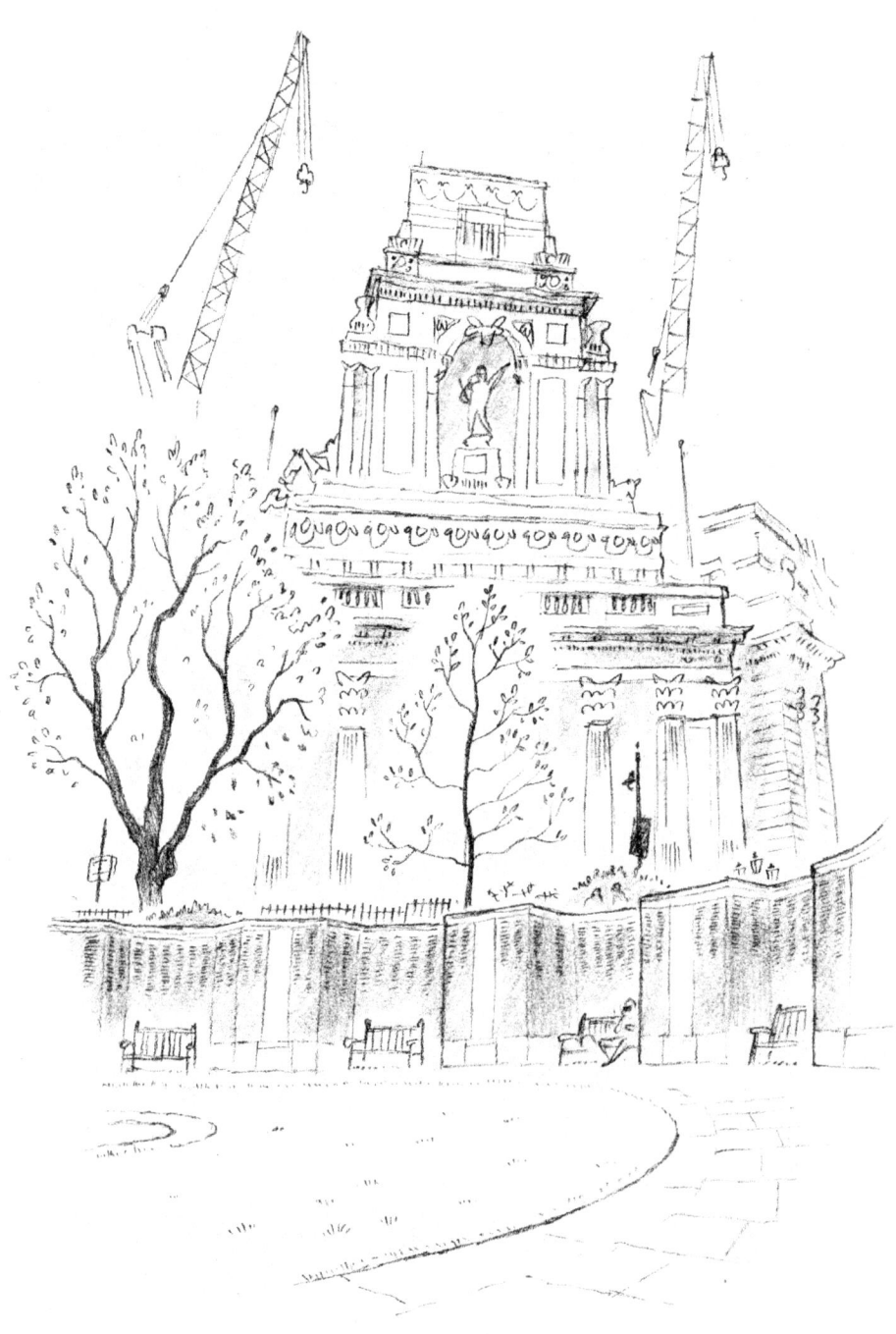

Opposite: 10 Trinity Square with the Tower Hill Memorial in the foreground

10 Trinity Square

Overlooking Trinity Square Gardens where many people lost their head (the last dropping off in 1747) is the former Port of London Authority, now being developed into a hotel and apartments. A bit of movie trivia, this building appeared in the 2012 James Bond film Skyfall.

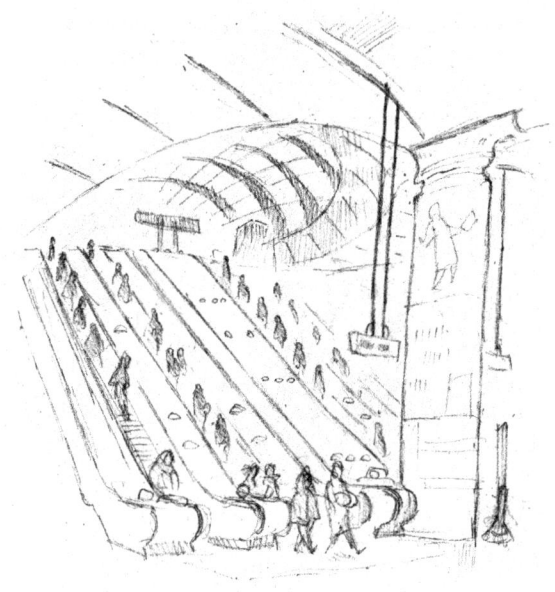

Canary Wharf Tube Exit

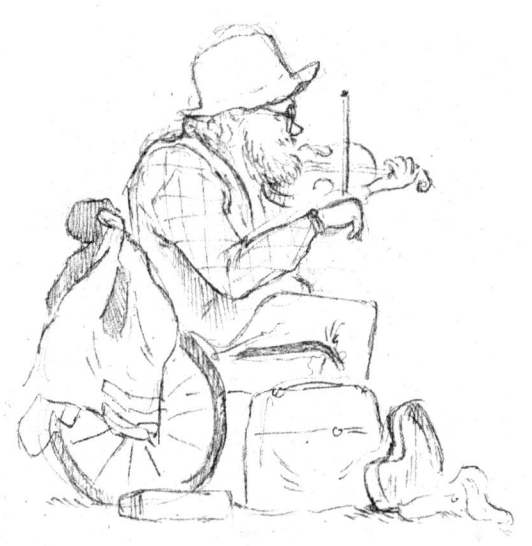

A busker at the Canary Wharf Tube Station.

Tower Hill Memorial 1939-1945

Tower Hill memorial commemorates the people lost at sea during both world wars. The northern section shown opposite focuses on the Second World War. Arranged in alphabetical order are the commonwealth ships and their crew. Nearly 24,000 lives are listed. Merchant Navy make up the large majority along with the light house & pilotage services and fishing fleets.

The Tower of London

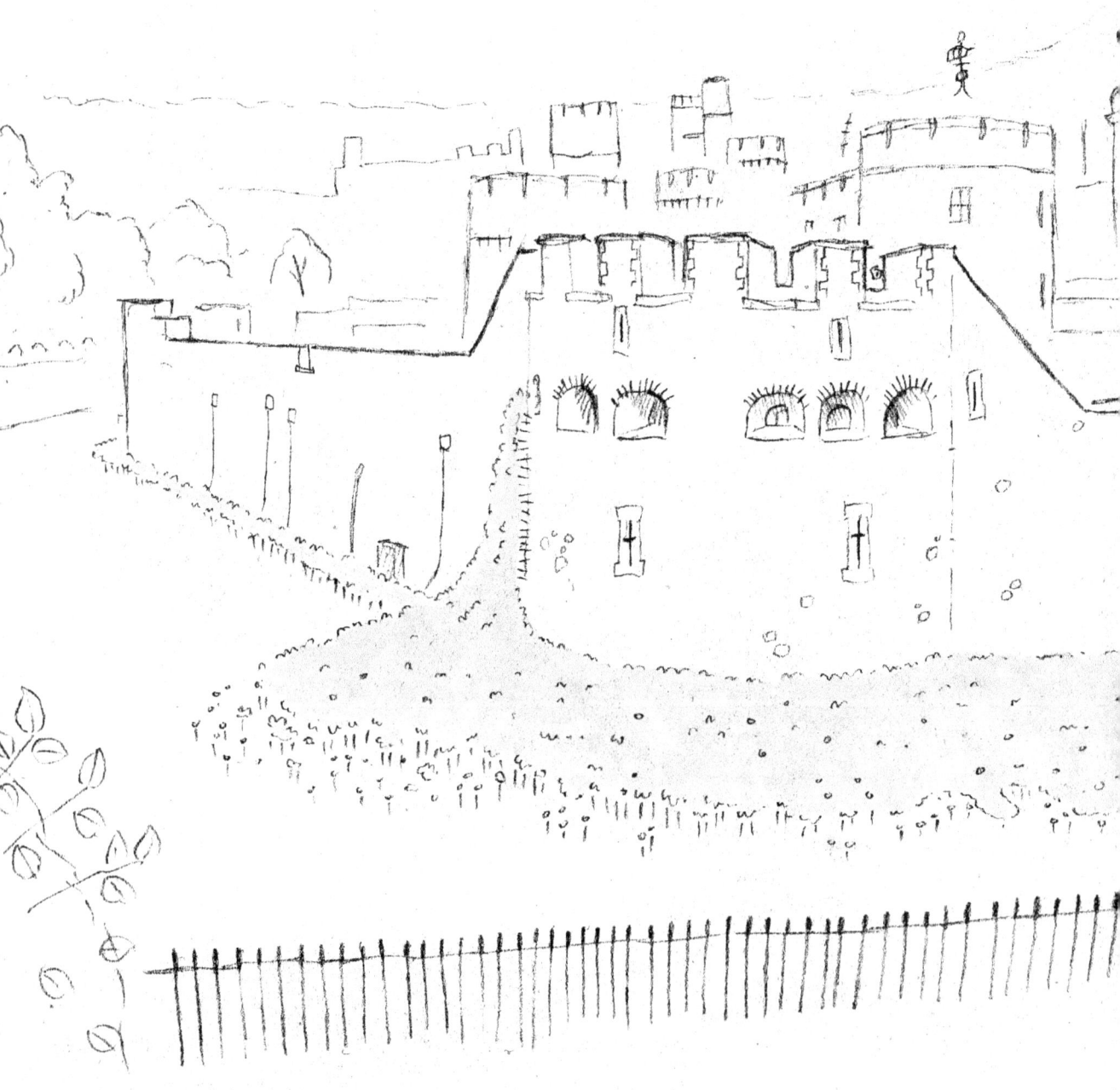

In August 2014 to commemorate the 1st world war, the art installation
'Bloodswept Lands and Seas of Red' was created by ceramic artist Paul
Cummins. In total 888,246 ceramic poppies were to be planted by the
11th November surrounding the castle, each one marking a life
lost from the British military during the conflict.

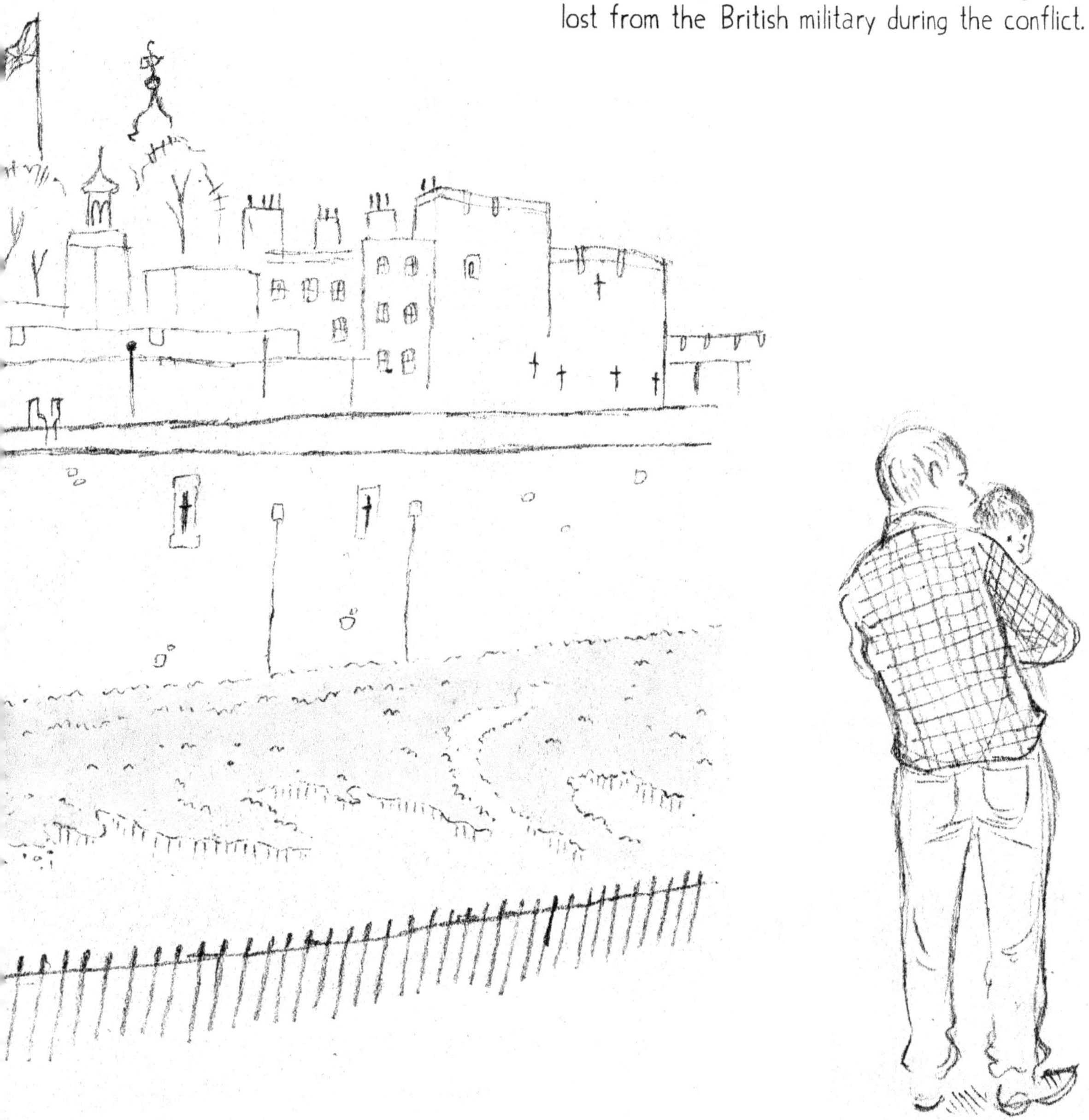

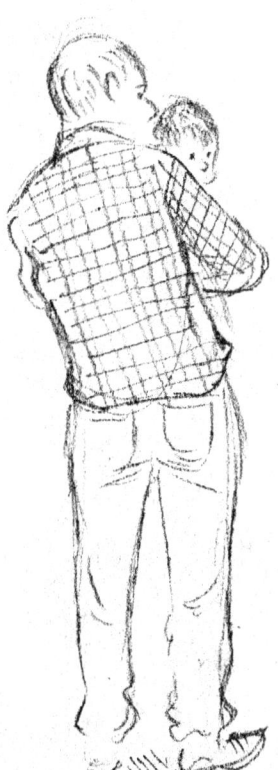

Tower Bridge

As the population of east London grew throughout the 1800's, there became an overwhelming demand for a bridge over the Thames east of London Bridge. There were multiple bridges west of London Bridge but for inhabitants in the East End this meant long journeys to get across the river. So in 1876 the City of London Corporation decided it was time for a new bridge. After more than 50 designs were considered, the current one was completed in 1896 with the now iconic bascule bridge (drawbridge) design.

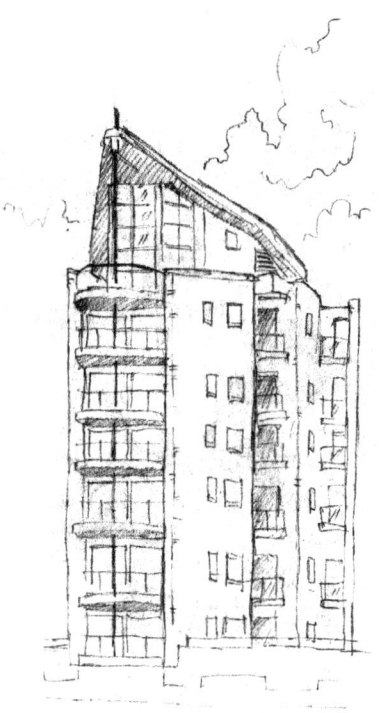

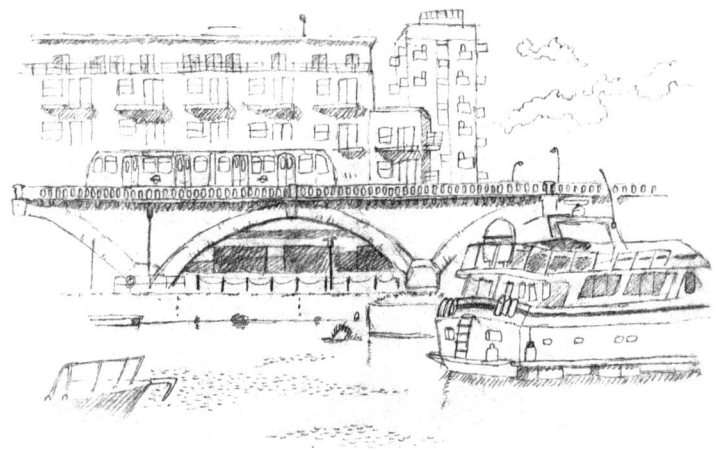

Limehouse Marina

Jubilee Park,
Canary Wharf

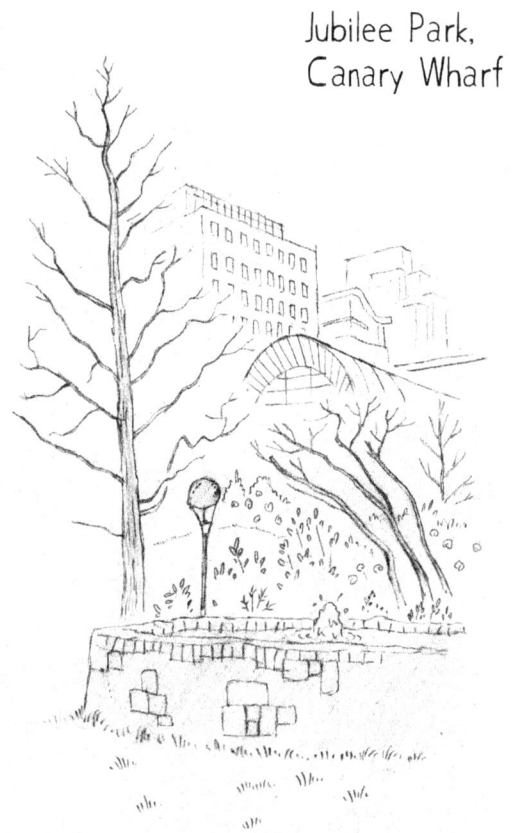

Unlike historic architecture, when sketching more contemporary buildings such as those in Canary Wharf, it can be hard to give them individuality. A good way to discover an objects characteristics is to draw it from distance. This can help your eyes pick up the features that distinguish it from other similar objects. For example, modern glass buildings when drawn close up can appear very uniform and lack character but from a distance you can identify patterns in their construction. This will help you leave out certain features from a building that would distract from it's uniqueness.

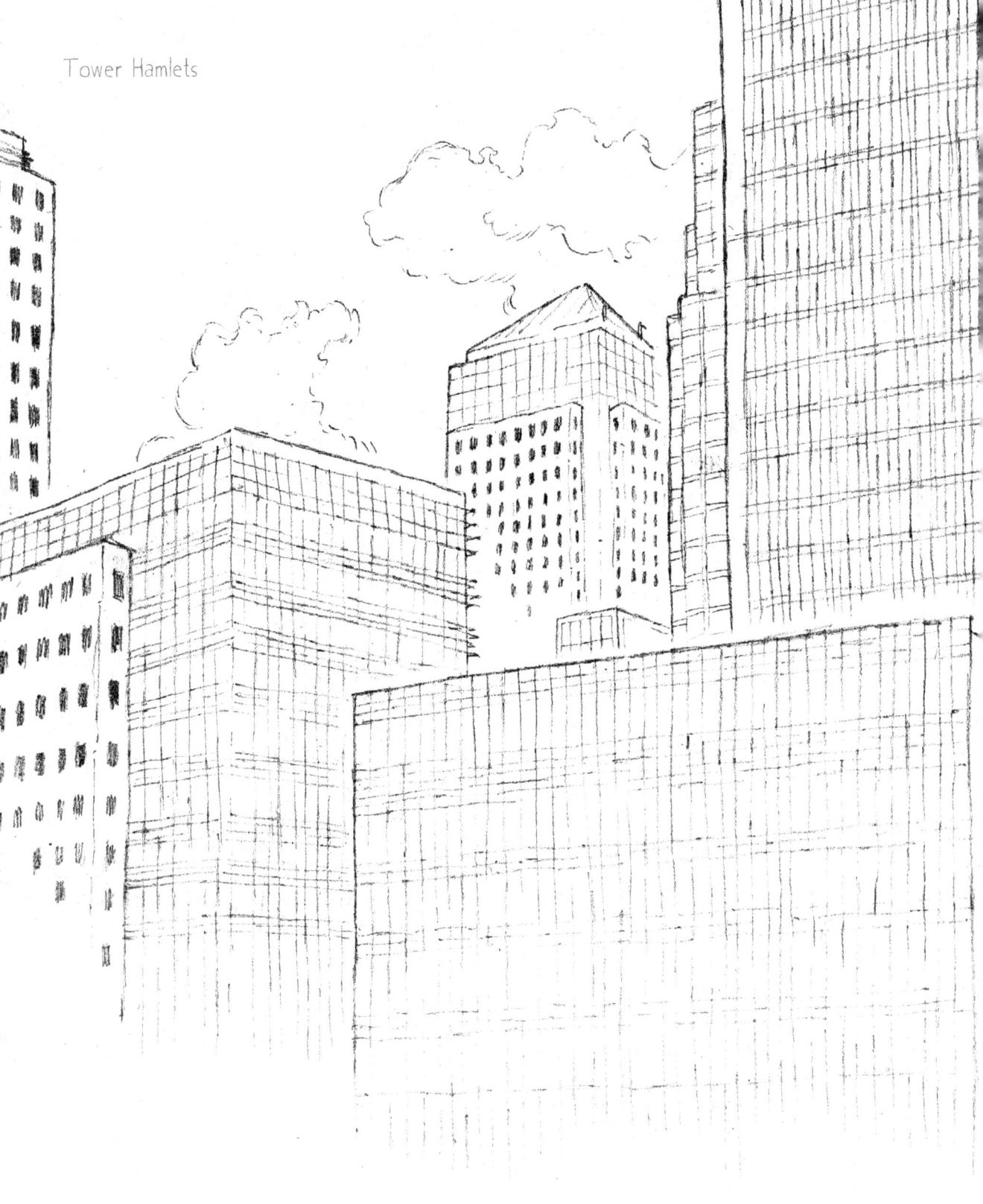

View of One Canada Square from South Quay, Canary Wharf

Coffee Break

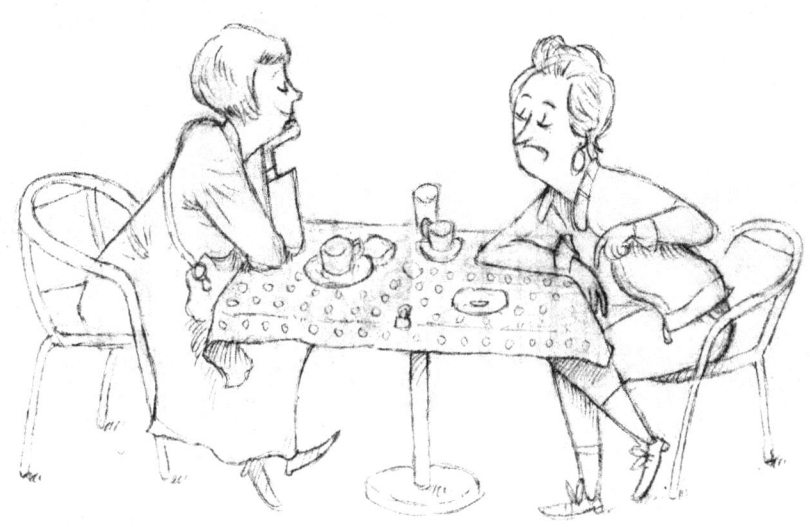

Coffee shops, pubs and cafes are great places to sketch people. Unlike studying people on the tube, they are usually so absorbed in their conversations they don't notice. It also gives you a nice cosy place to escape. Especially useful in the winter.

Coffee Break

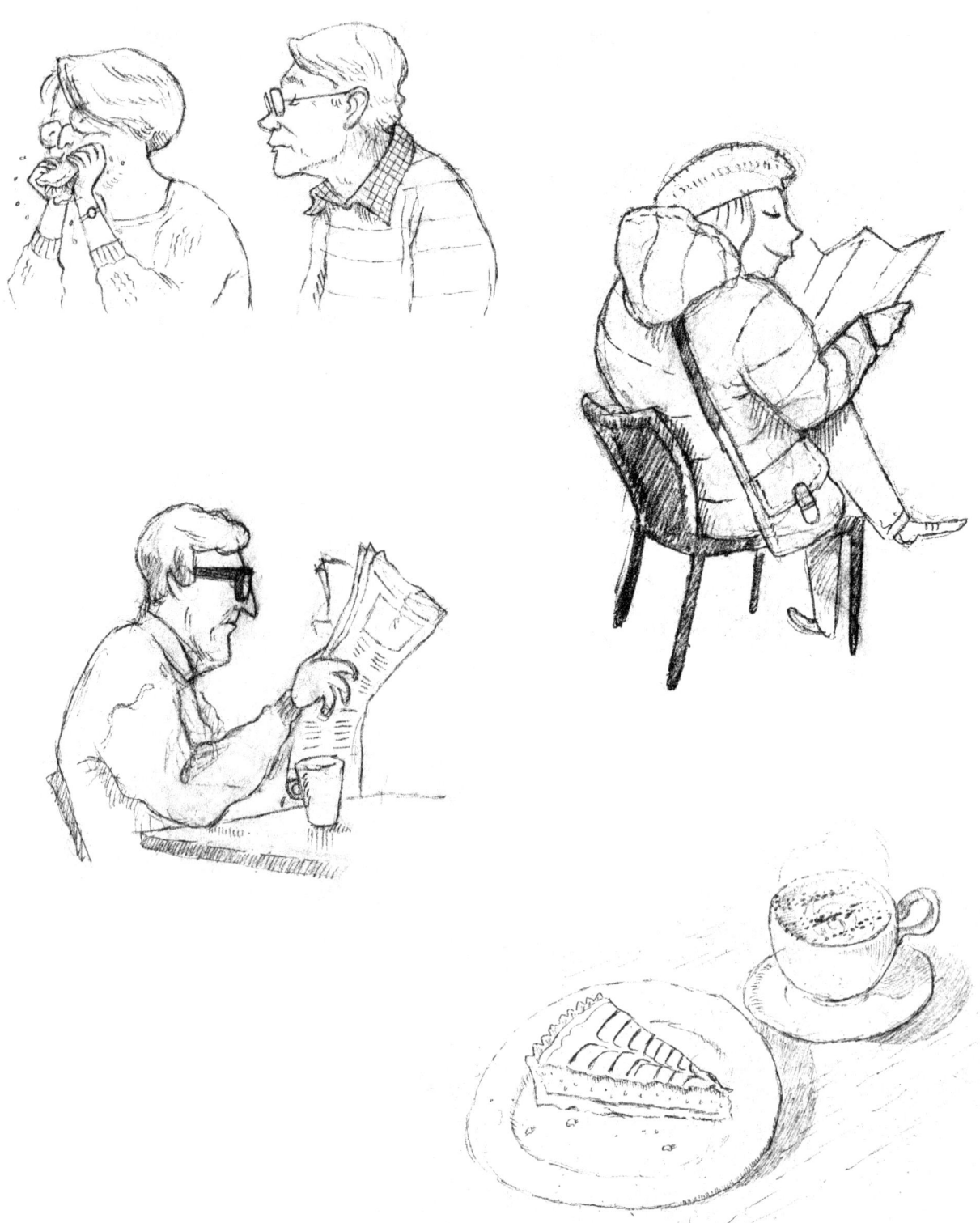

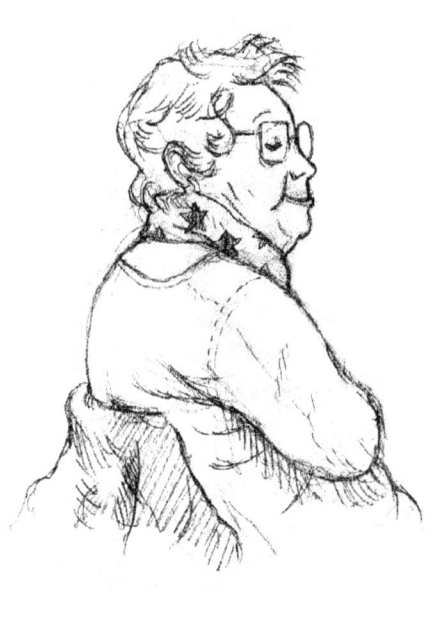

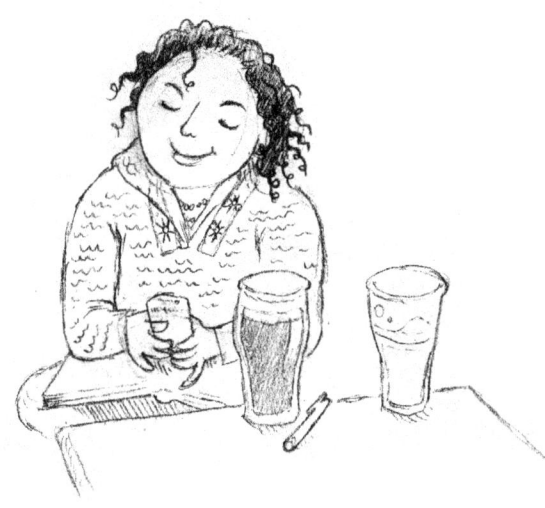

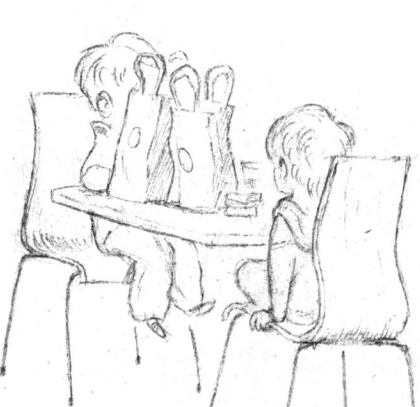

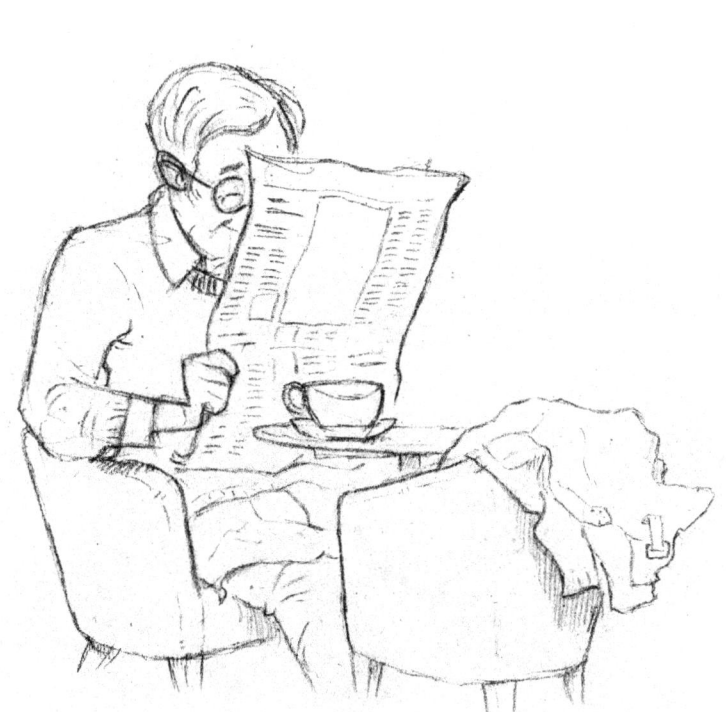

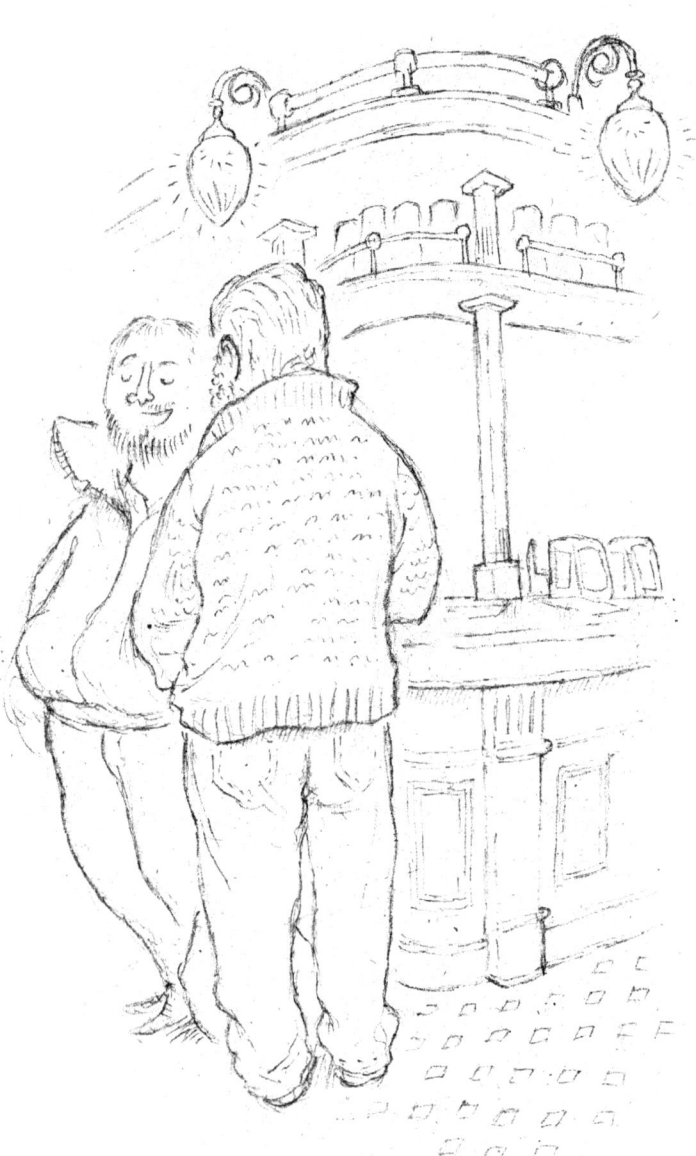

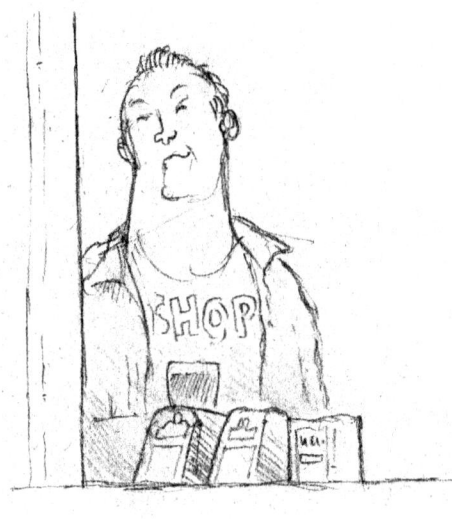

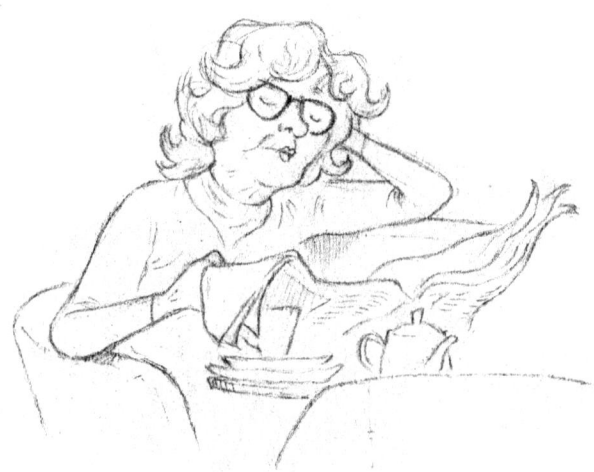

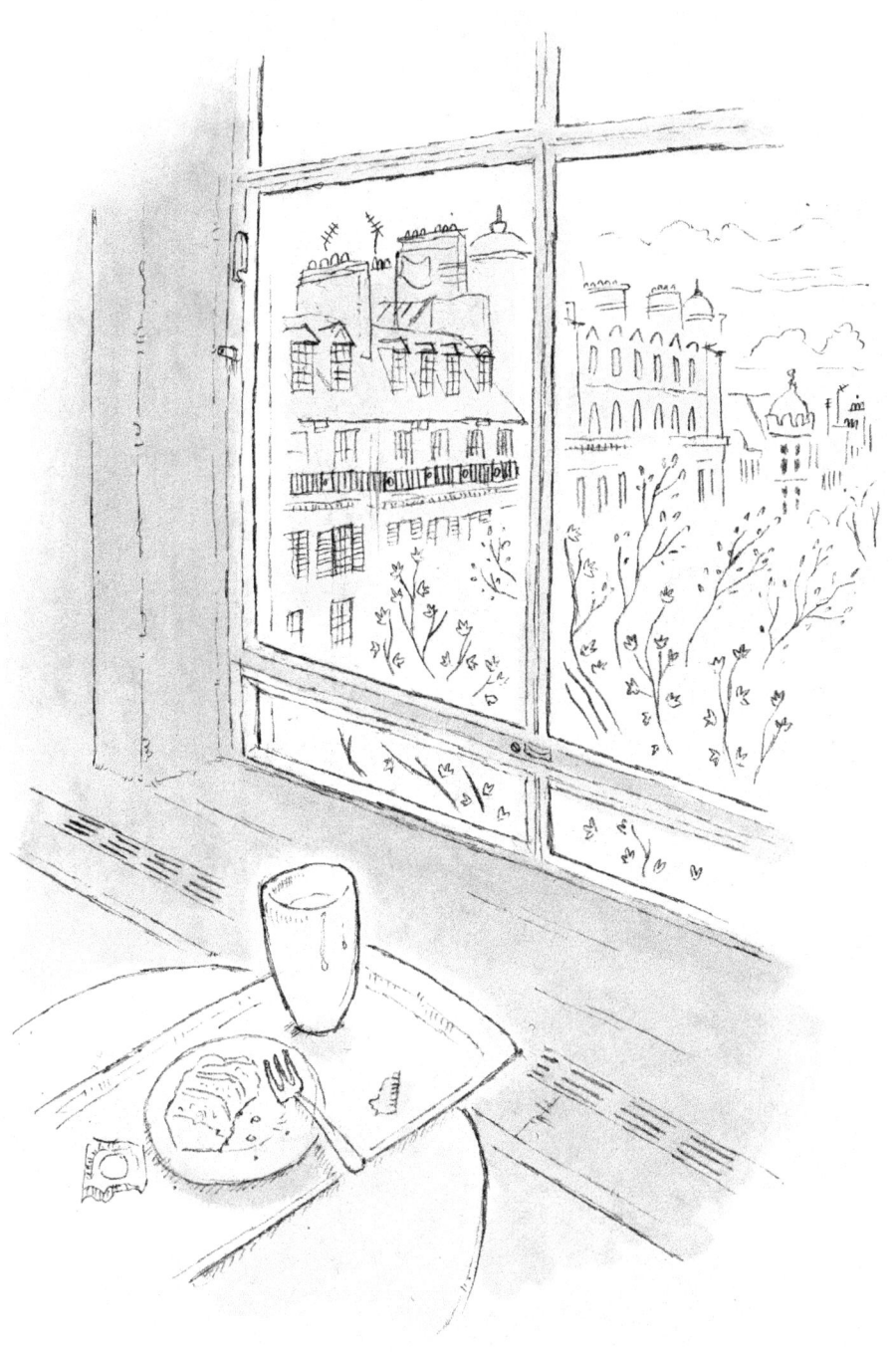

View from the John Lewis Cafe on Oxford Street overlooking the Royal College of Nursing and Cavendish Square.

Greenwich

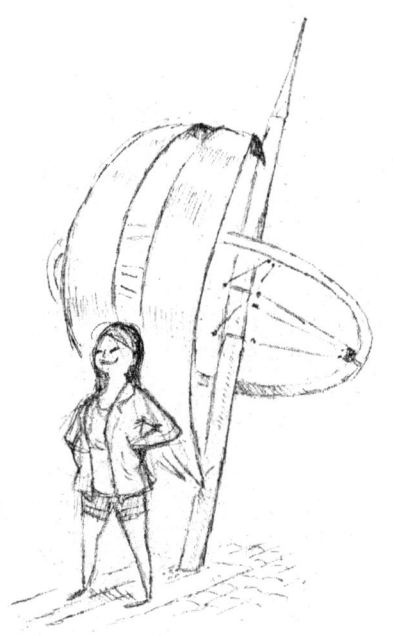

Girl standing on
the Meridian Line

I remember going to Greenwich as a child. I think like most tourists
the only thing I remember from that trip was standing either side
of the time line. The significance of which I'm sure was lost on
my young brain.

The Cutty Sark had an extensive six year restoration which was completed in 2012 (small fire interruption included). It now sits (somewhat controversially) raised 3m off the ground within it's dry dock. Surrounding its upper hull is a glass structure resembling the rolling sea. If you press your face up to the glass you can get a pretty decent free view around the ship. Obviously you have to pay the entry fee to get a proper look though.

Cutty Sark

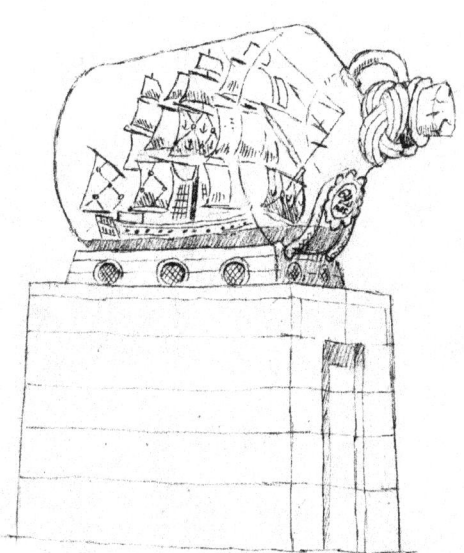

Ship in bottle outside the Maritime Museum

Royal Naval College

As part of Maritime Greenwich, this former college trained naval servicemen between 1873 and 1998. Designed by Sir Christopher Wren with two domes (one sketched), it was originally used as a hospital from 1712. UNESCO describes these buildings as 'the most outstanding group of Baroque buildings in Britain'. Since the Royal Navy left in 1998 it has served a wide range of uses for community projects and education and you can often hear musicians practising as you walk around the grounds. The site is also a popular location for TV series and films.

Dining Hall

Free to enter, this huge dining hall was designed by Sir Christopher Wren and Nicholas
Hawksmoor. The painted walls and ceiling were by Sir James Thornhill and took
19 years to complete. In 1806 Horatio Nelson's body was brought here
to lie in state following the Battle of Trafalgar.

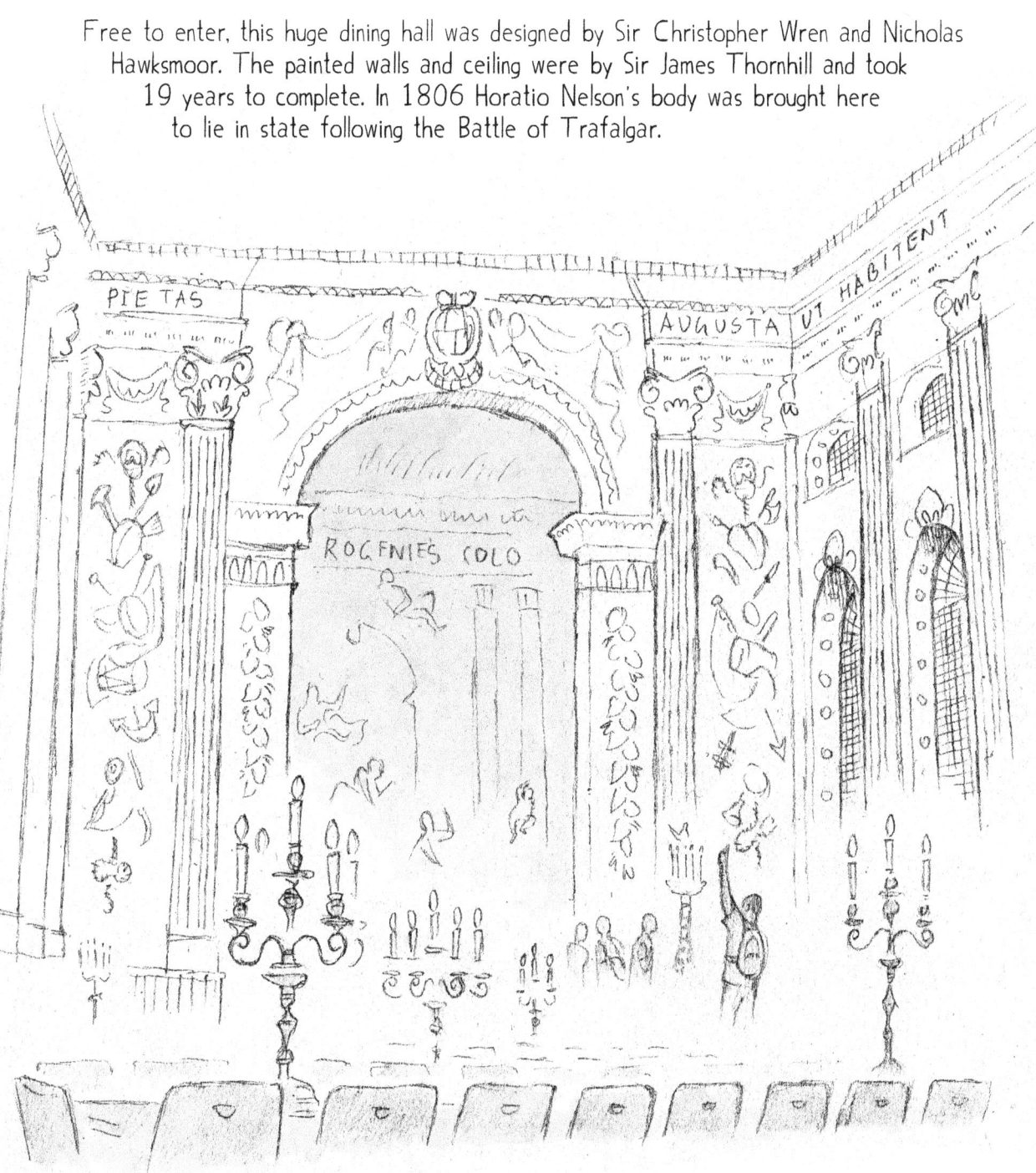

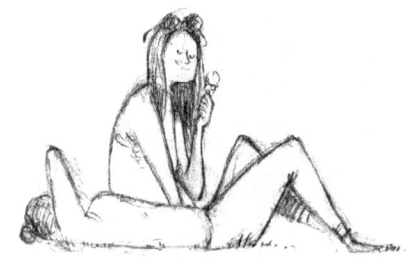 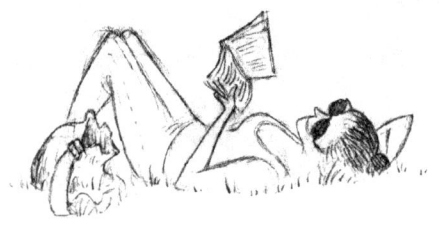

Royal Observatory

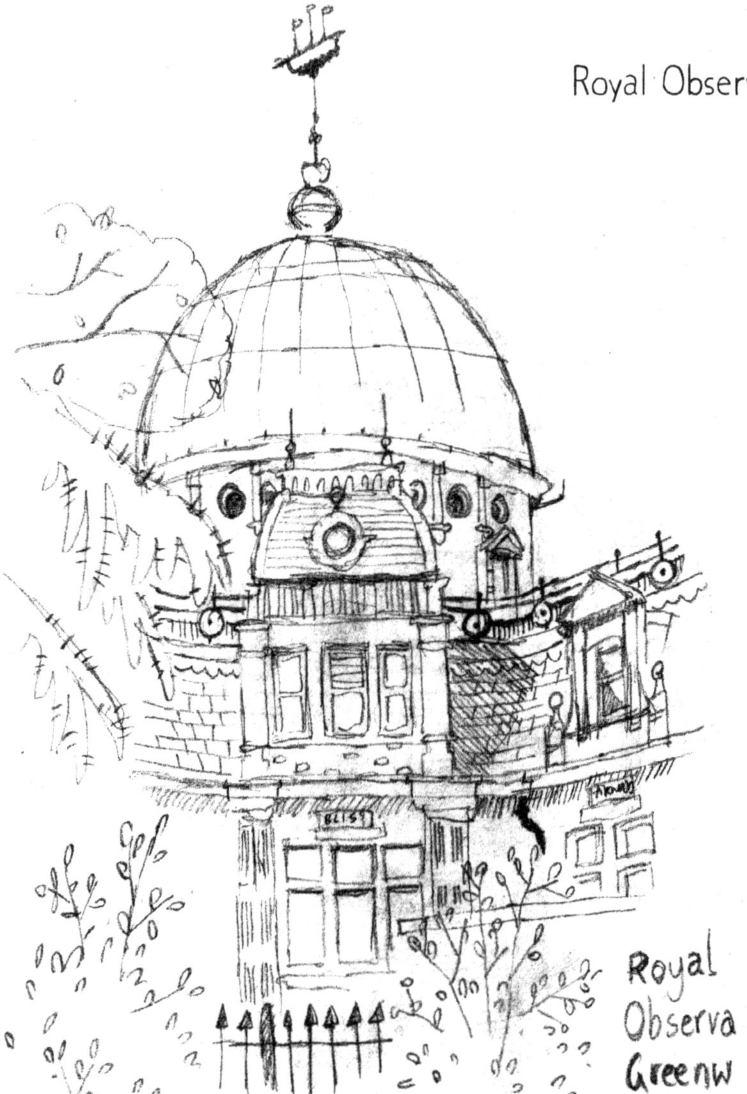

Royal
Observa
Greenw

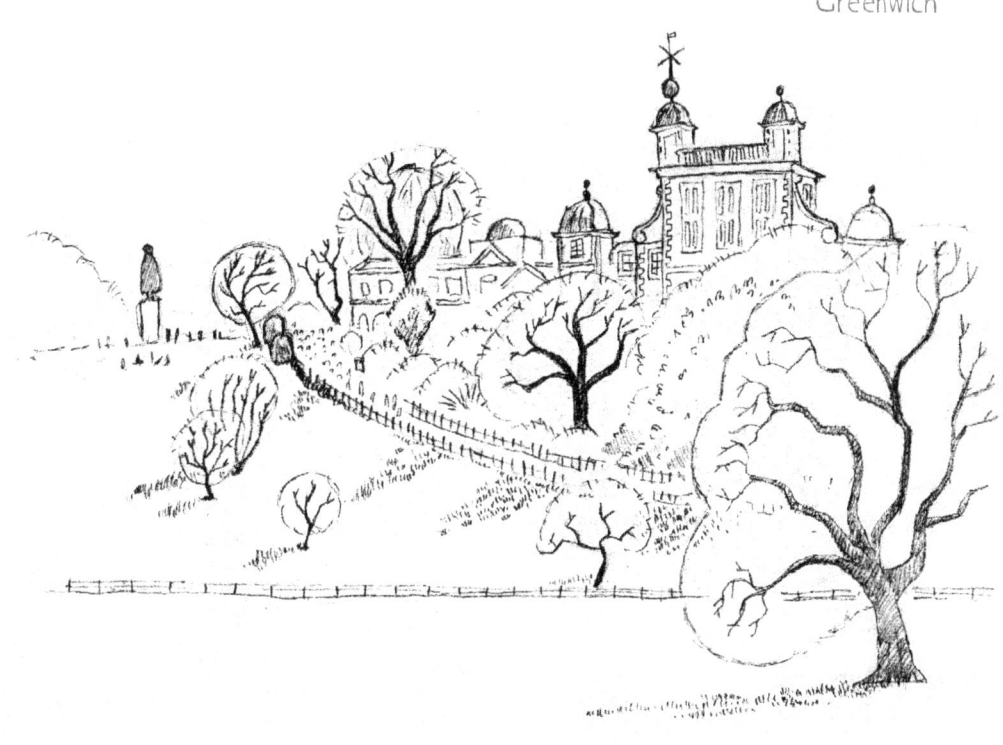

Looking up towards Greenwich Park & the Royal Observatory

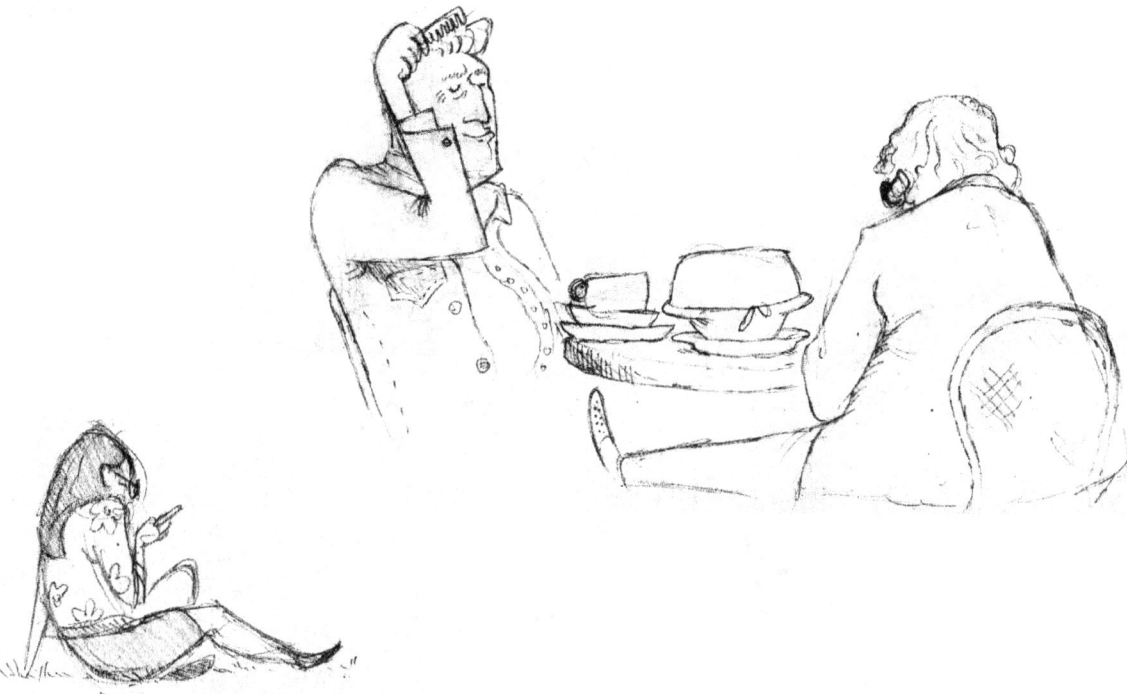

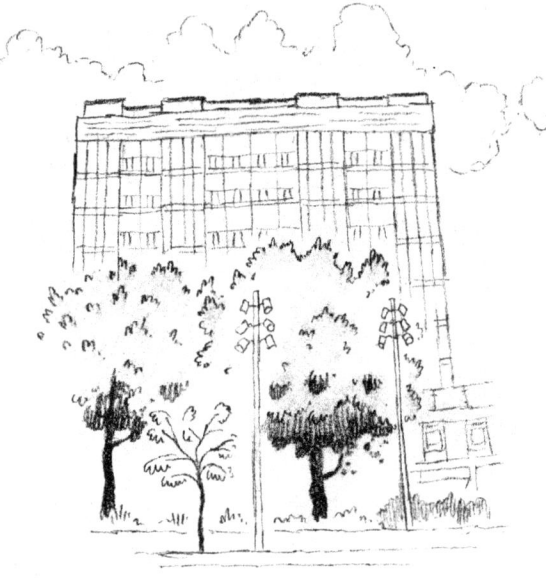

Woolwich Arsenal
Tower Block

Woolwich Central Tesco
Store with Apartments

In 2014 this building was awarded
the Carbuncle Cup by the architecture
website Building Design. It's the
architectural equivalent of a razzie,
given to the worst new building in Britain
each year. I can't help feel it's a bit
undeserved. The judges labelled this building
'oppressive, defensive, arrogant and inept'. I
thought it looked a bit depressed but sitting on
top of a giant Tescos
probably doesn't help.

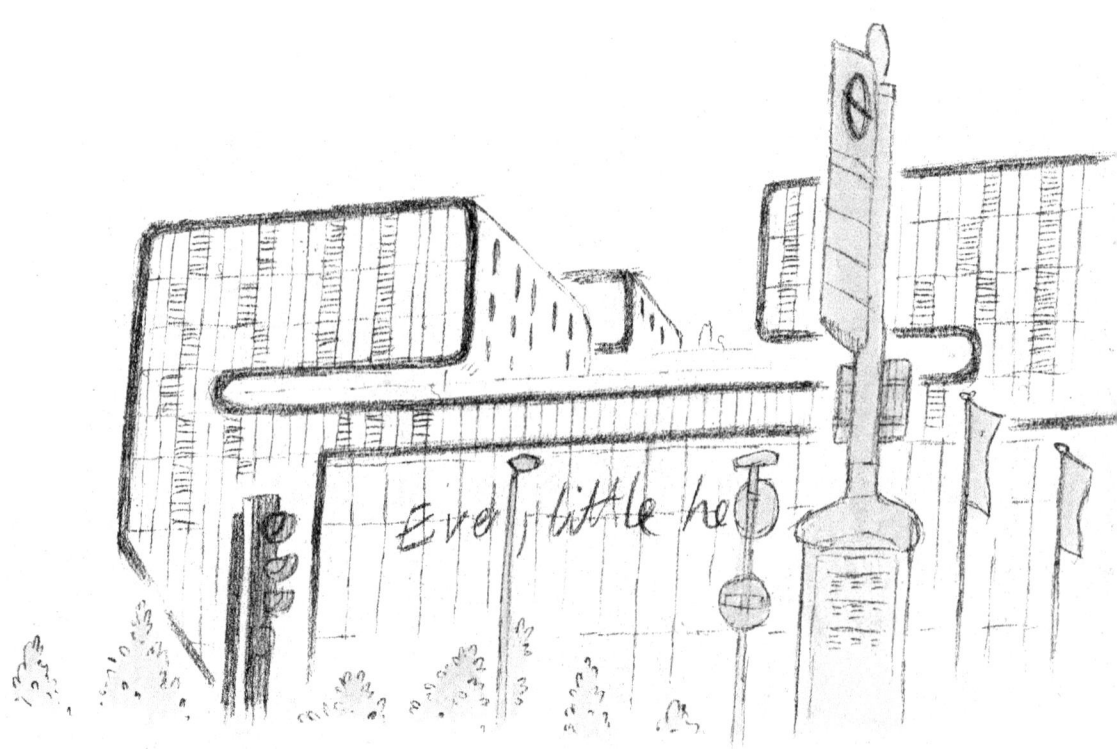

Lewisham

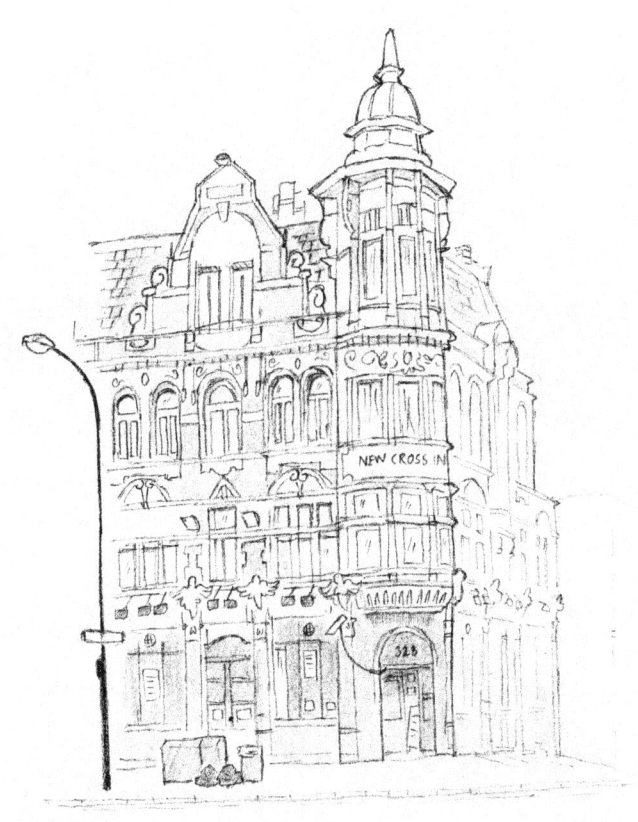

New Cross Inn Hostel

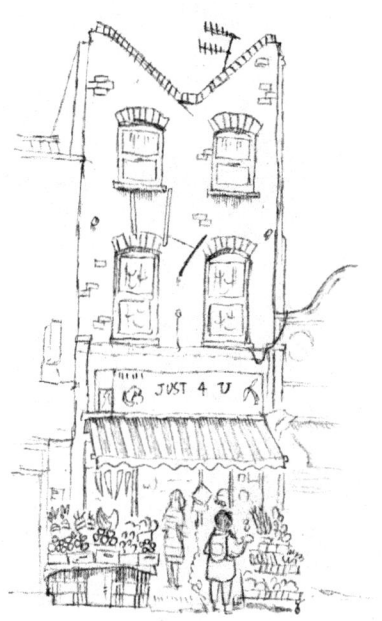

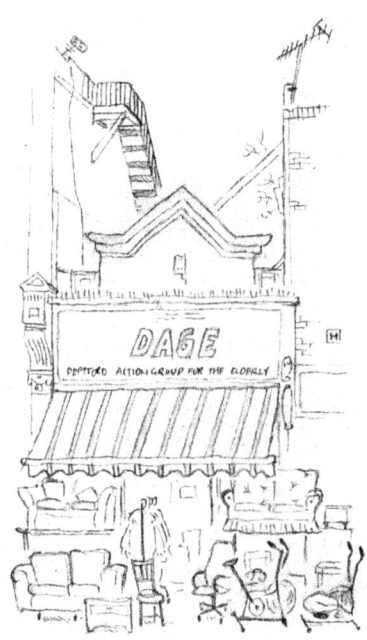

Shop fronts on Deptford High Street

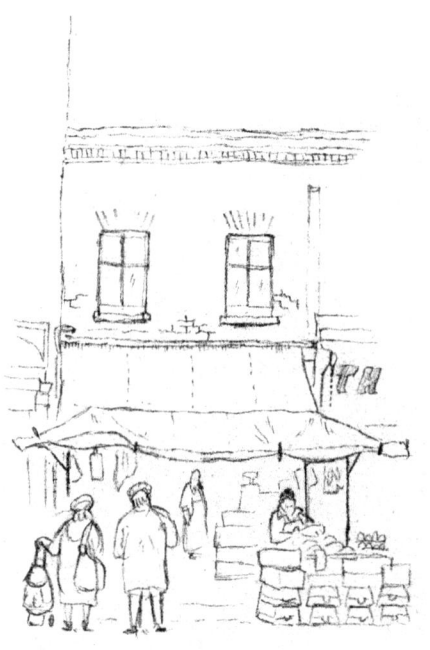

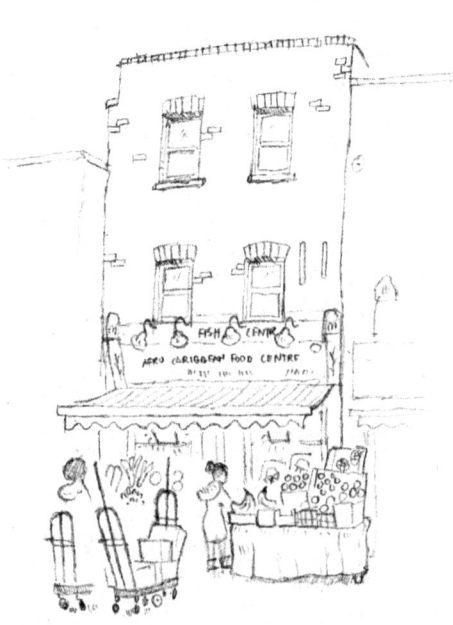

As well as the interesting shop architecture along Deptford high street, the Saturday market has characters to match. There was one guy selling jewellery, the special offer being free bracelets only available that day. His pitch seemed to be they would make a great Mothers day present and as he threw them onto the pavement he cried "Pick 'em up and sort'er aat". It seemed to do the trick. You also get the odd person asking if you have found Jesus, I think I spotted him in the local Cod Fathers.

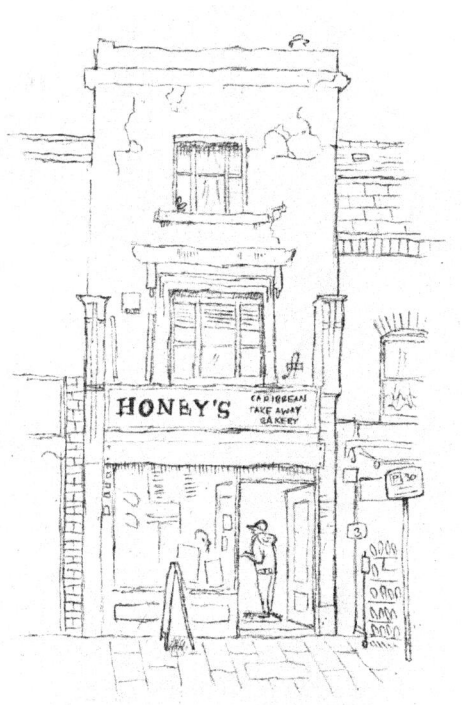

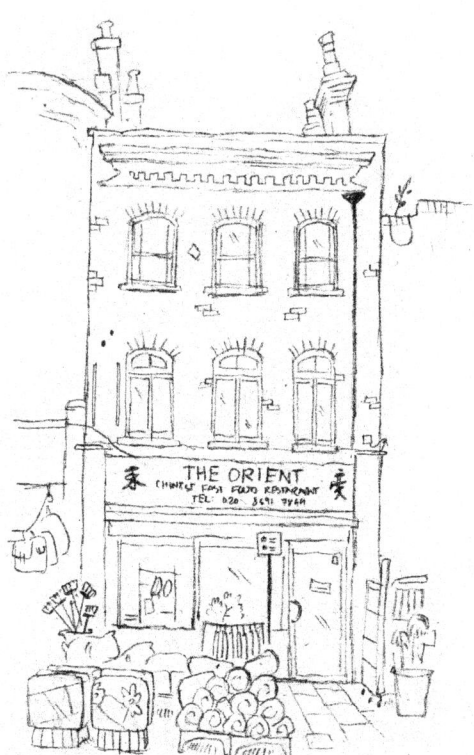

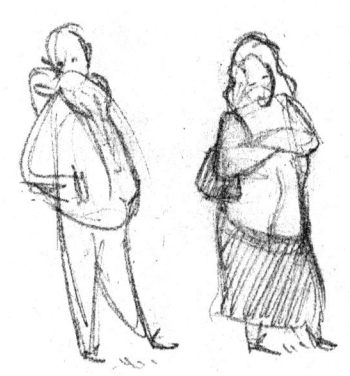

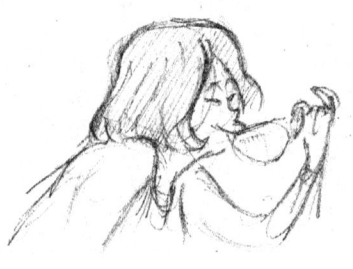

Cafe Selecta Sandwich Bar, Deptford High Street

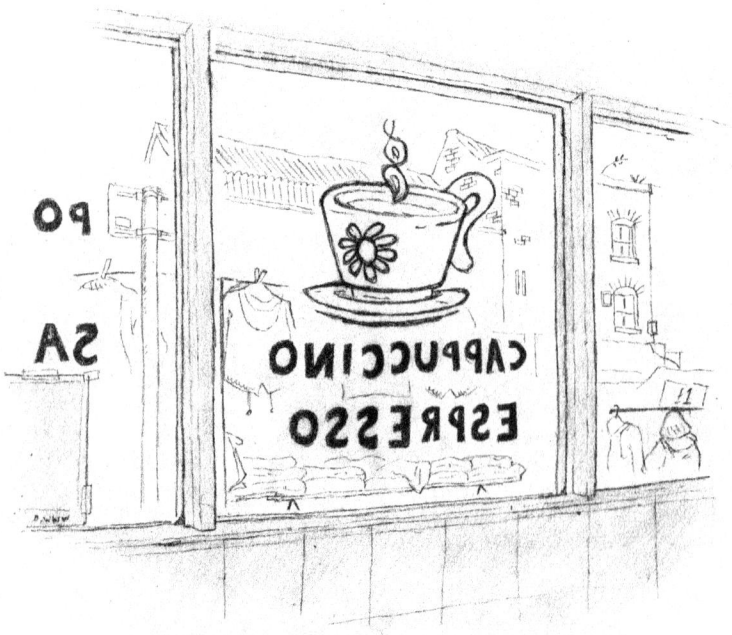

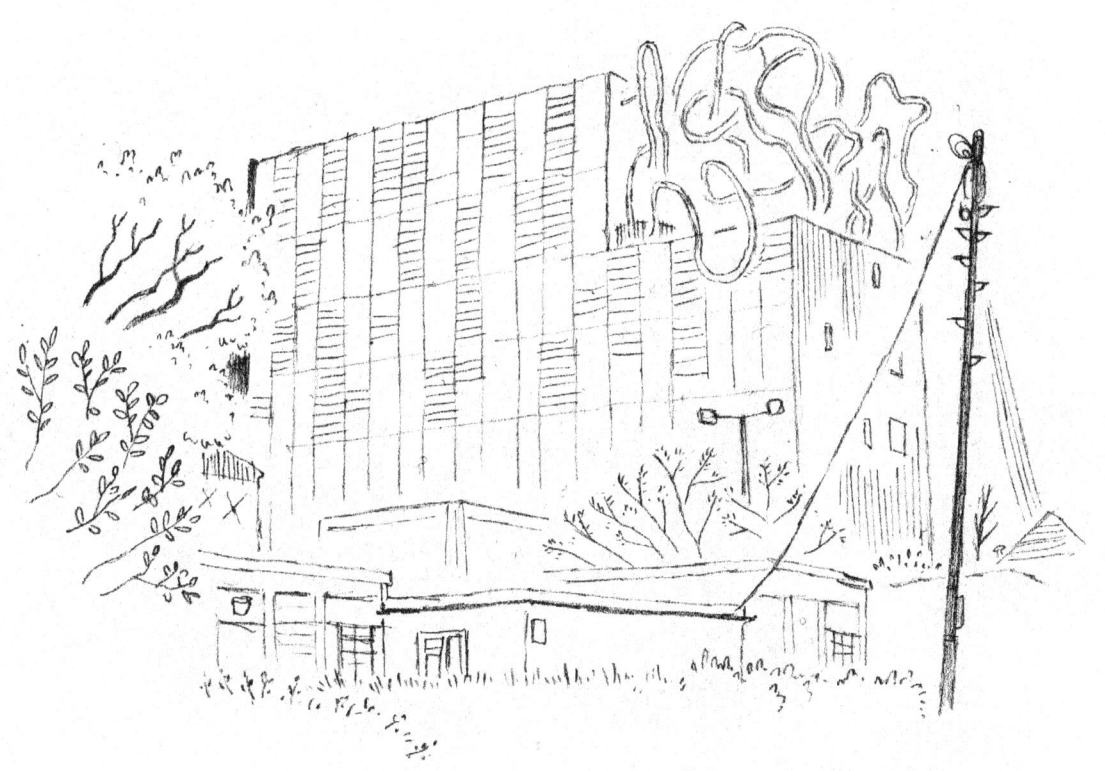

Goldsmiths College, 2005 Ben Pimlott building with scribbly sculpture

Another Coffee

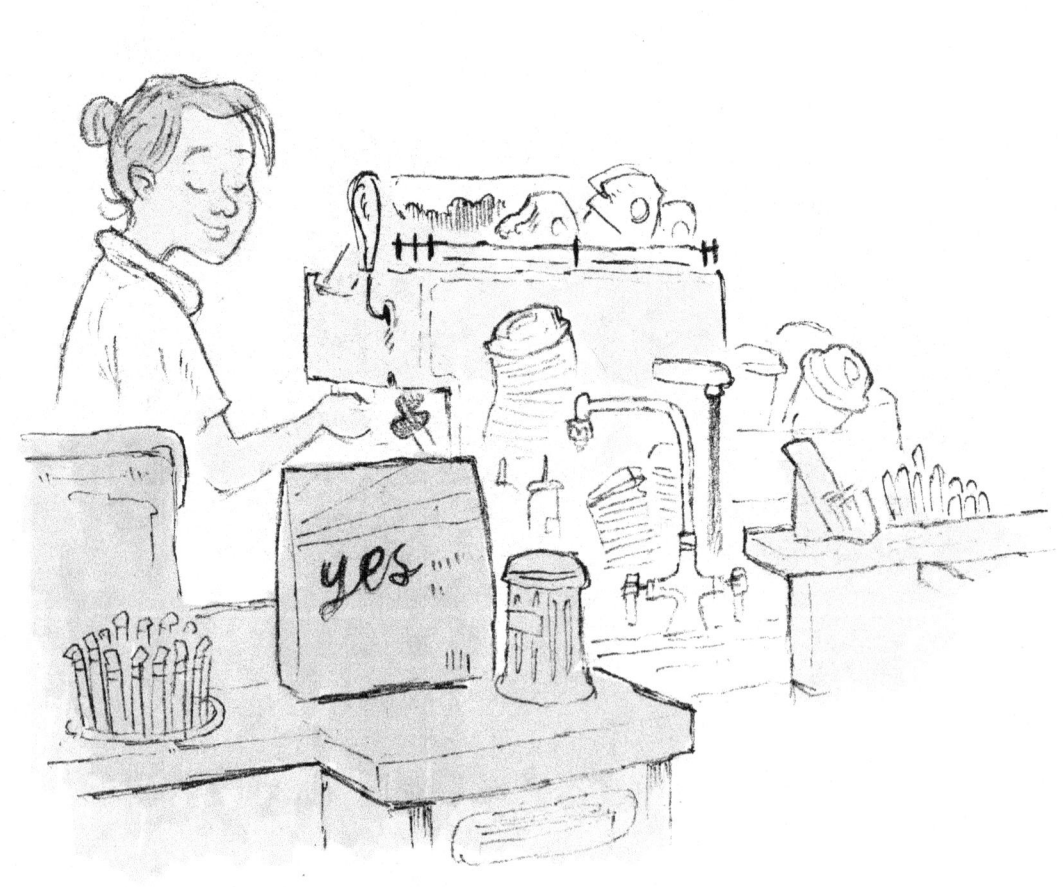

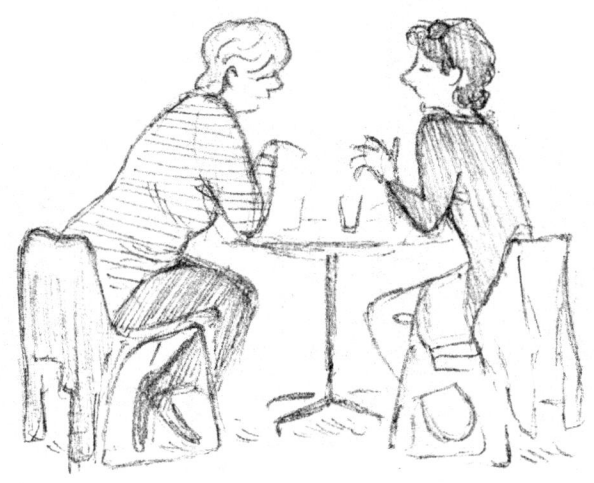

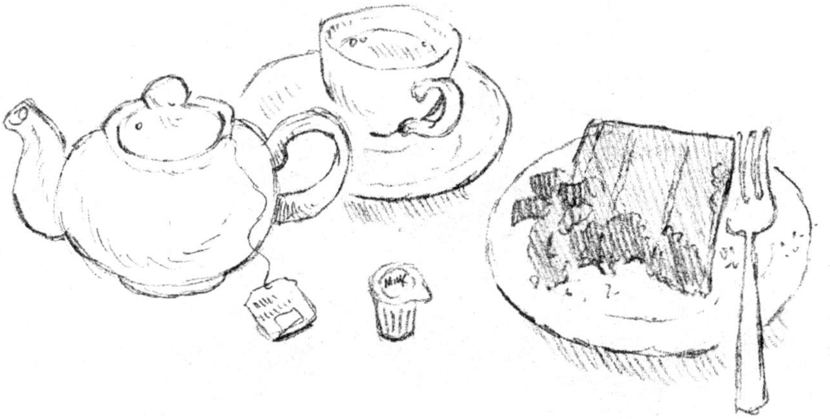

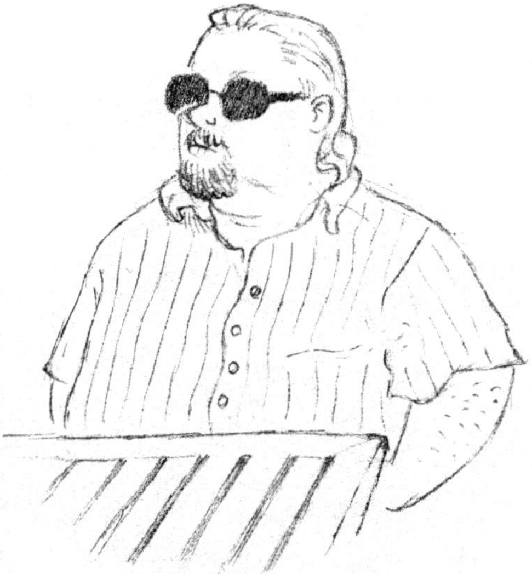

Or perhaps a pot of tea.

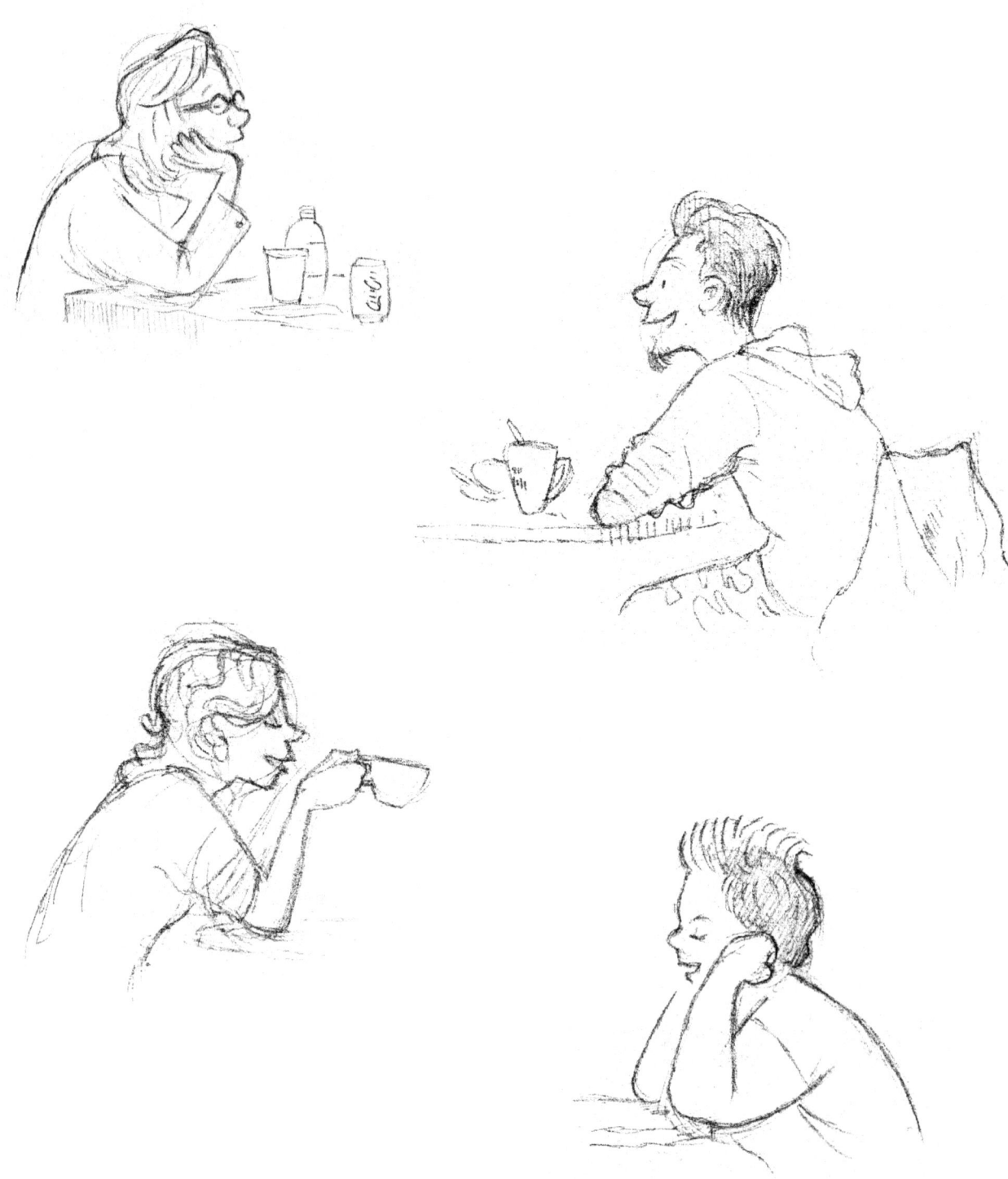

Another Coffee

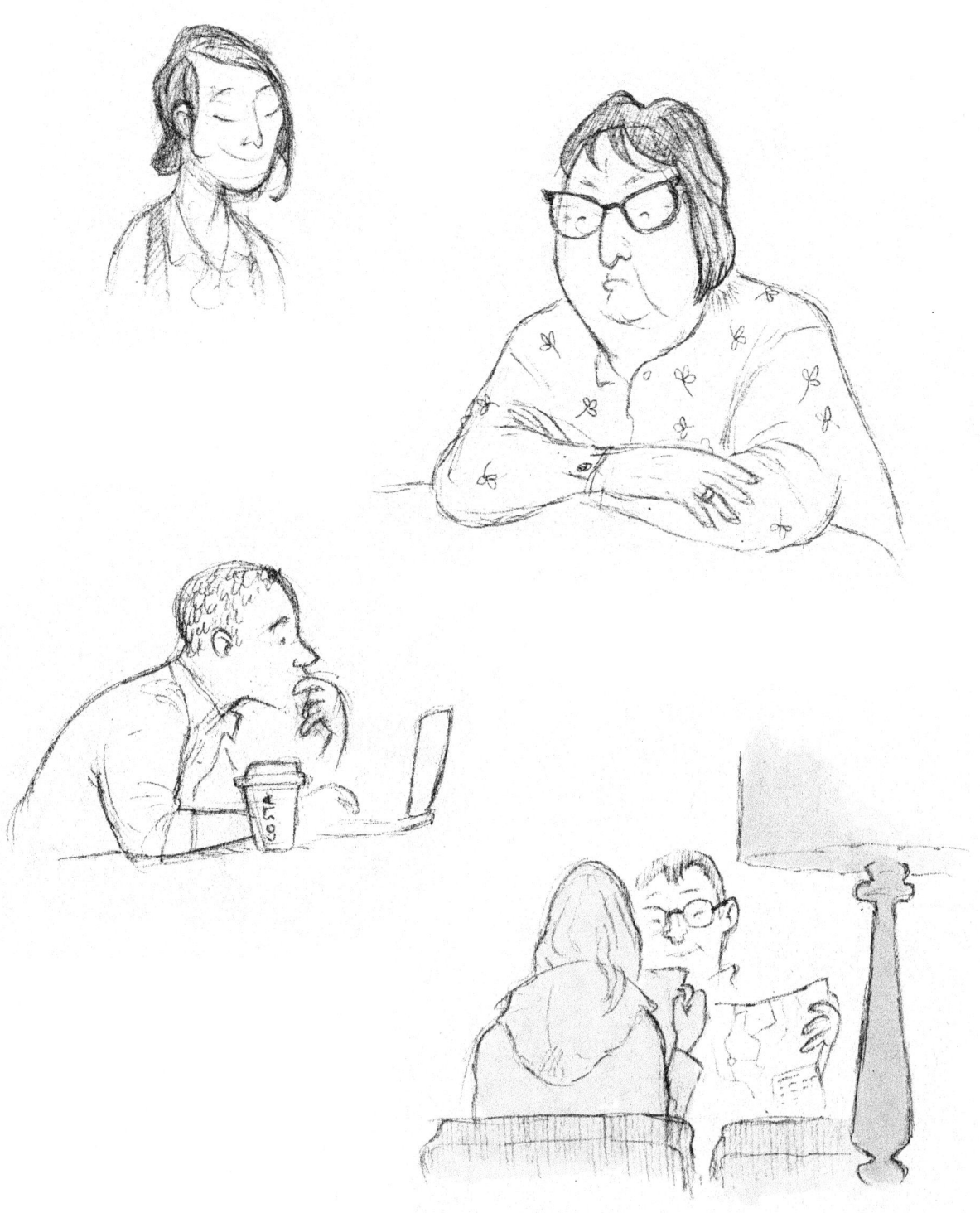

103

Pigeons!

I know a lot of people don't have much time for pigeon's, flying rats perhaps. I however see a lot of character in them, strutting around the place nodding their heads and doing very pigeony things.

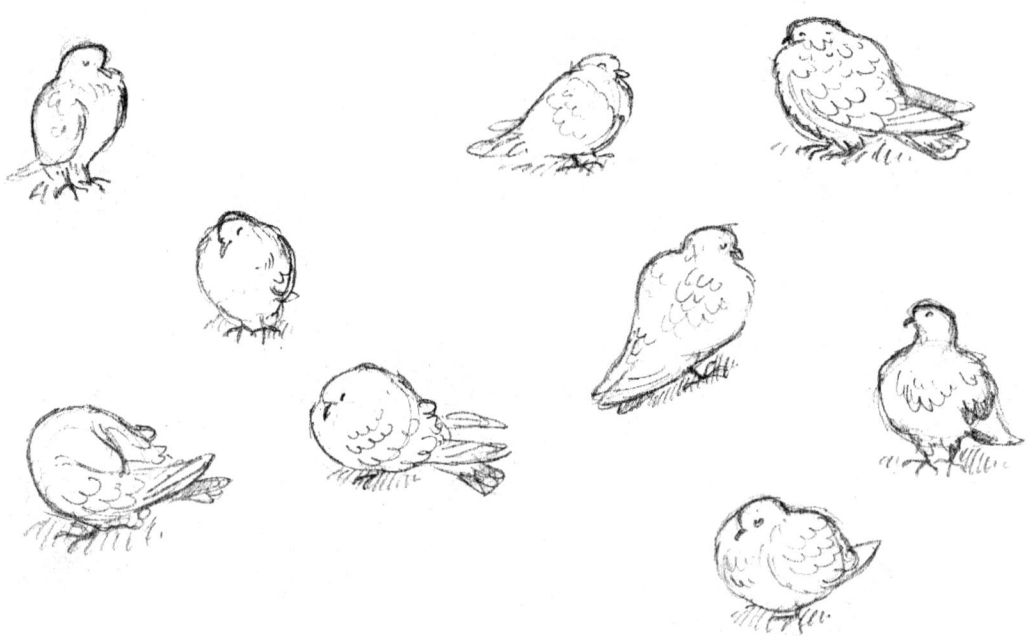

Southwark

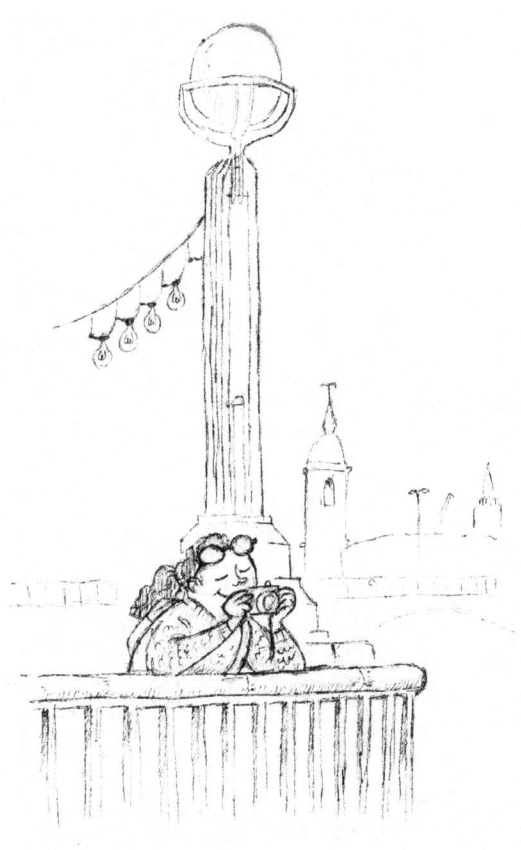

Southwark

Shop in Borough Market

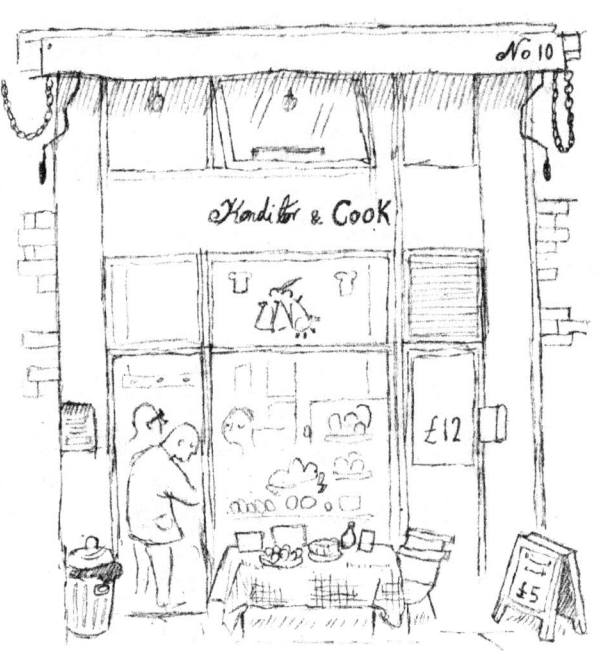

Boat in Greenland Docks

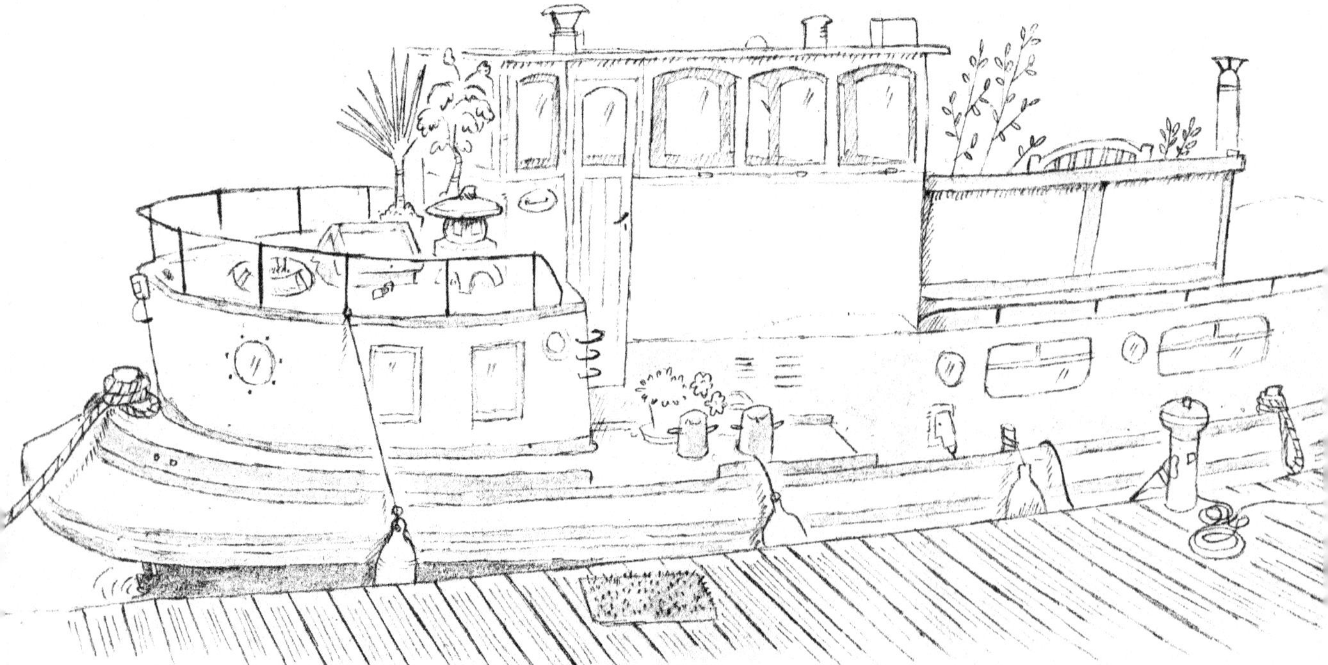

The Shard.

Opened in 2013 the Shard
stands at 306m, making it
the highest building in the
European Union at the time
of completion.

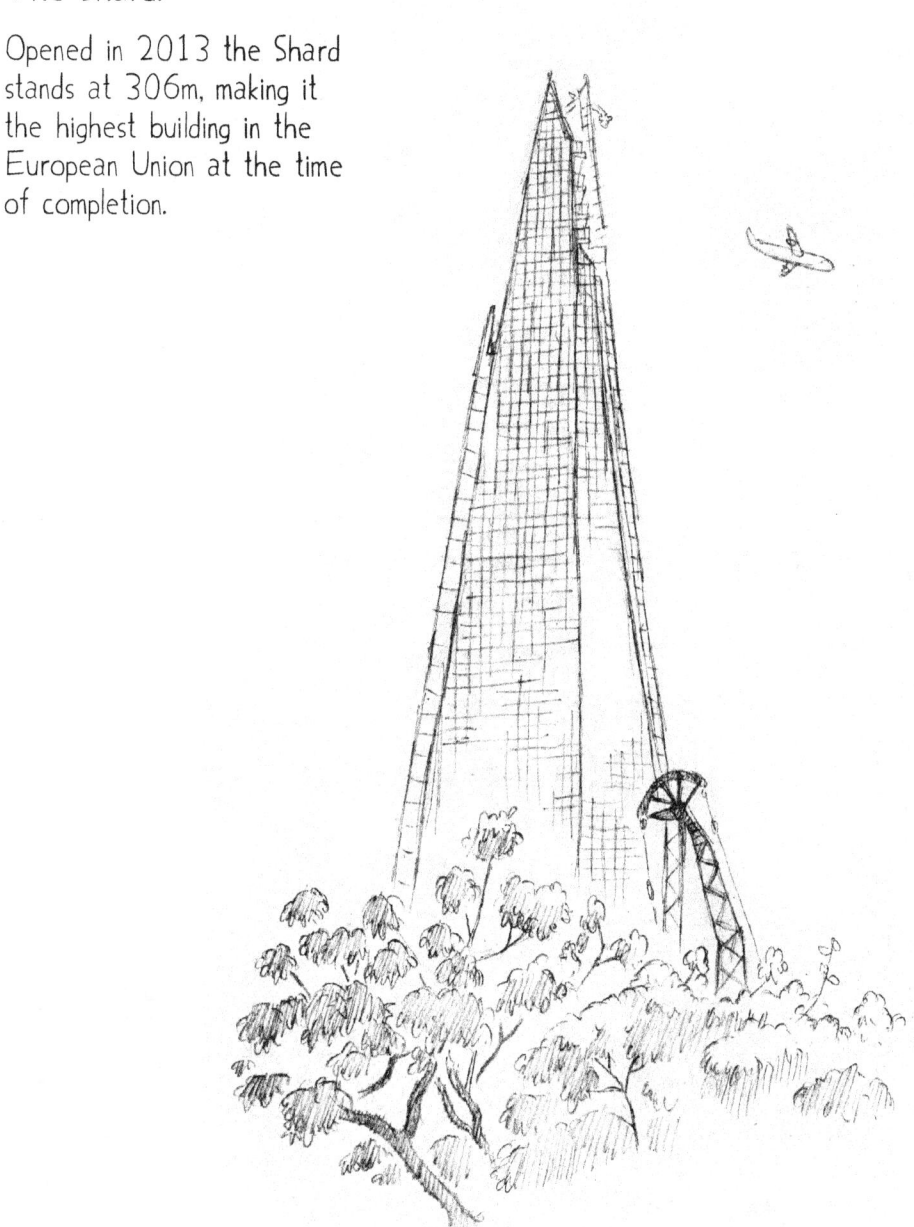

The Old Operating Theatre Museum

Housed in St Thomas Church, this museum has the oldest operating theatre in Europe and an interesting array of old fashioned and some less than convincing medication.

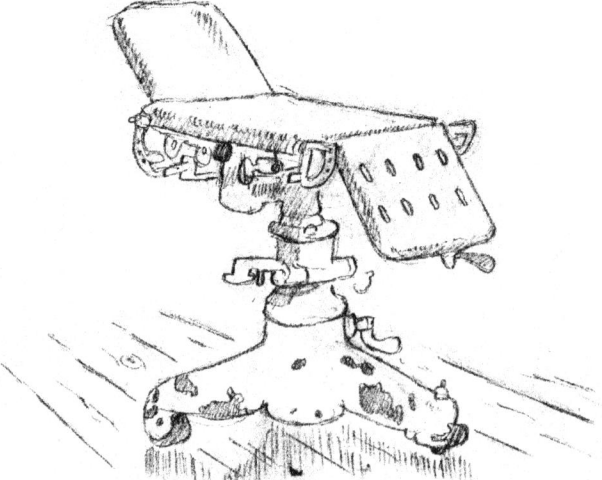

Operating table from the Evelina London Children's Hospital, 1905.

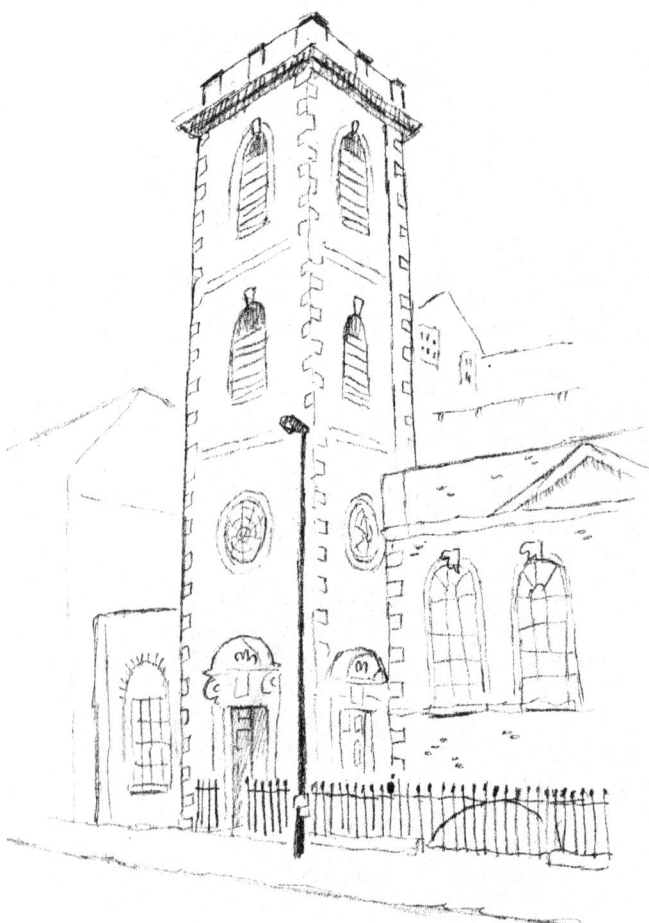

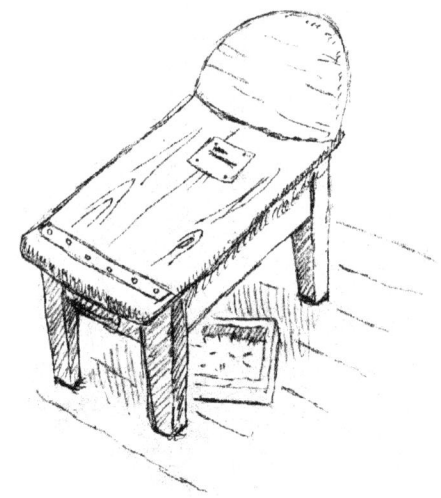

Early 14th Century Operating Table

Along the South bank of the river

City Hall, 45m

Home of the Greater London Authority and London Mayors since 2002. This Foster & Partners design stands at 45m tall.

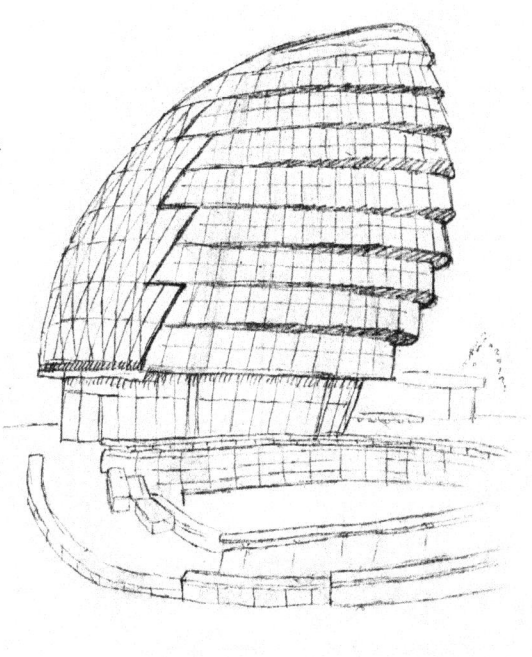

HMS Belfast

Launched on Saint Patrick's day in 1938, Belfast was the largest and most powerful cruiser in the Royal Navy. After a premature hiccup in her service when she collided with a mine, Belfast went on to protect supply conveys to Russia and play a part in the D-Day landings during WW11. She retired in 1963 and is now a permanent museum ship, moored on the Thames just west of city hall.

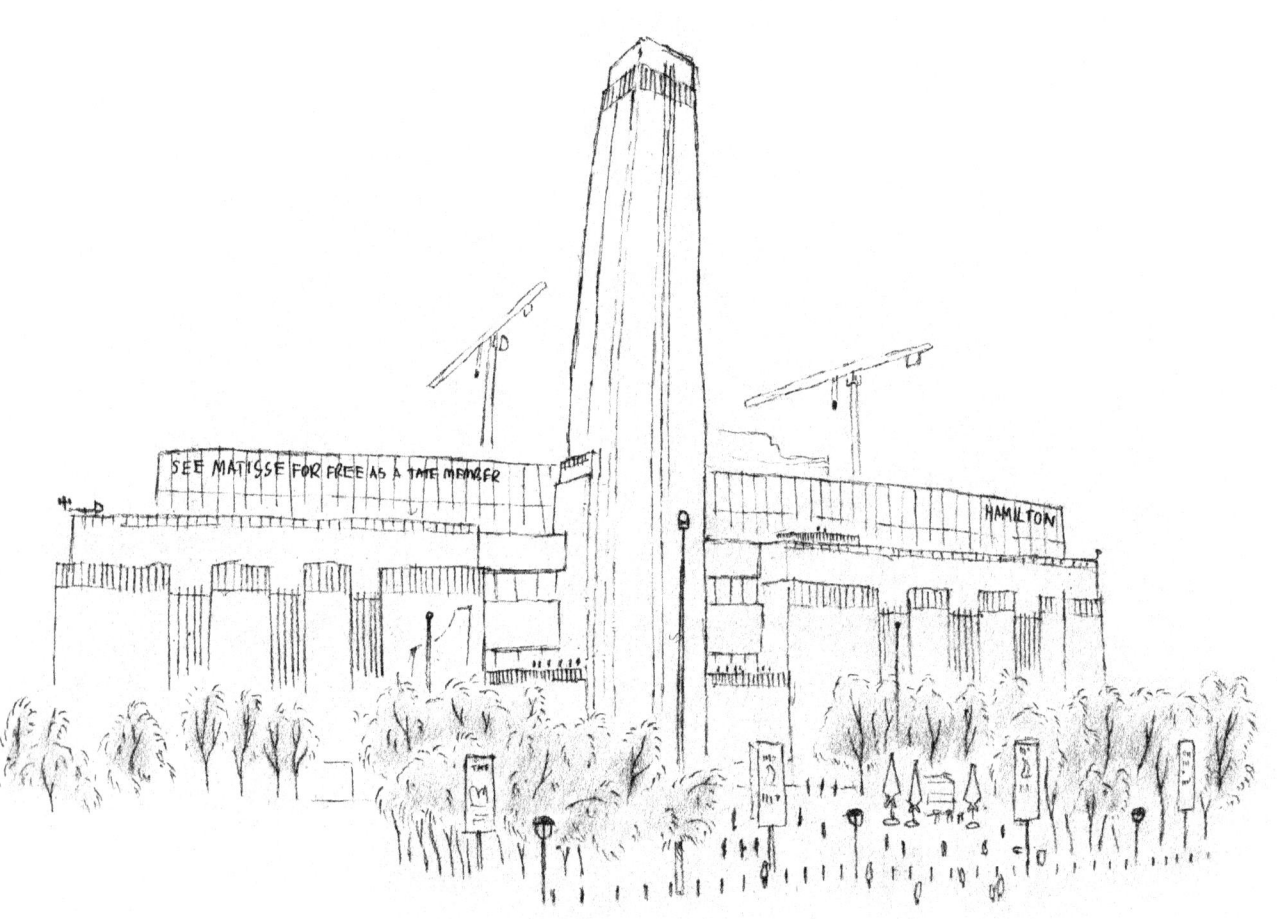

Tate Modern

Previously the Bankside Power Station, this became the home of the national modern art collection in 2000. Modern art in this case being anything created from the start of the 20th Century onwards. Makes you wonder when modern will become old fashioned.

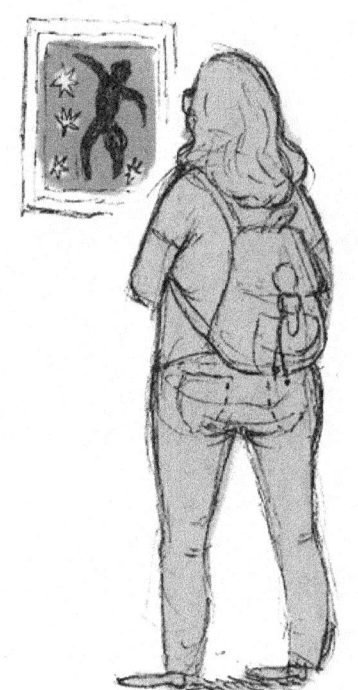

Lady studying 'Icarus' in the 'Henri Matisse: The Cut-Outs' exhibition, June 2014 at Tate Modern.

'I Don't Know. The Weave of Textile Language' by American sculpture Richard Tuttle, October 2014.

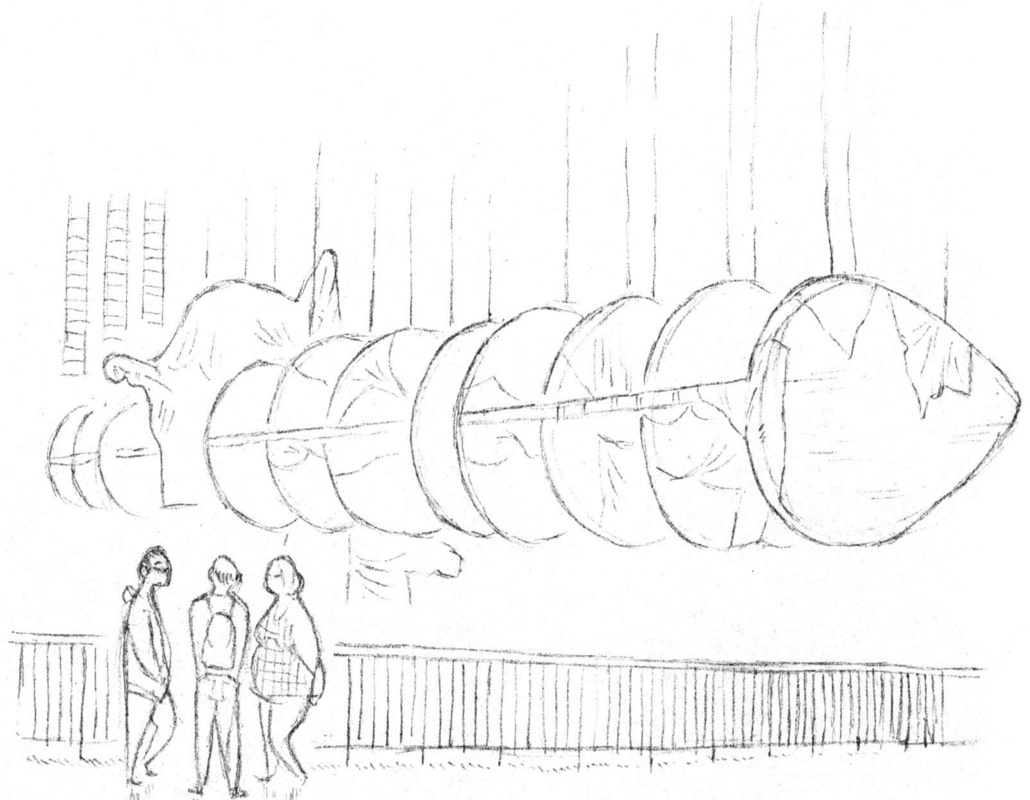

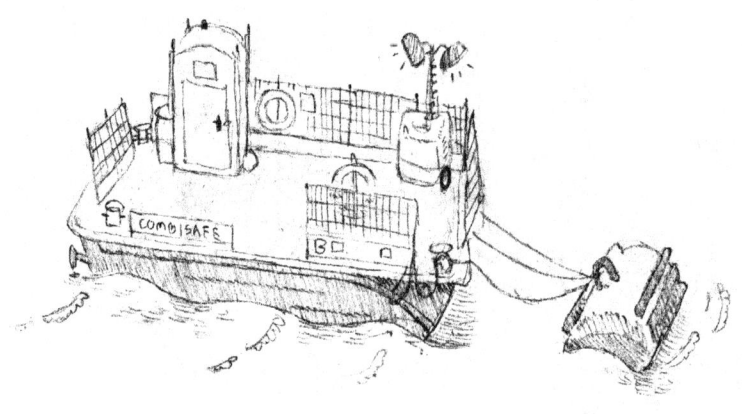

Floating jetty on Thames with toilet.

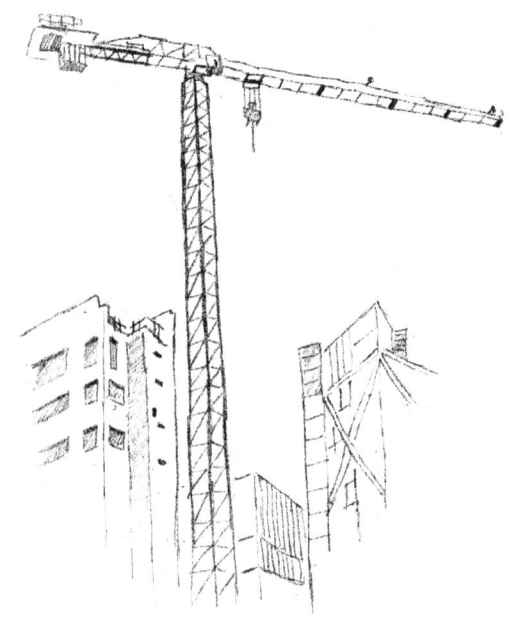

Crane on the building site for the Tate Modern's western block, March 2013.

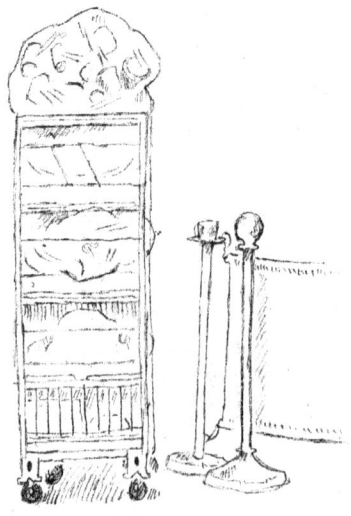

A waste bin at the Tate Modern (not part of an exhibition).

Christ's Chapel,
Dulwich

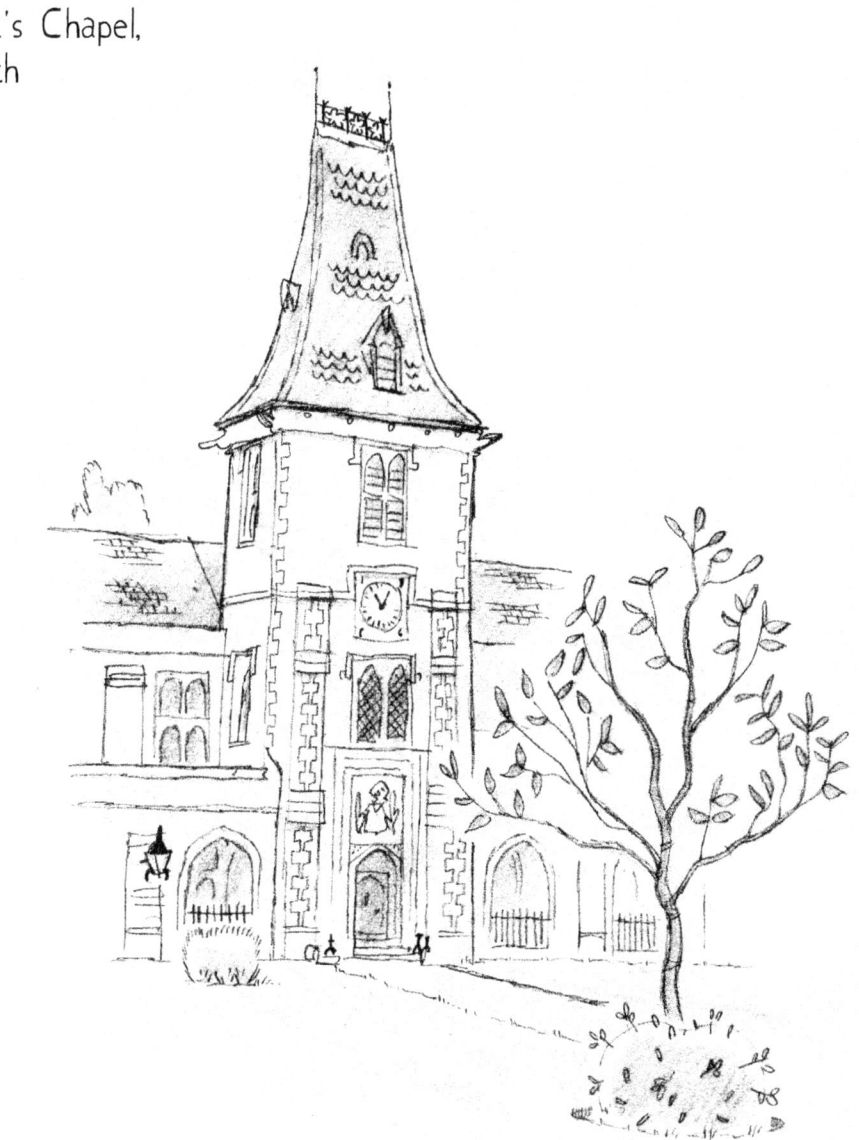

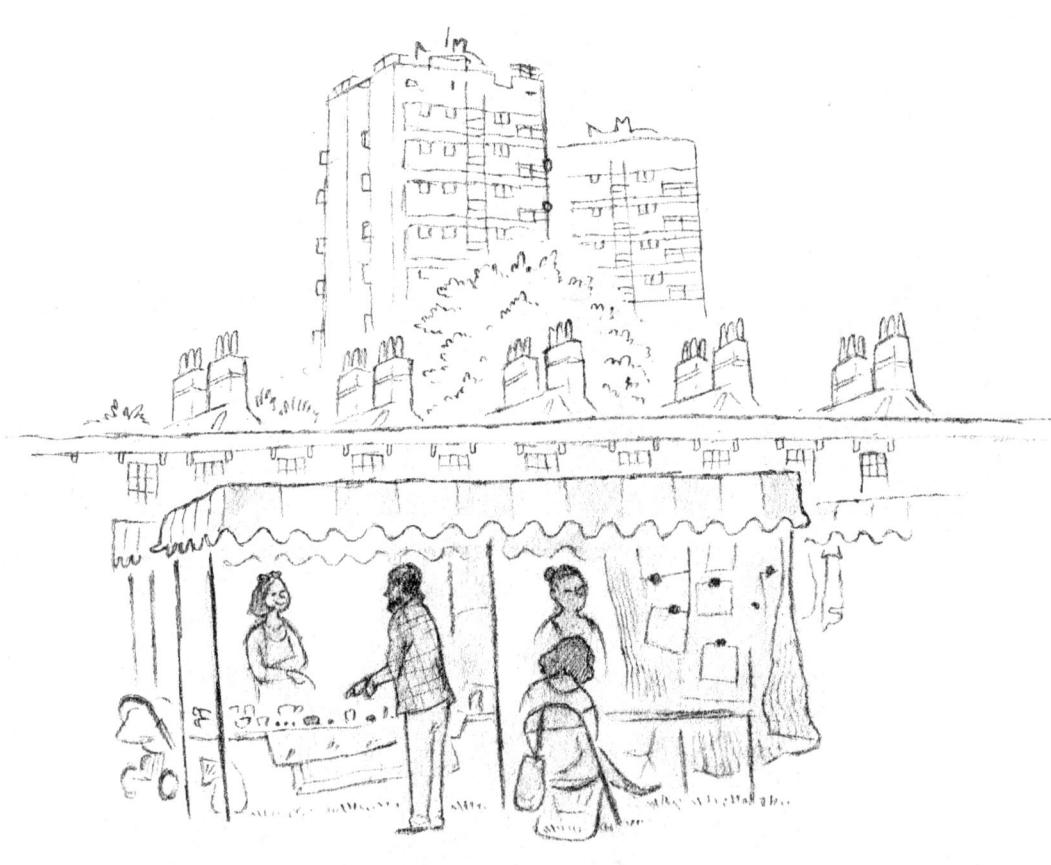

Stalls at Brimmington Festival, June 2014

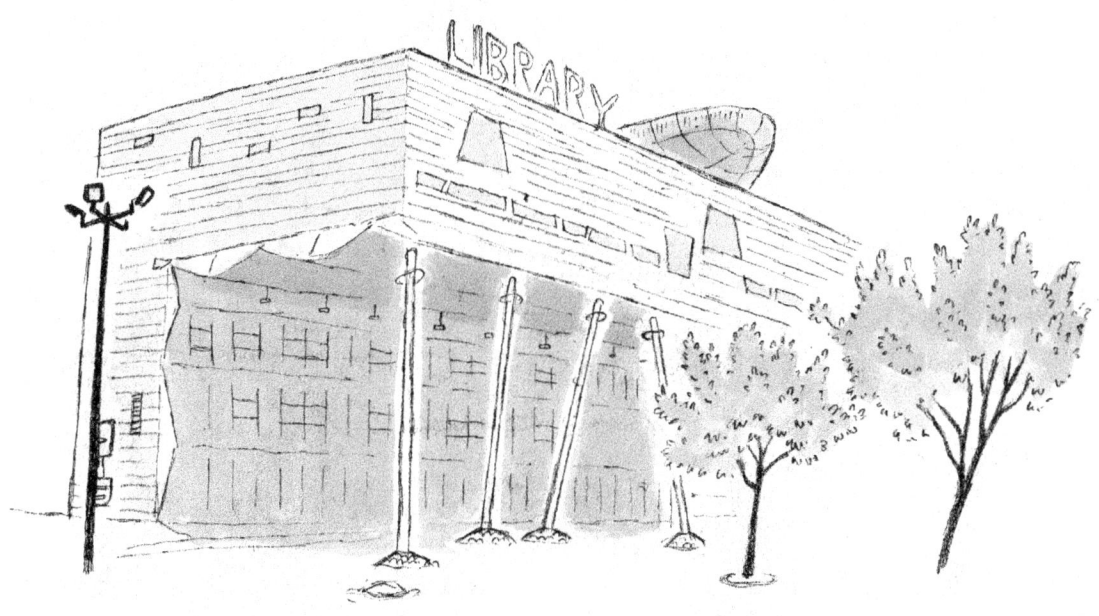

Peckham Library

Designed by Alsop and Stormer, this building won the 2000 Sterling prize for architecture.

Imperial War Museum

Since 1936 the home of the London IWM has been in Southwark. The building having previously been the Bethlem Royal Hospital for mental illness from which the term Bedlam came into use.

The two huge 15-inch guns guarding the front are from separate war ships and have seen action in both world wars, the right hand gun being used on D-Day. Each barrel weighs nearly 100 tons with a range just over 16 miles. They could comfortably reach Wembley Stadium.

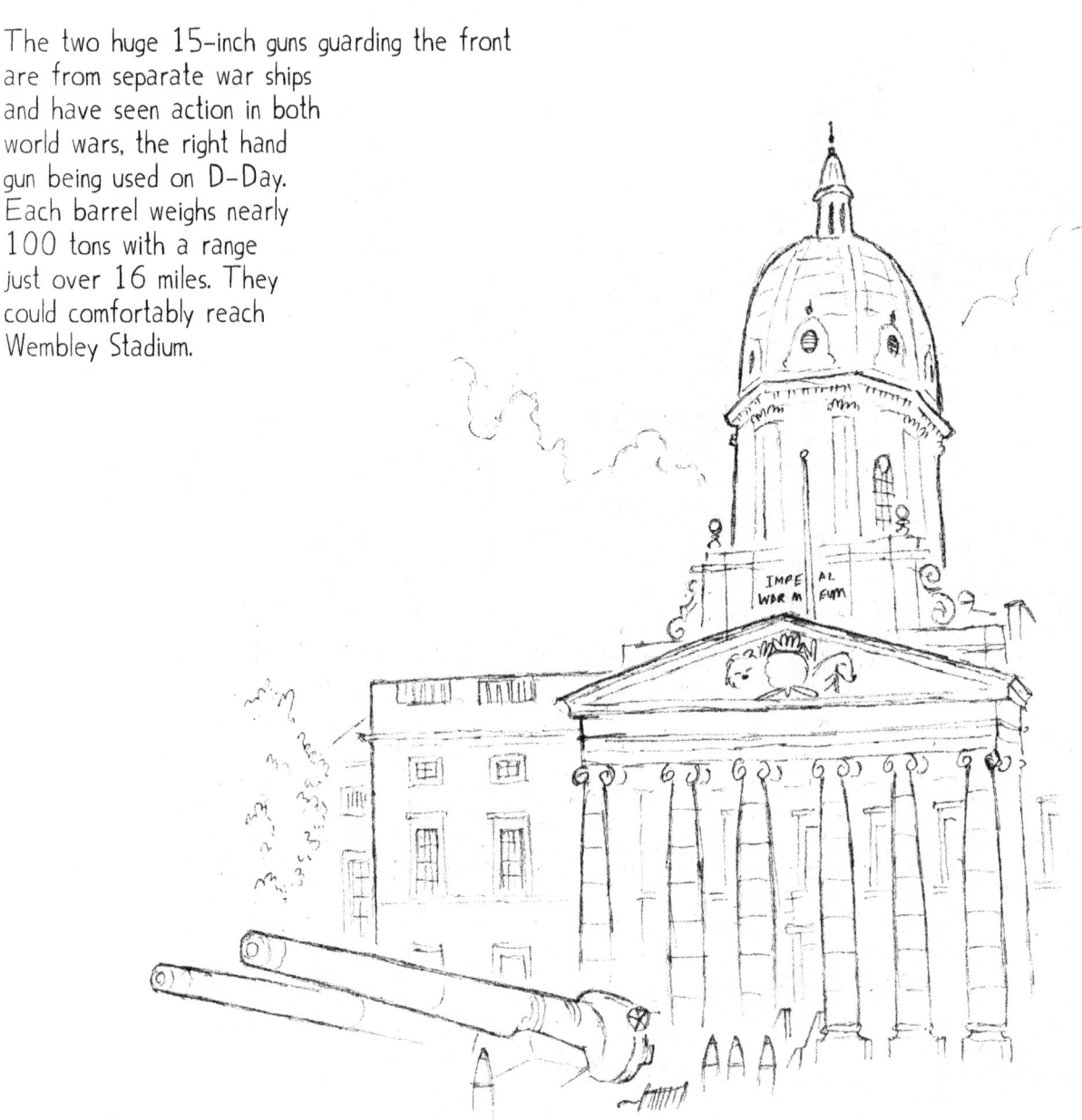

United States Jeep

An instantly recognisable part of
American military and cultural history.
This was developed in 1940 to be
a light, general purpose vehicle for
the Second World War. Used by
every allied army during thewar,
by the end of the conflict
nearly 640,000 had been
produced.

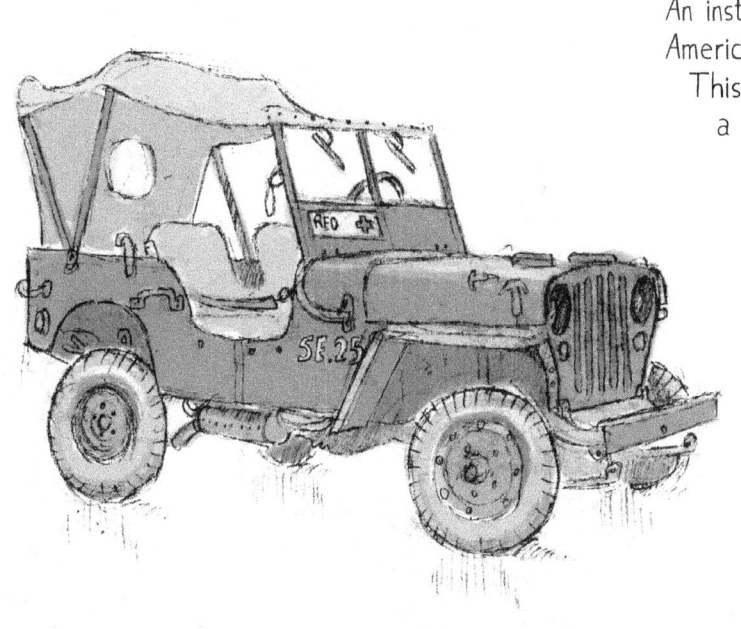

Argentine 20mm Anti-Aircraft Twin Gun

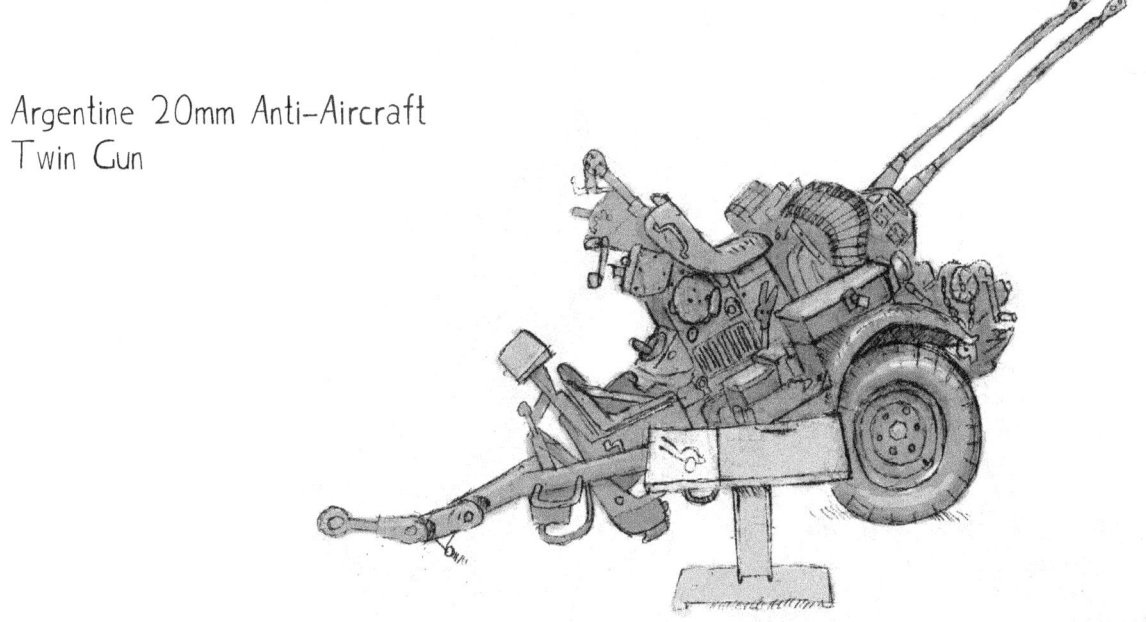

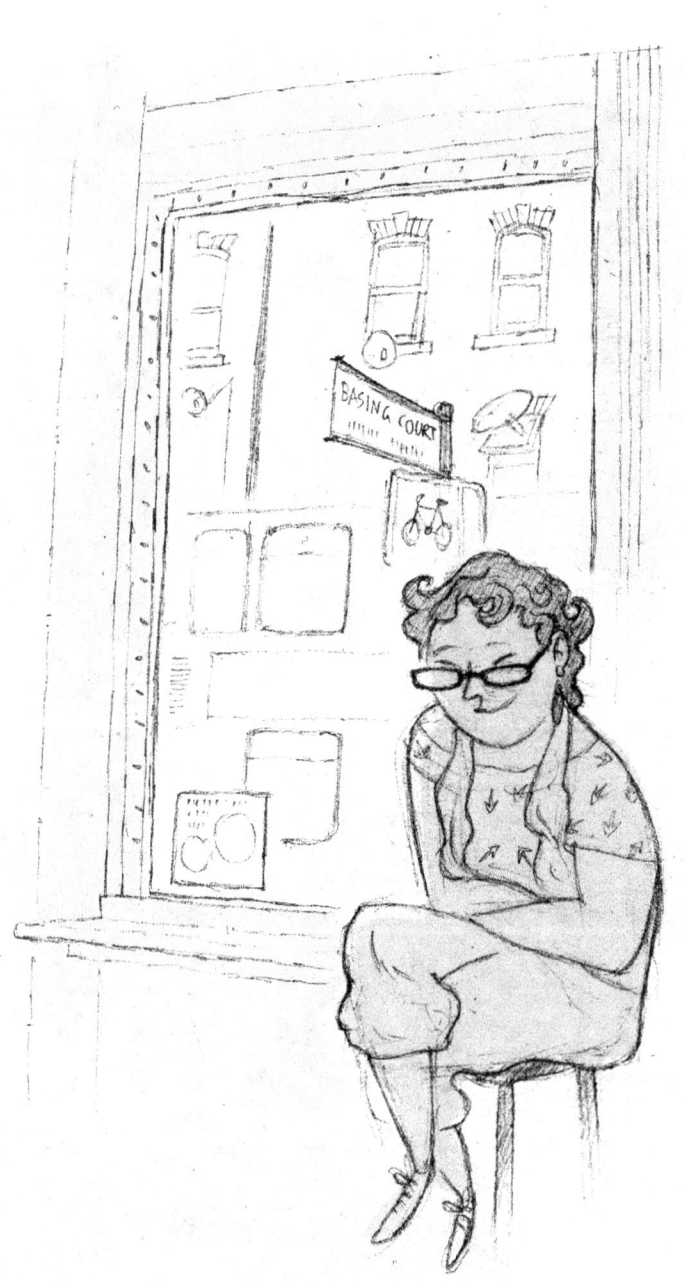

Inside cafe, Peckham

Everyone Can Draw

It's far too easy for people to believe they can't draw. It seems society largely views drawing as a traditional skill and therefore should produce results that fit with traditionally held artistic values, if the work is to be of high value. So many 'How to Draw' or 'Learn to Sketch' books just teach you to observe and copy what you see. Although this is a skill and can give much satisfaction it often discourages people from picking up a pen or pencil, knowing that when they try and draw a face, for example, what ends up on the paper doesn't look realistic. Well the thing is it probably looks more like a face than you think, by this I mean that it's more 'facey'. It embodies the essence of a face if you like. Think about it, when a child draws a picture of a house, you know it's a house, even if it doesn't look like any house that has actually been built. It has the spirit and character of the house in spades. It has a door, big windows maybe a chimney on top. All the things that define the essence of a house.

Well you were young once too and you probably didn't think twice about drawing, only later when thoughts begun to enter your mind like 'that doesn't really look like that house did you become self conscious about your work and stop. This fear is only reinforced by the prominence of teaching you to draw exactly what is in front of you. The real treasure out there is more creative, more exciting than producing a photo realistic copy of a house. Anyway please save yourself the agony of counting how many bricks there are on a wall or the number of windows on a skyscraper, leaving the audience with just an impression is, in my opinion, even better. I should add that I do fall into the accuracy trap, it's something I have to resist nearly everytime I draw.

So get out there and sketch, free from any pressure to produce something that contains exactly the right number of bricks!

Unless you enjoy counting bricks :)

Concentration

Concentration is usually a given once you start drawing but making a sketch successful is all about maintaining focus.

For people to believe in the work and for it to have harmony it has to consistently keep to a set of rules. These can be thought of as your natural style, something that you may not consciously consider while working and a seemingly unquantifiable expression. The qualities of your style can be quantitative though. If you like to draw cars with small wheels and tall windows, your buses, trains and bikes have to fit ergonomically into that world as well. The way you represent form and texture with your medium has to in some way be consistent across all subjects, regardless of their substance, for example hair vs. leaves or a doormat.

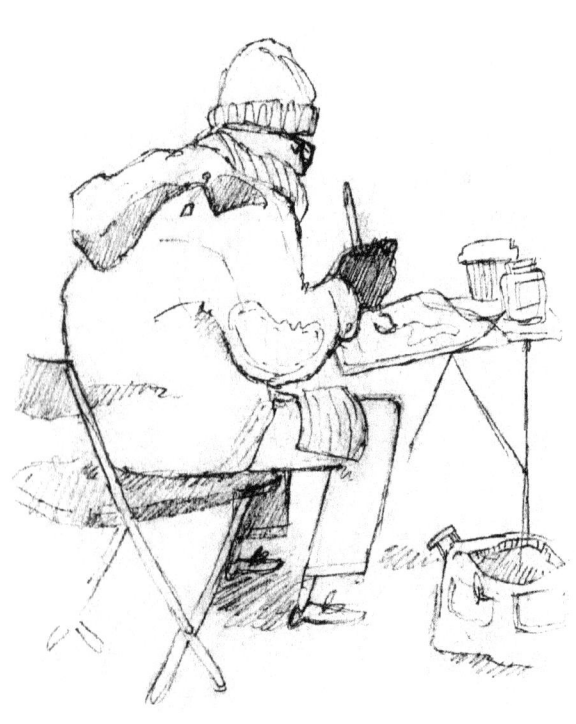

Another aspect that requires concentration is keeping in mind a certain narrative or story for the work. Perhaps people arguing over dinner, an awkward meeting on a street or someone calling for assistance at a Boris bike station. It doesn't have to be explicit, a lot of the interest in looking at pictures is joining the dots as it were; layering a scenario on a scene as the observer. However there has to be a certain amount of 'push' from the artist to make this possible. Any narrative needs to be kept in mind all the time while sketching to properly convey the intended actions or context.

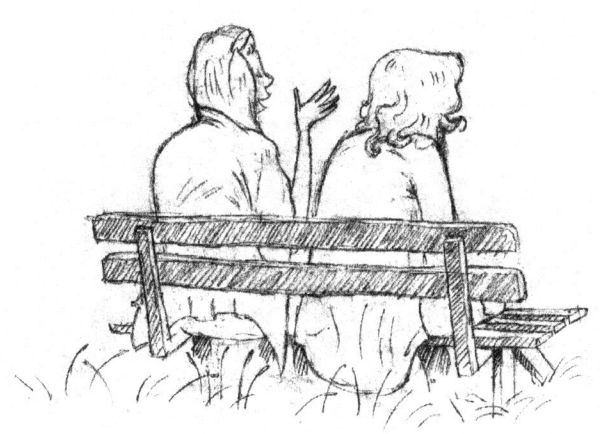

Ladies Chatting in Hampstead Heath

When your concentration wanders, the pictures story and consistency, it's believability let's say, can easily be lost. Worse, if you become aimless in your sketching you end up doodling. This is not necessarily a bad thing per-say, it can be very relaxing but it is probably going to counter any constructive message your work was trying to convey. It is also counterproductive to improvement. Doodling is what you do when on the phone, or thinking about tomorrows problems; your mind is not focused on the subject you are working with. You're not thinking about the aim of the piece, not learning and (here comes the school teacher bit) therefore not improving.

This is a not an easy thing to always keep in mind, I often slip up having committed a technique to memory that I can then just repeat. All the images in this book have a degree of this, when concentration drifts and I fall back on some comfortable compromise to the problem. Of course you can't be at one hundred percent all the time but the higher it is the more rewarding the final piece will be, generally, ignoring the unavoidable mistakes :)

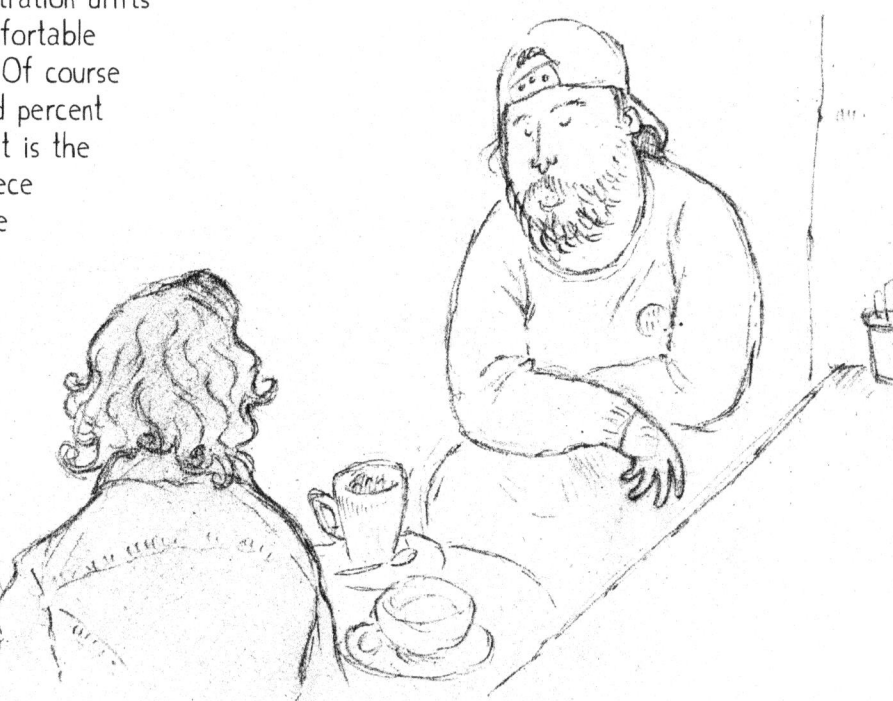

Getting Through the day

Maintaining a high concentration while sketching does mean you often get tired. As with any physical exercise, mental exercise also requires fuel to keep you at or near your best. I guess it's a bit like taking a test or writing a book, you can tell when your mind is struggling to keep all the pieces together. Along with the endless coffee and snacks I did end up with a good recipe for a bespoke sandwich, after attempting to save a few pence buying lunch. Dinning out every-time does little to help the struggling artist. So here is the sandwich recipe...

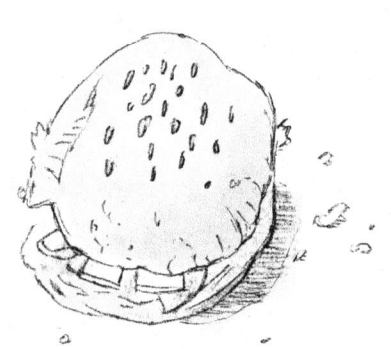

1 Brown Roll
1 Slice of Ox Tongue
1 Slice Honey Roast Ham
Cheese of your choice
Sliced Red Pepper
Sliced Avocado
Victorian Chutney

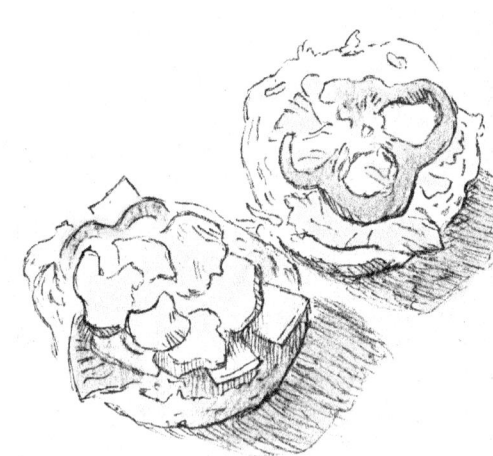

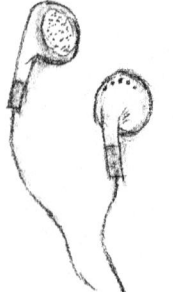

Although taking in the sounds of your environment might be a virtuous thing for the 'artist' to do, sometimes I just need to listen to something out of context. I have spent many glorious hours sketching in the sunshine listening to music or podcasts. The Bugle podcast was a personal favourite and with over 250 episodes there is plenty of material to keep me amused.

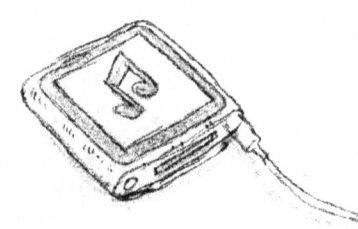

Lambeth

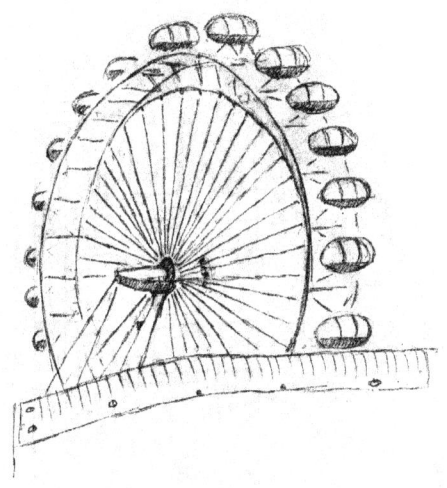

London Eye, 135m

Next page: The Shell Centre, 107m.
Built in 1961 and designed by Sir
Howard Robertson

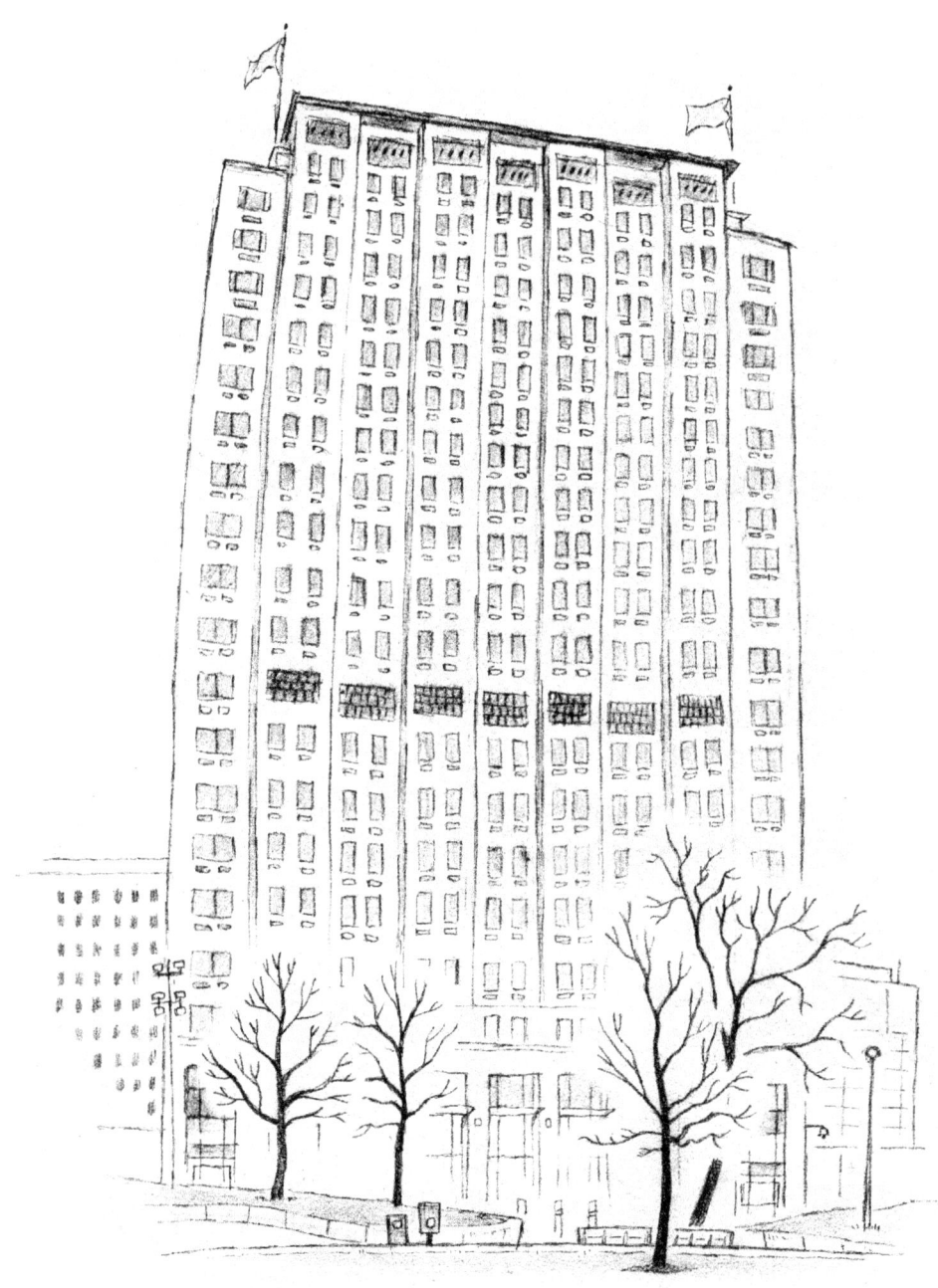

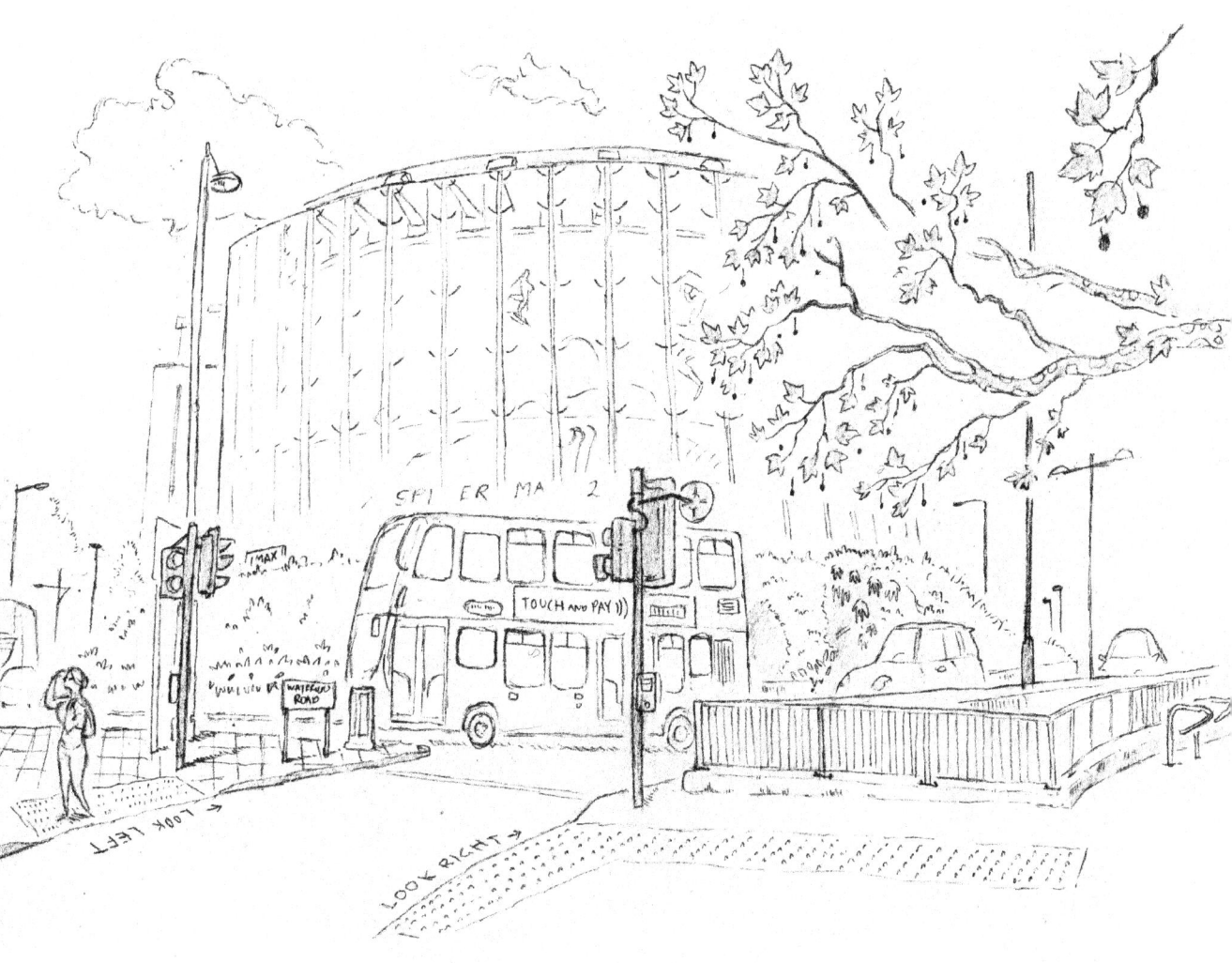

If you are going to a movie that's best viewed on a big screen, there is none bigger (in Britain at least) than the British Film Institute's IMAX at Waterloo roundabout. Standing next to this busy roundabout sketching was not a pleasant spot, having to breathe in all those car and bus fumes. A hot air balloon would have been much better, or maybe perched up a tree,

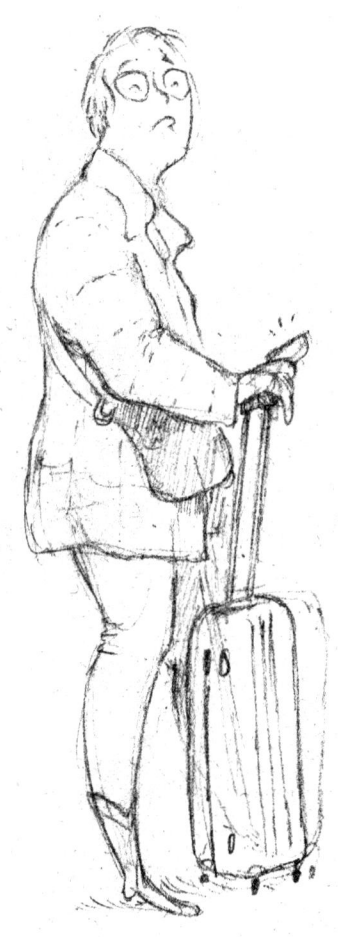

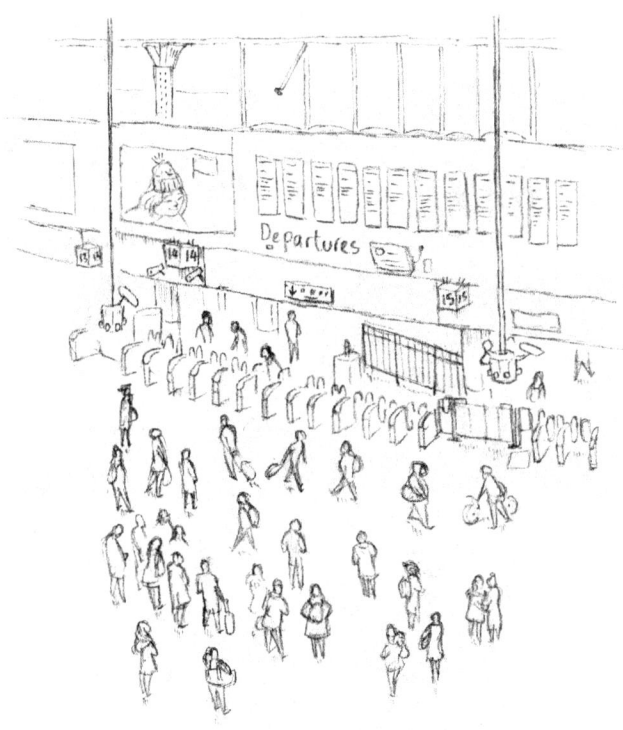

Commuters at Waterloo station waiting for their train home on a Friday night.

If you want to practice drawing people in public without them noticing you, try the ones absorbed by the train departures board.

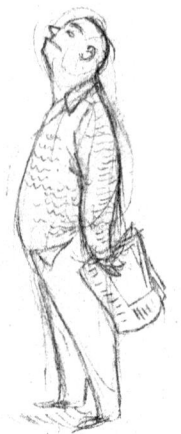

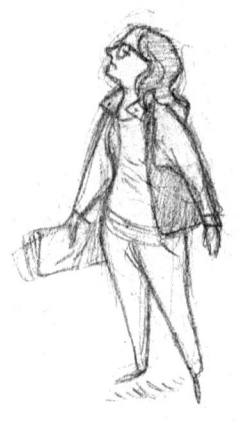

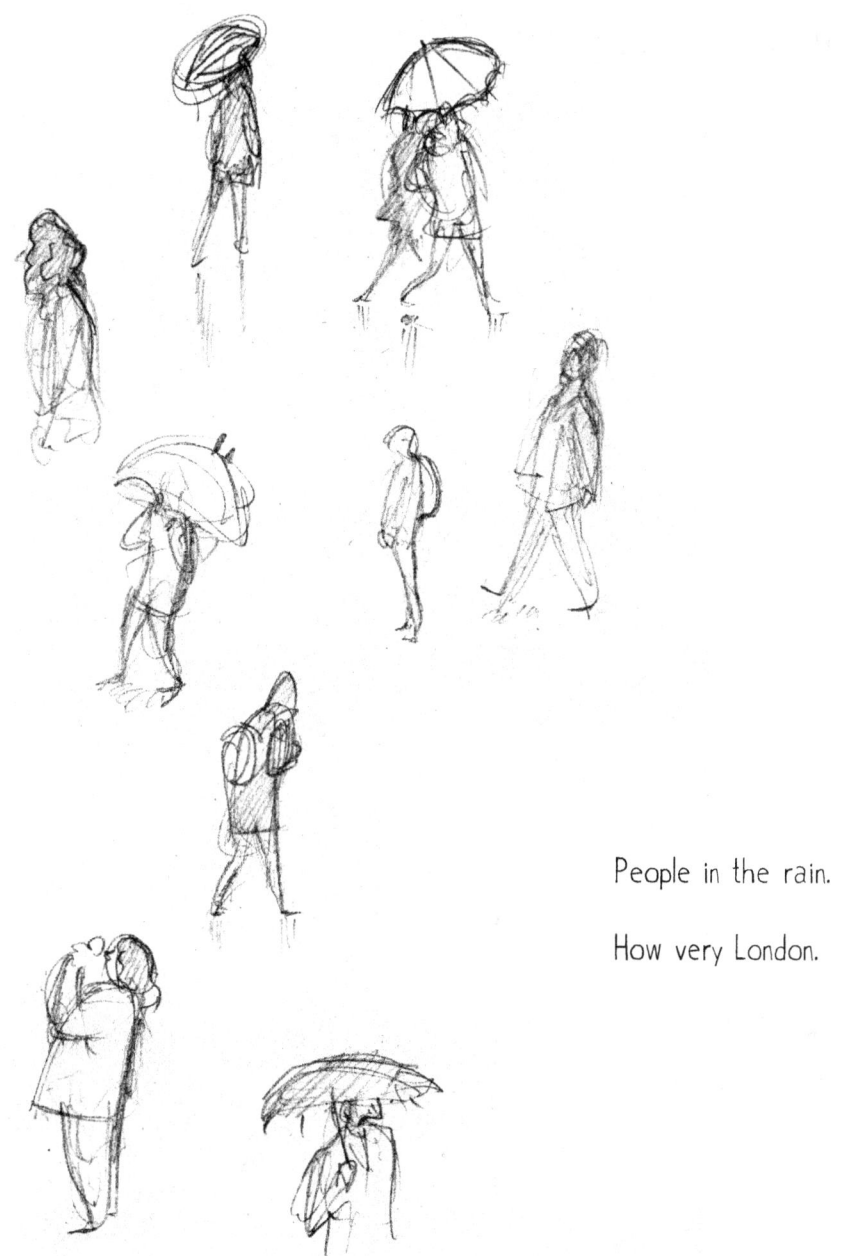

People in the rain.

How very London.

Vauxhall Bus Station

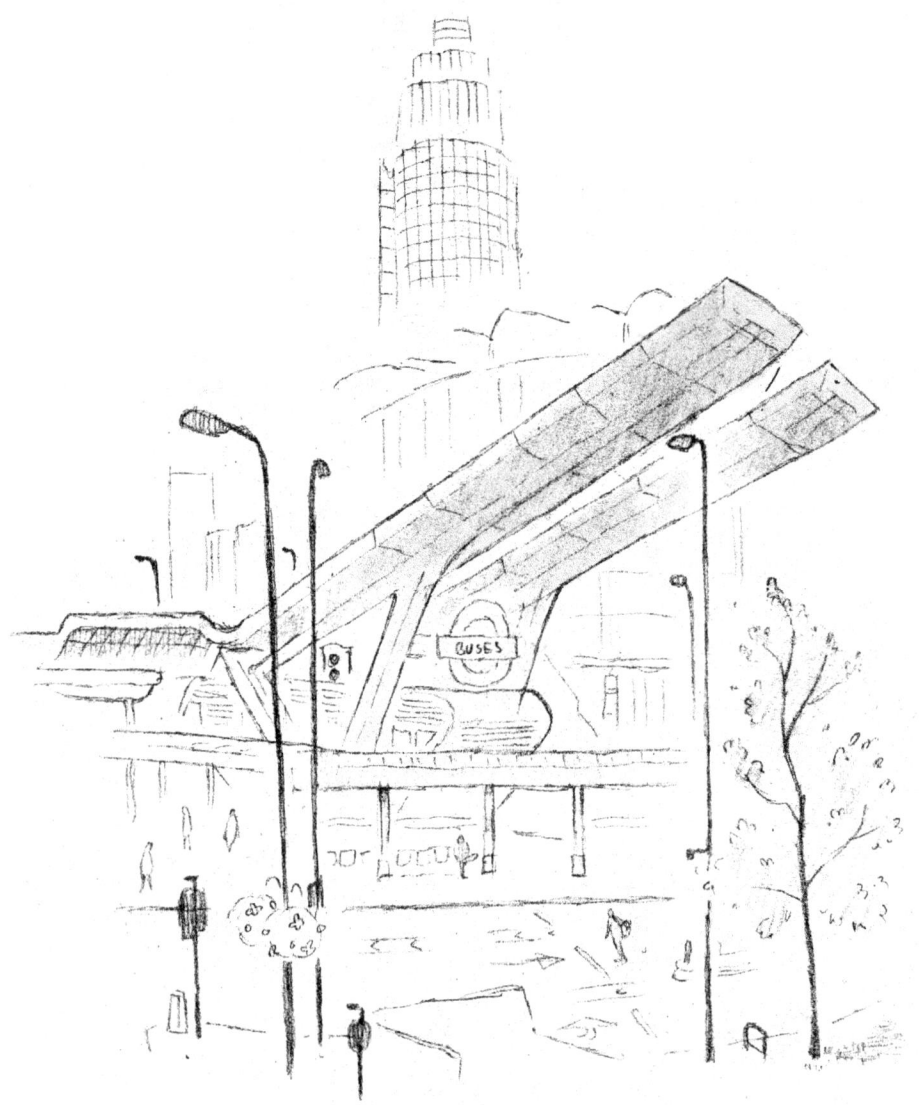

The Tower One, St George Wharf
180m, residential, completed 2014

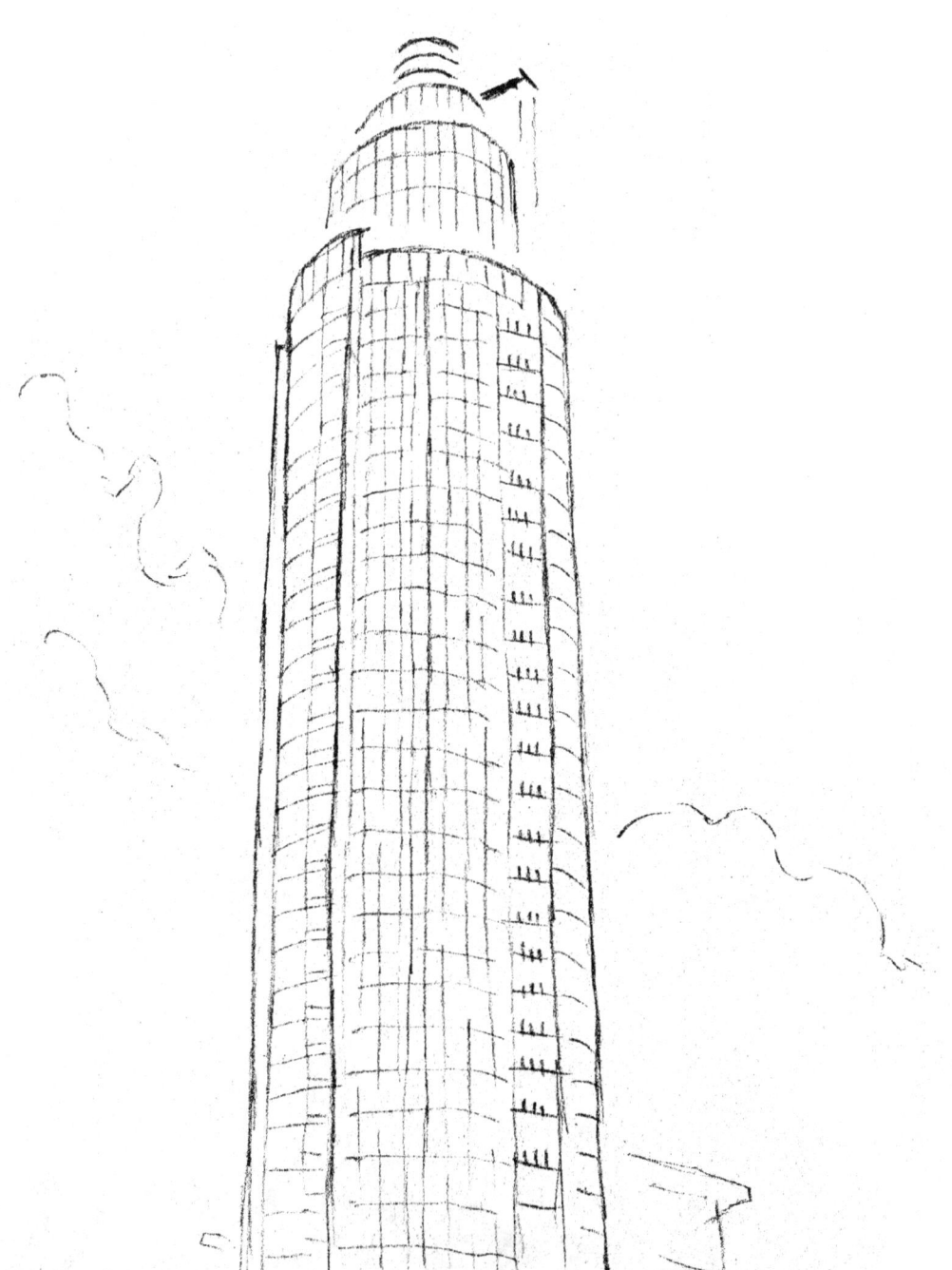

On The Tube Again

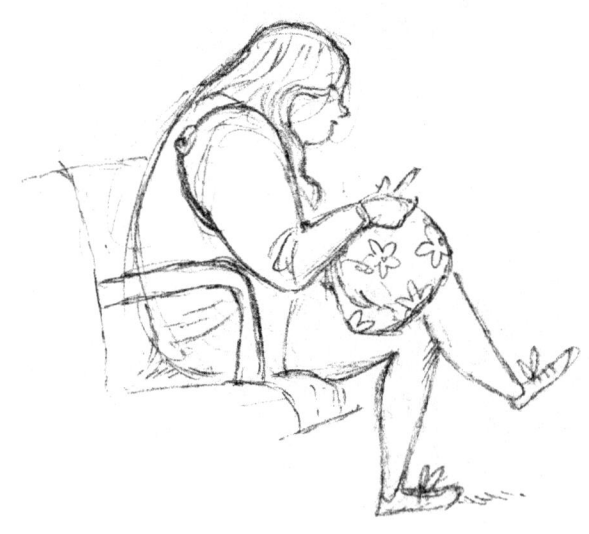

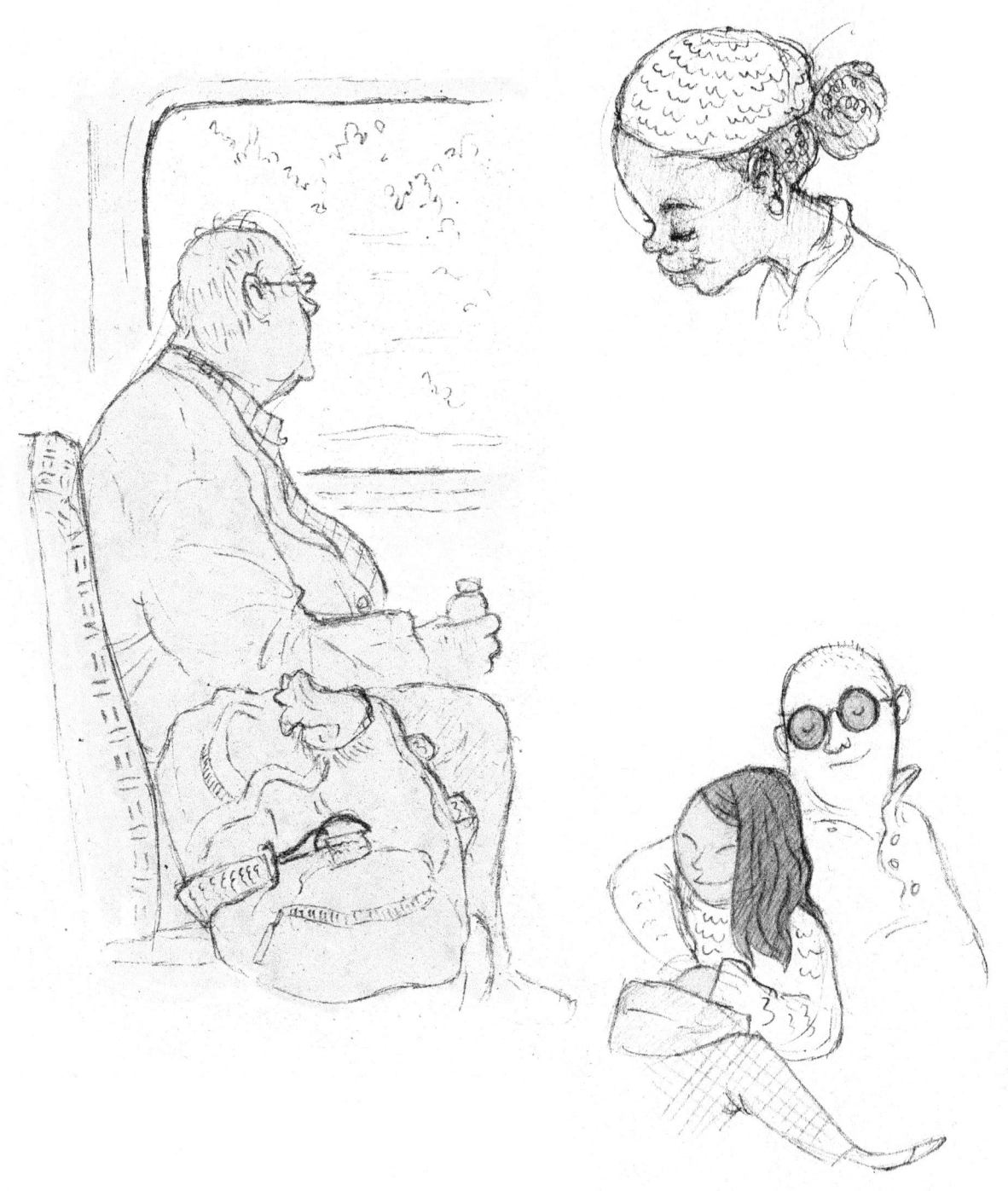

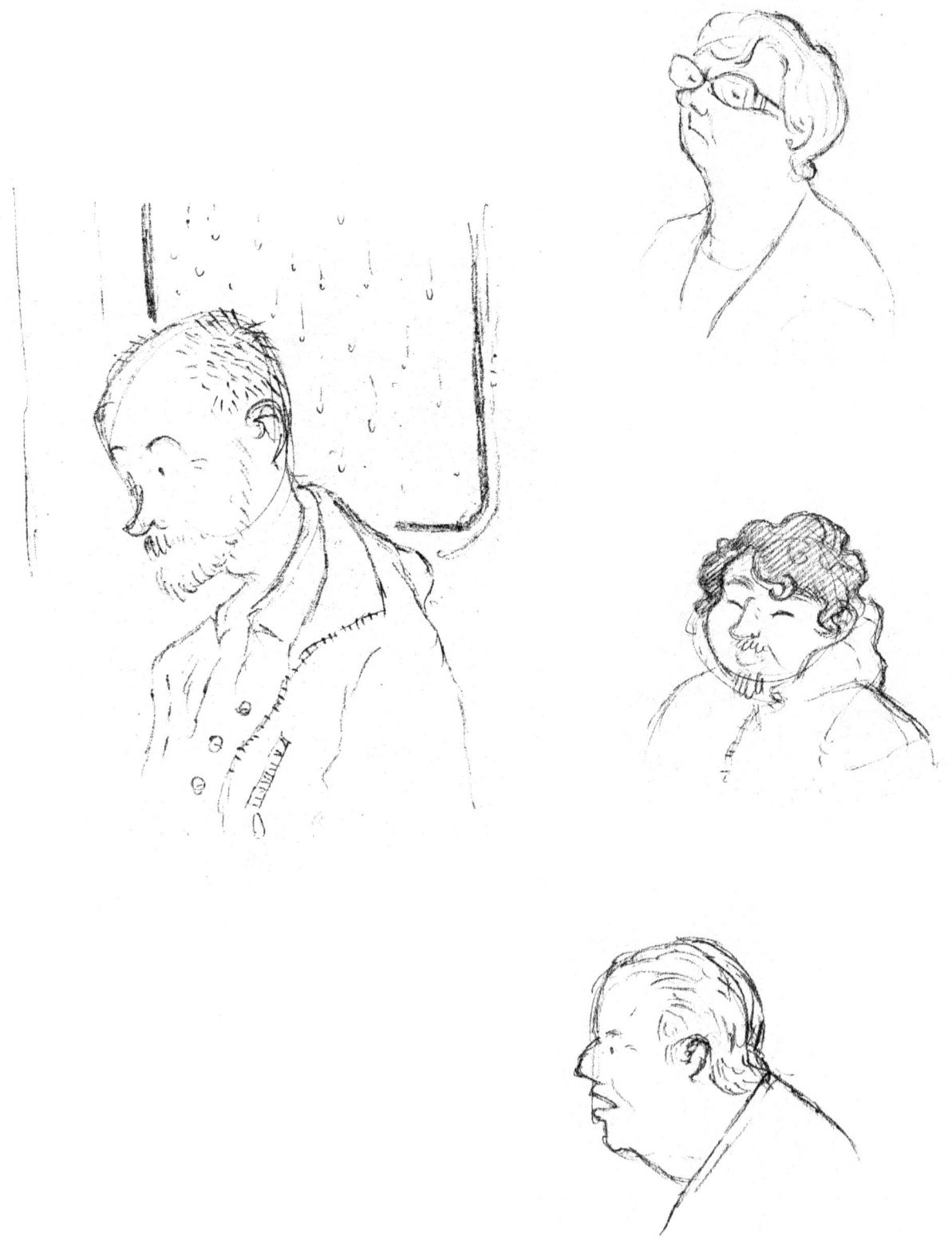

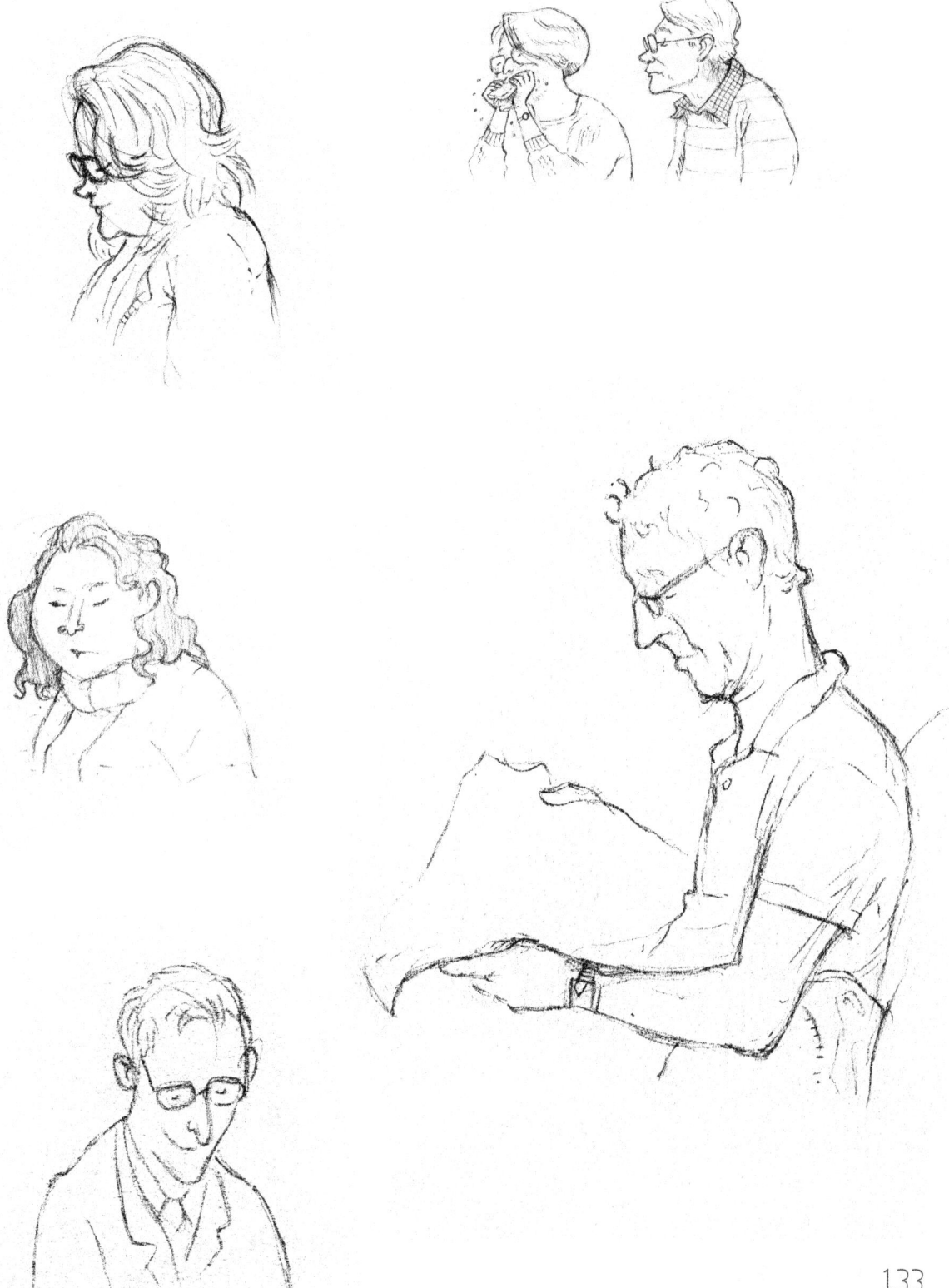

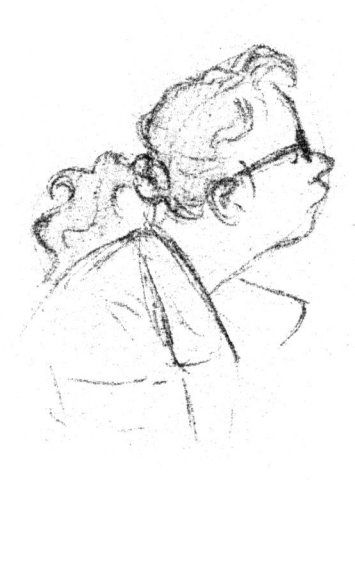

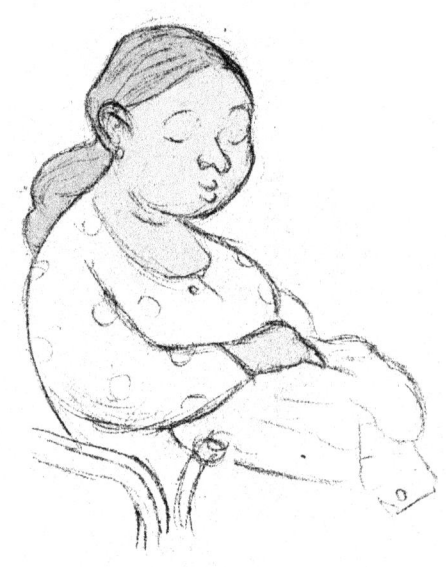

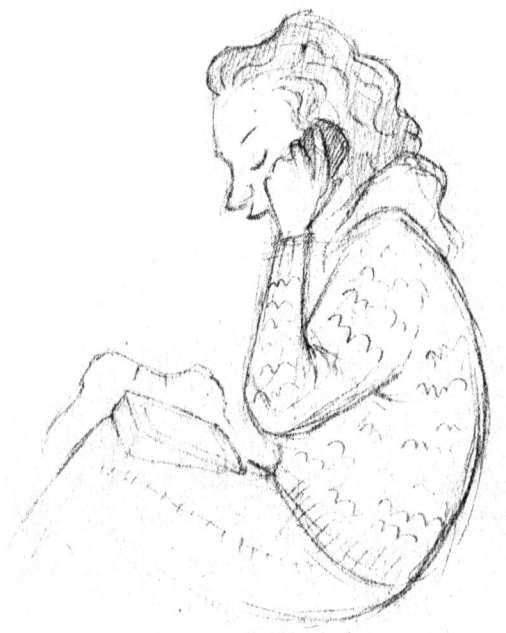

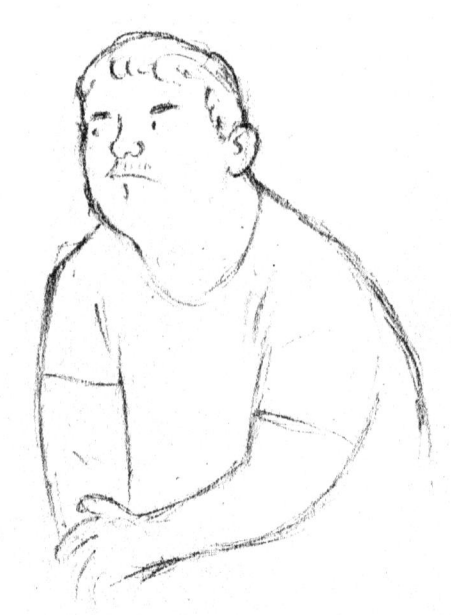

Wandsworth

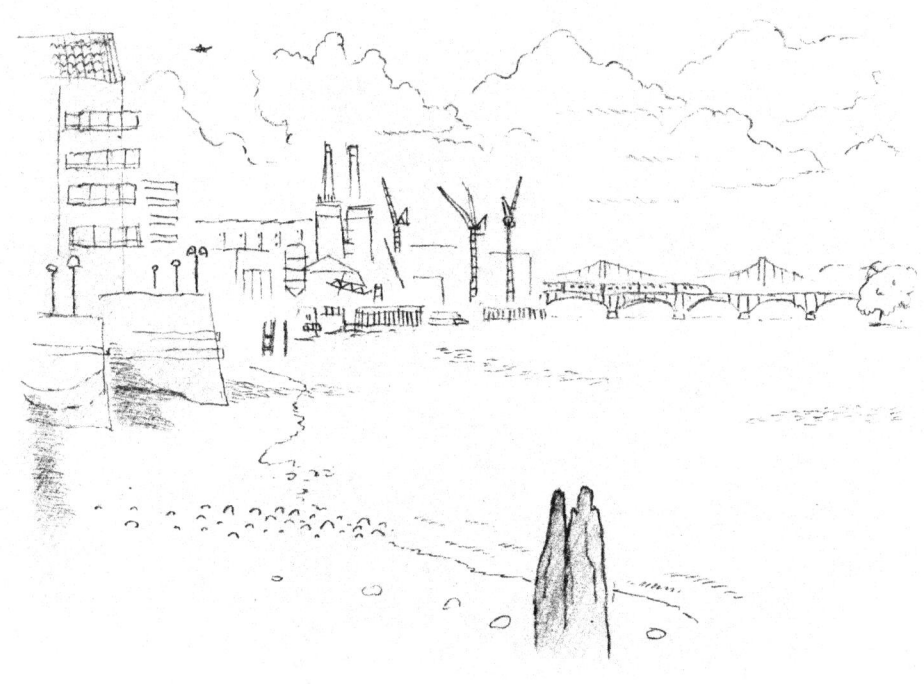

Battersea Power Station & Chelsea Bridge from the Riverside Walk

Battersea Park

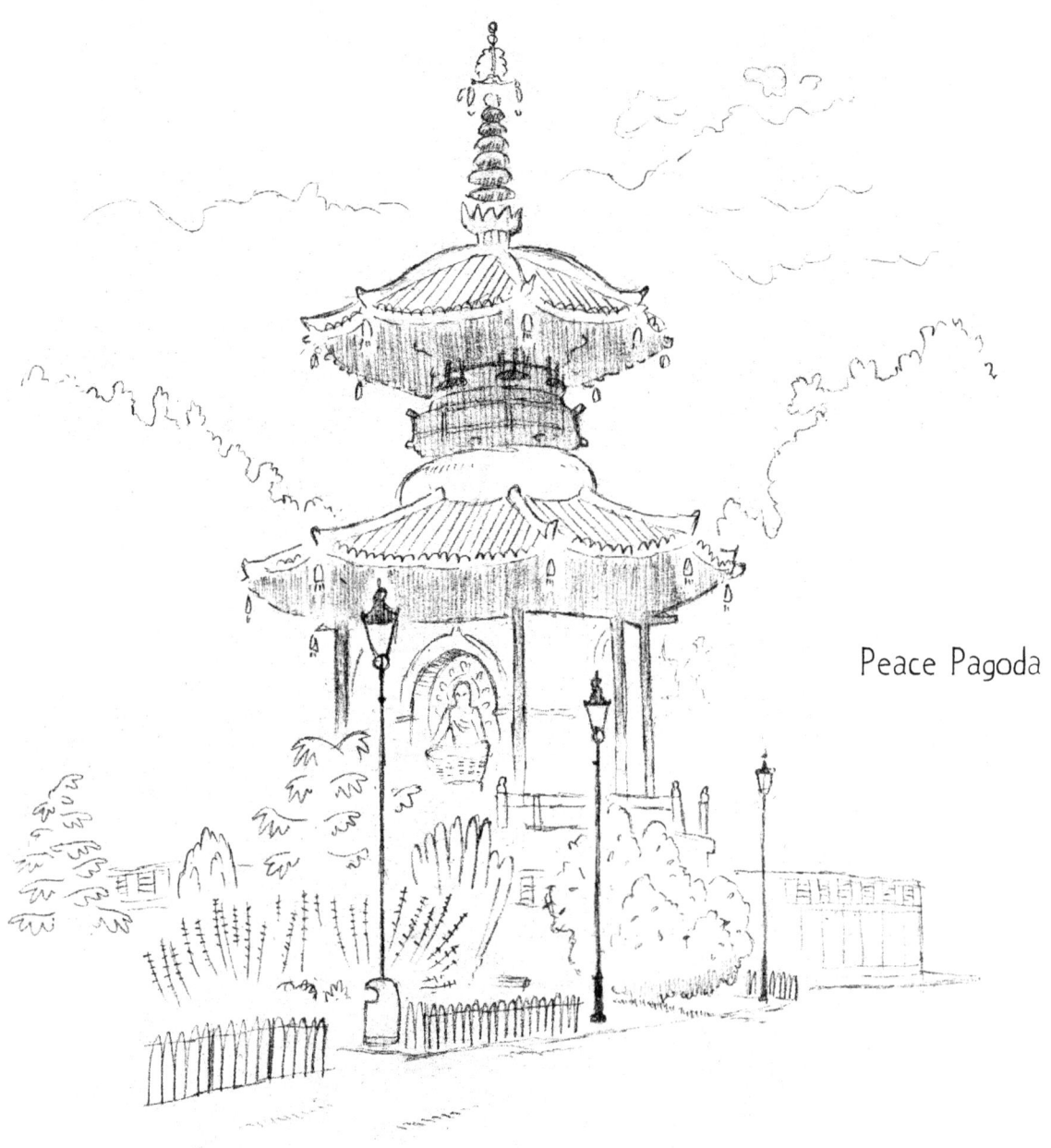

Peace Pagoda

Before being transformed into a park in 1858, this area was an expanse of marshland popular with duellers looking for some pistols at dawn action. It has been listed as a grade II Historic Park by English Heritage since 1987.

Amongst the many features within the parks 200 acres is the London Peace Pagoda that sits on the north side over looking the Thames. These Buddhist monuments promote world peace and there have been over 80 built across the globe. That gives me an idea for a long holiday challenge, to sketch them all! This one was gifted to London in 1985 by the Japanese Nipponzan Myohoji Buddhist Order.

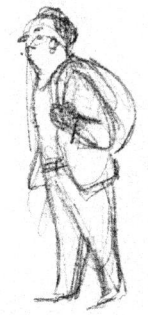
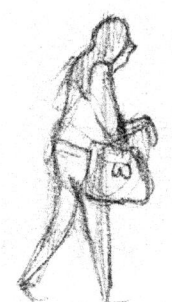
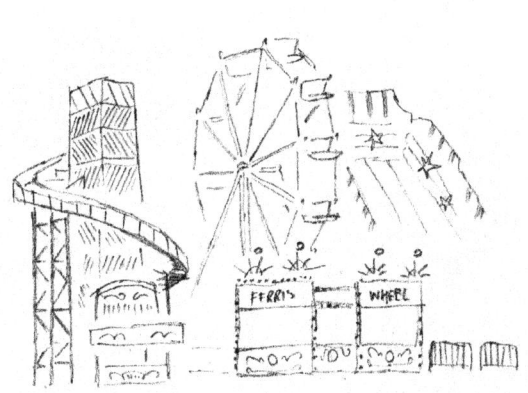

Fun Fair

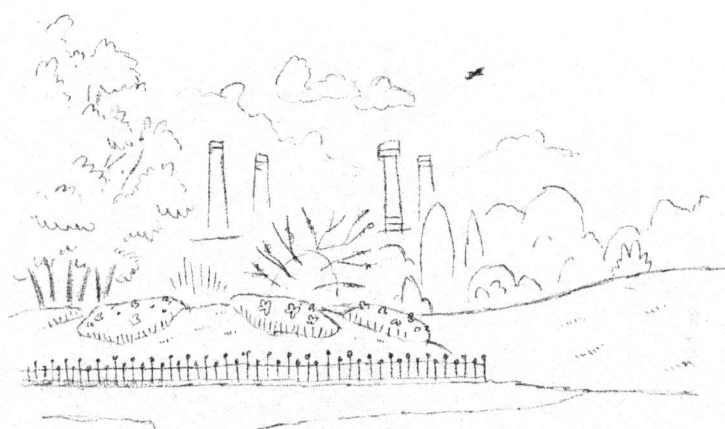

Battersea Power Station from the park

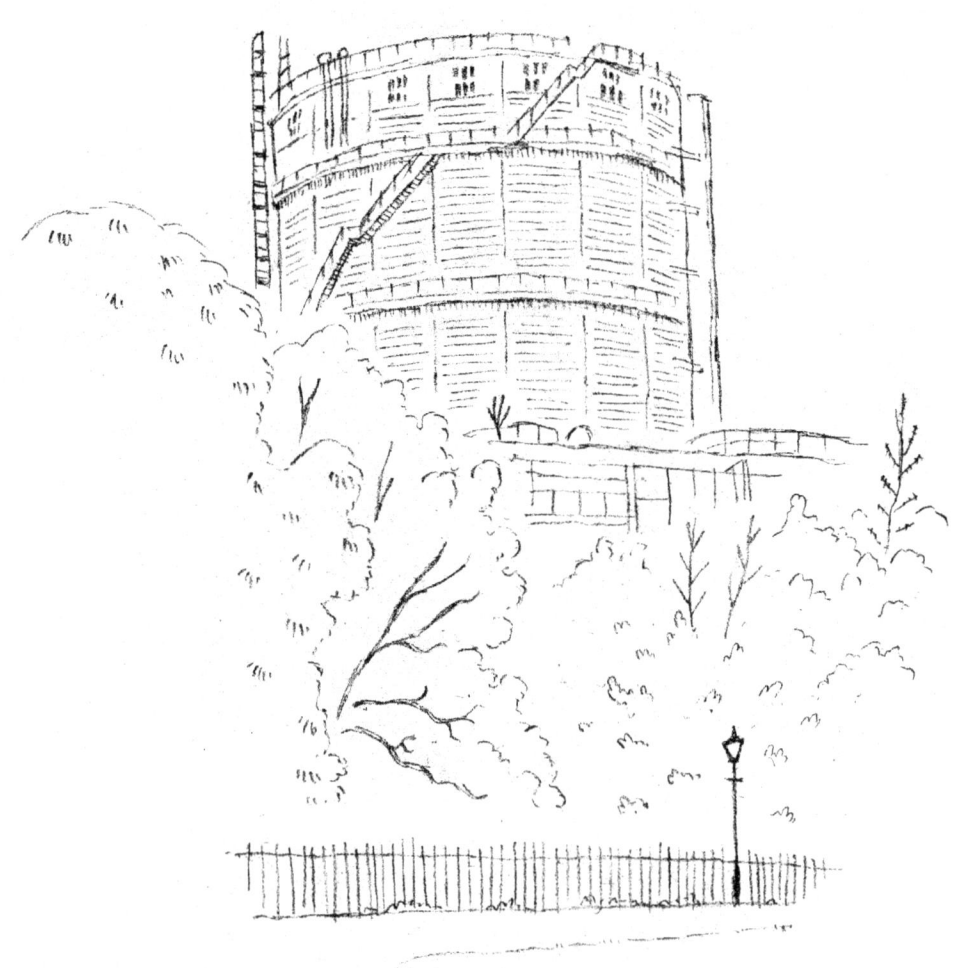

A Victorian Battersea gasholder viewed from Battersea park.
Sketched in mid 2014 this beautiful structure was demolished
before the end of 2014 to make way for the Battersea housing
development surrounding the power station.

Tower blocks, Grant Road, Battersea

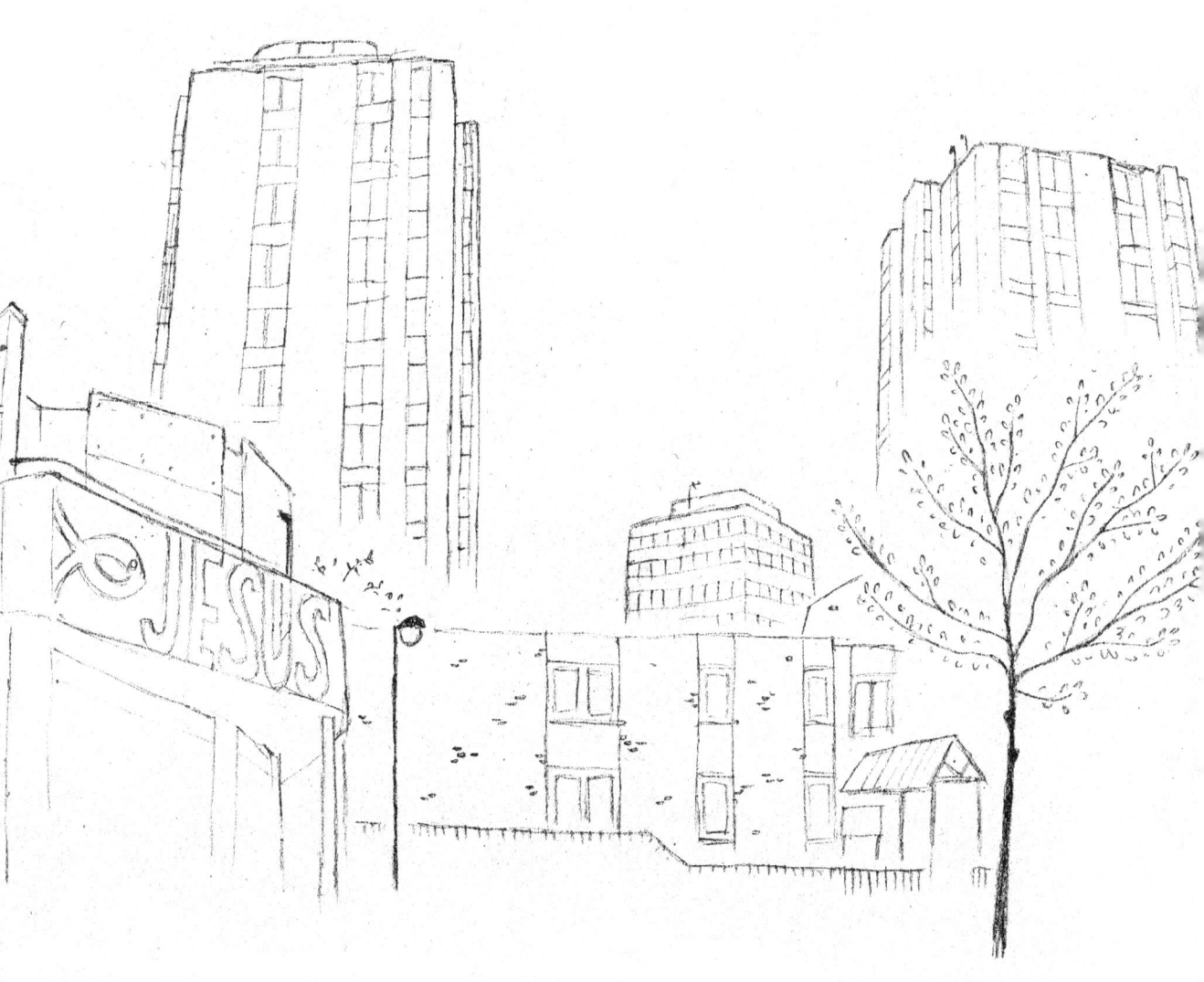

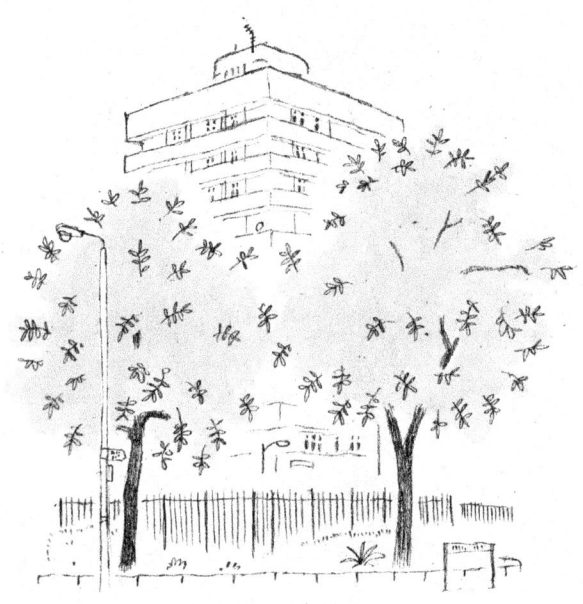

Sendal Court, Grant Road,
Battersea

Roundabout road
works at the South
East corner of
Battersea park

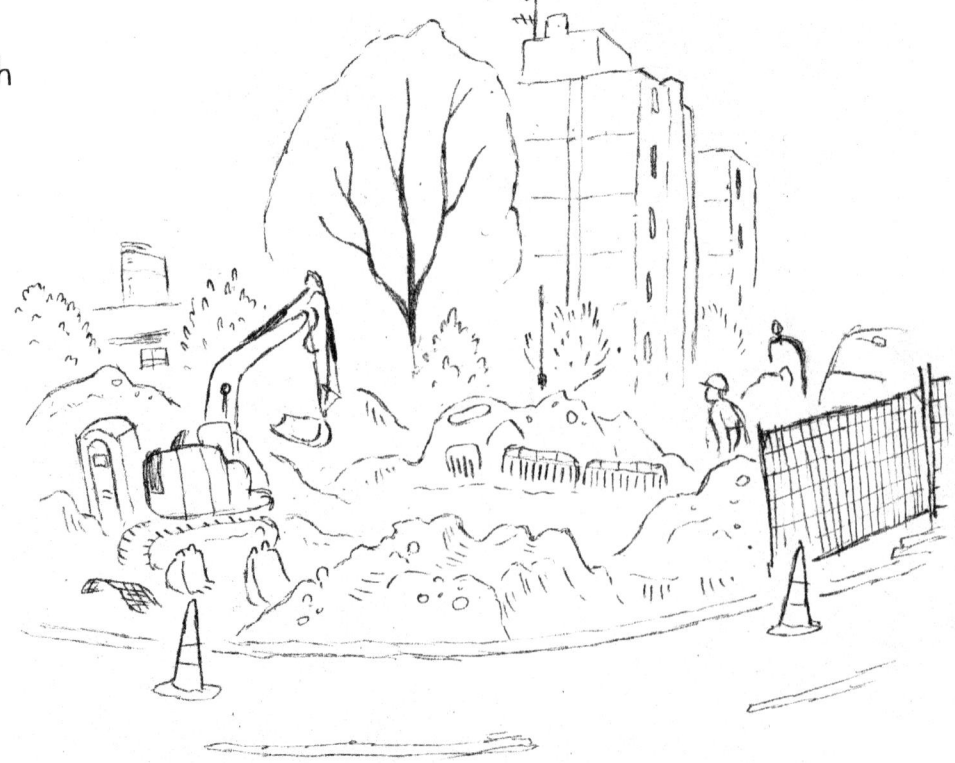

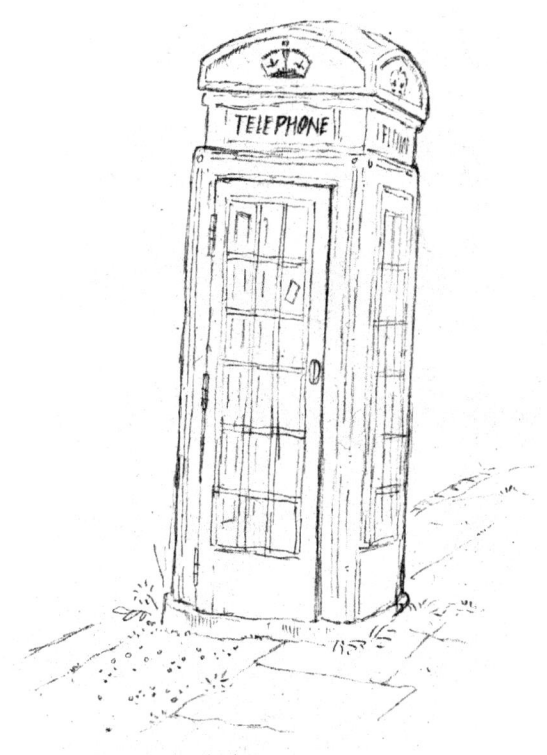

A Little About Mike

After studying Illustration at university many moons ago, I now work as a User Experience Designer. Though a different discipline to illustration, good UX requires many of the same qualities to be successful. Layout, focus, empathy, and simplifying the message to the user, boiling it down to the essentials.

Away from work I regularly sketch in and away from London, attend life drawing classes, paint (occasionally) and take part in exhibitions (even more occasionally). Along with all the other things life has in store, these all help in the search for creative inspiration.

If you would like to see more of my work, I also post on things like Instagram etc. (see handle on back cover), So go check it out, free art!! :)

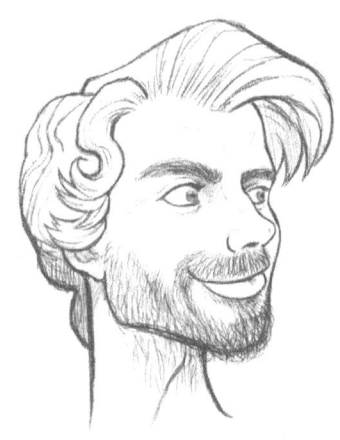

www.ingramcontent.com/pod-product-compliance
Lightning Source LLC
Chambersburg PA
CBHW081150180526
45170CB00006B/2018